A Look Back in Time

By Bernard N. Lee, Jr.

This work has been self-published by:
Bernard N. Lee, Jr.
2300 Mallory Circle
Conyers, GA 30094-8201

Photography by Bernard N. Lee, Jr., unless otherwise noted.
Cover Design by Dwayne Johnson
Book Interior Design and Layout by Michele Barard

Printed in the United States of America.
First Edition: Volume I

ISBN: 0692313044
ISBN-13: 978-0692313046

DEDICATION

To my mother, Helen F. Lee,

and

my sister, Bernadine F. Dickerson,
who were both accomplished writers, and inspired me to follow in their footsteps.

To my wife, Edwina,
who encouraged me to write and waited patiently for me to follow through.

To our children, Erik A. Moses and Angela F. Bostick,
who always kept me honest about my mission, my role and my purpose.

To my sister, Almaneta G. Kennedy, and my brother, Mercer W. Lee,

and

to the grandchildren, godchildren, nieces and nephew
who are the next generation of our family; may knowledge of this history make you
proud.

Table of Contents

FOREWORD

Bernard Lee has written a memoir about growing up, a "negro" boy during a unique, difficult, challenging, rebellious and turbulent time in history. It was a time when the United States was embroiled in trying to negotiate all the rights that people wanted, deserved and needed, were denied, never had. He begins writing a memoir about a boy coming of age in the midst of the turbulence so well documented in the historical works about this period. His story is set in the same time frame, but it is played out on a parallel stage that is as universal and ubiquitous as any story I have read.

Amazingly, Lee, who has traveled many roads during his decades of adulthood, has managed to preserve the heart, mind, and spirit of the young Bernard we meet in this memoir. By some unique or supernatural process, Lee shares his life from five years old until junior high school in what seems to be real time for his readers. He recounts conversations, situations, emotions and emotional events that are sweet, bitter, and bittersweet with the vividness of recall as if they happened yesterday. His stories of past decades rekindle memories as one can stoke a smoldering ember and return it to life. I meet the young boy that he speaks through and I want to follow him, to befriend him, and to see his world through his childlike eyes.

This boy, this young Bernard, takes us to his time and shares the experiences of a normal boy, in a normal family, in a world of normal people, places, things and experiences

Yet, "normal" is not usually what books are about; books, even memoirs, are about mysteries, histories, romances, serendipitous childhood fantasies, not normal little boys growing up in a normal world. So what makes Lee's book about normal so much of a gift to his readers? It is because his normal is all of our normal.

As the world around that era was boiling over in that cauldron, the Young Bernard, of the 1940s through the 1950s, shares his emotions, his inner soul, and his experiences in extraordinary detail with candor, honesty and openness. As his stories unfold, the readers find that they could tell many of them. They want to say, "You too!" His stories will resonant and bring a smile, a laugh or a silent pang to readers of all ages and backgrounds. We have all been there.

Somehow, along the way, in the days and years the reader spends with Young Bernard, the Lee family, the friends and communities become our childhood memories, our neighborhoods, our families, our youthful friends and classmates, our schools, our neighbors, and our churches. He takes us to "normal" and that is what makes this memoir a book I could not put down. Bernard and Bernadine's stories are a look back in time for a reflection on today.

...And there he was this young boy

A stranger to my eyes

Telling my whole life with his words

I opened this book and was beckoned in by a young, brown boy with the luminous white eyes and bright, dark brown pupils that is the special gift of youth. He had the sparkle in his eyes and the smile that lingered as he spoke just as he would have in adulthood. He stood with me silently as I read the first chapter that established the setting, plot, and characters I needed to meet before he took me on the trip to his youth…his normal youth. I did not know that he would also take me to mine. He smiled at me and opened a door that took me to his world that still exists just beyond the threshold of our minds.

He shared stories that speak to two very different audiences. The children and adolescents of today will be enchanted by this long ago time of innocence with little insight to know that it was not that long ago nor that innocent.

Adults who lived through the marches, wars, freedom rides, war protests, women's protests, segregation, desegregation, integration, assassinations of that time will see this young boy's youth as a time of parallel reality. We will acknowledge the turbulence, inequities and unrest, but we will still sit awhile with Lee's memoirs and feel the simplicity and sheer joy of laughing with friends. As you enter that parallel reality, you will recall leaning against your mother in church, sneaking out of church with your friends only to return just before the benediction, standing with your best friends in the school yard before the bell rings, sliding into base, counting your marbles, jumping rope, and hoping someone will dance with you at the Valentines' Day party. It takes you back to normal.

Normal for Young Bernard was moving to military bases across the country, meeting new friends and families, joining new churches, enrolling in different schools, experiencing the unique beauty of different states and cultures, and then leaving it all behind to begin the process again…lucky them. In the book, Lee says that he did not realize how lucky he was to have lived the life of a military "brat" until he looked back as an adult.

As a reader, I am pleased that he shared his family and their way of life with me. I played with Bernard and Bernadine, I admired his parents and their values and lessons on raising children, and I did not want to relinquish my place in the family when the book ended.

Thankfully, Bernard Lee has written a memoir that takes everyone who reads it to a place and time that is as comfortable as a gently swaying porch swing on a warm evening with fireflies twinkling in the night.

Bernadine Duncan

ACKNOWLEDGMENTS

My many years of traveling around the world and seeing the love and affection people have for their permanent hometowns inspired this book. That feeling was missing from my personal life experience. I felt a need to share what it was like as I was growing up, always moving and experiencing life as a child whose parent was in the military.

I owe much of the memories of my great-grandparents, grandparents, aunts, and uncles to the recollections of my mother, Helen Lee. She spent many hours with me recalling the experiences she had as a child, a parent and, later, as the matriarch of our family. I would not have been able to share those memories without her input. I also benefited from the historical records preserved in our family Bible, which contained the names, dates, and places of our extended family's births, deaths, and marriages. My mother diligently recorded those entries for sixty years.

I am grateful for the encouragement I received from my wife, Edwina, and her aunts, Lillian Humphrey and Winona Fletcher, who chronicled the life of their family in Offshoots: The H.F. Lee Family Book. Their work inspired me to want to share similar stories of my family.

I received inspiration and encouragement from a former neighbor and friend, Ernest Gilchrist, who published Fusion of Cultures: The Spirit of ArgyllAmerica Revealed. His fondness for the people and places where he spent his childhood prompted recollections of my own.

I would like to acknowledge the dedicated and highly professional assistance I received from my editor, Michele Barard of Urban Book Editor LLC. Her disciplined approach to producing this manuscript for publication allowed me to write without worrying about sacrificing the quality of the final product. I would also like to thank Bernadine Duncan of Virginia Beach, Virginia, for her review of the manuscript and her kind, insightful comments in the Foreword.

I appreciate the assistance I received from members of the research communities of the Rockdale County Library in Conyers, Georgia, and the Bedford Circuit Court in Bedford, Virginia. In particular, Bedford Deputy Clerk Karen Rowlett was very helpful in verifying the chain of ownership of the Mitchell family home in Big Island, Virginia.

I would like to express my appreciation for my cousin, Arleen Holmes, and my friend, Jasper Fletcher, whose enthusiasm for my efforts to share my family history motivated me to press on. I would also like to thank my brother, Mercer Lee, and my sister, Almaneta (Lee) Kennedy, for their willingness to share their versions of our family's stories with me.

Finally, I owe the wonderful memories of traveling during childhood to my father, Bernard N. Lee, who left for his Heavenly home in 2002. I owe my perseverance for writing to my sister, Bernadine F. Dickerson, who joined him in 2005. Memories of their lives are an inspiration for us all.

If you knew your light was dimming,
But had memories left to share,
Would you take the time to write them,
Or wonder who would care?

If you found your past was fading,
And your present fleeting too,
Would you capture it for those you love,
As I have tried to do?

We are here for precious moments,
Very soon we will be gone,
So I choose to share my memories,
Maybe they will linger on.

The Question

"Where am I now?" is a question I asked myself in February of 1982. At that time in my life, it was one of the many questions I had that begged for an answer. I needed to try to understand why. My response was to begin recording my thoughts and, in so doing, compile a record of where I had been. I hoped that in the journey of reflecting on my past I would be able to better understand *where I was* and maybe, see clearer into the future.

It was a genuine attempt at finding *my purpose*. I needed to believe that all of my experiences up to that point in my life were not unrelated and insignificant. I truly wanted to succeed in my life, and I believed that my definition of success should be the one chosen for me by God. I didn't feel comfortable anymore just plodding along day-by-day, and hoping for the best. I wanted to believe in myself, my dreams, and my future.

I always had been comfortable expressing myself. I had even found some success in writing. In college, I had contributed pieces to a poetry anthology. In junior high school, I was awarded a regional prize in literature for a biographical review. In 1982, I was a contributing sports writer for our local newspaper. Given that background, it should have been easy to put my thoughts and observations into words. I started, but then I failed to follow through. The pages I had written lay dormant and forgotten for the next thirty-one years.

"So, where am I now?" I am finally able to answer that question.

The Answer and the Journey

I am living in Georgia, approaching nearly seventy years of life, having retired from the military services and a career with the telephone company. I have had many wonderful experiences in my life. I finally have started sharing them. This time I intend to follow through. I hope you will enjoy going on the journey with me to take a look back in time.

I am taking this journey to remember all of the wonderful people and places I have experienced. I invite you to go along so that you can experience what it was like for a young man of color to grow up in the U.S.A. during the fifties and sixties. I am excited about the chance to share these memories with you. I hope you will find significant reflections of your own childhood among them. Let's begin.

Chapter 1: Life on the Farm

I was born in Garfield Memorial Hospital in Washington, D.C., June 1945, near the end of World War II. My birth certificate listed my father as Bernard Nathaniel Lee, colored, age 21, occupation - clerk-typist, and my mother as Helen Lee, colored, age 19, occupation - domestic. I don't believe there were many colored housewives in those days. I spent most of my early childhood, from ages one to five, in Waugh, Virginia, which is better known today as Big Island, Virginia. We lived on a farm in Waugh with my grandparents just a stone's throw from the mighty James River, the same river on whose banks early American settlers built the Jamestown settlement of 1607.

Bernard Lee met Helen Mitchell during an afternoon walk to the local drug store in Alexandria, Virginia. He was wearing his army uniform and sporting a freshly spit-shined pair of shoes. She noticed him as he went into the store and was so impressed by how sharp he looked that she waited for him to come out. My father was soft spoken and polite. He told Helen that he worked at the National Guard Armory in Washington, D.C., and asked if he could call on her. She agreed and after a few dates, he invited her to bring a friend and to join him at a local club. My mother accepted his invitation. She went with her best friend, Cordelia Freeman, who knew both of them through social contacts in Washington, D.C.

This handsome young soldier, who carried

Bernard Lee, Sr.

himself with an air of confidence, impressed Helen. His comrades treated him with respect and the ladies couldn't seem to leave him alone. Bernard and Helen courted until Helen decided she wanted the field all to herself. My dad was a talented dancer. He could empty a dance floor with his smooth dance steps. My mother, who had learned to dance in secret as a child, was determined to impress him with her own abilities. Her plan worked. Soon, they were inseparable. Bernard Lee wed Helen Mitchell on February 5, 1944, at 138 U Street, NW, Washington, D.C., the home of Bernard's aunt, Daisy Shorts. After the wedding, they lived with his aunt. I was born the following year in June.

Soon after my birth, my parents took me to see my maternal grandparents in Waugh, Virginia. It was a wonderful time for the Mitchell family. My grandparents were overjoyed to see all of us. My parents, who could only spend a weekend, were able to show me off at Sharon Baptist Church on Sunday morning before they returned to Washington, D.C. late Sunday evening. Only a short time later, they would receive a telephone call that would redefine their future. Grandpa Mitchell was ill and Grandma Mitchell was unable to take care of him on her own.

Sharon Baptist Church

My mother did what all faithful daughters do; she left her job to take care of her parents. My father joined her soon afterwards, but found he could not get comparable work in Lynchburg. It was a dilemma that he understood well and he knew exactly what he had to do to resolve it. He had joined the Marines at sixteen years old to feed himself before. Now, he was forced to re-enlist, this time in the Army, so he could feed his family. The choice that kept his family from starving put his life in jeopardy in the Korean Conflict. For that unselfish sacrifice, we owed him a debt of gratitude that we could never fully repay.

Helen and Bernard Lee

During those early years, our family consisted of my sister, Bernadine, who was born in Lynchburg, Virginia, in 1946, my mother, and me. With my dad away in the service, my mother was left to care for Grandma Mitchell, the family farm, and the two of us. Being separated from our father was hard for her.

Mother and Son

Our dad was stationed in Alaska when Bernadine was born. A mother doesn't forget an event so important, but she does learn to forgive a husband who said he would always be there for her. As her ailing parents struggled with their challenges, our mother took charge and did her best to save the farm.

The Mitchells were a resourceful, well-respected, and proud Negro family. They heralded from a storied past, as did many Negroes during their time. The family tree included an interracial marriage on Great Grandpa Mitchell's side of the family. Thomas "Jake" Mitchell of Amherst County, Virginia, married Emma Davis of Amherst County, Virginia, on July 6, 1887. From that union eight children were born. My grandfather, William Howard Mitchell, born in 1889, was the second child born to them. Grandpa William married Alma Eubanks; who already had a daughter named Gladys and a son named Jimmy. From that union came four children: my mother, Helen Mitchell, and my uncles, Isaiah, Henry, and Joe.

Grandpa Mitchell owned a farm and, by most people's standards, "did all right for himself." He raised hogs and chickens, planted corn and potatoes, and hired himself out as a handyman when he could. During good times, he worked at the sawmill a few miles down the river

from the farm. During hard times, he sold honey from the oak tree boughs, caught possum, squirrels, rabbits, and slaughtered hogs for the few white folks who could still afford to raise them. "Bitty" was his nickname and people said that "his word was as good as gold."

Grandpa Mitchell and Emily

Bitty was a proud, black man. He had a reputation for fairness but packed a gun when necessary. He had a temper, which he did his best to contain, and a shrewdness, which helped him survive when his temper flared. He had very little formal education and didn't spend much time reading the Bible. He cursed and "swigged" his liquor with the best of them. If times got too hard, he crossed the railroad tracks with his cane pole over his shoulder, trekked down a well-worn path that ended beside a boulder of Virginia granite, slumped down, cast out, lay back and let the Good Lord do his fishing. Although I never had the chance to know my Grandpa, I loved him. I cherished all the wonderful things my mother told me about him. I was only five weeks old when he died.

Maybe you have lost a grandparent or have an uncle or aunt whom you have never met. Maybe you have a father or mother who is always gone. If so, then you know how important it is to learn as much as you can about them. My grandpa was very special to me. I had pictures of him, but I wasn't able to touch him or walk with him by my side. Still, I have a strong memory of all that he stood for. That has served me well. I didn't go fishing with my grandpa, but I can feel his presence in my solitude. I take him with me whenever I find the time to get away from it all…and go fishing.

Grandpa Mitchell lived during hard times. He was a colored man in Virginia during the Great Depression of the 1930's. The Great Depression had a profound effect on everyone who lived through it. If your great grandparents are alive today, they can probably tell you all about it. Millions of people lost their jobs. Thousands of people found themselves homeless. Many thousands more waited for hours in block-long bread lines outside of soup kitchens to get something to eat. Unfortunately, if this scenario sounds too familiar, it's because the entire world recently suffered through a similar financial "meltdown" like the one in the 1930's.

We called the most recent one the "Great Recession." Yes, I believe history does repeat itself, and the lessons you don't learn the first time will almost always come back a second and third time to bite you in the behind.

I was not there to see the Great Depression of the 1930's, but the fall-out from the stock market crash rippled across the country for years afterwards. Now that we have all lived through the Great Recession, I don't have to explain how devastating the loss of homes, savings, jobs, and family security can be. Everyone feels it. No one escapes it. That's the way it was for us in the late 1940's.

I remember walking along the railroad tracks and wishing that I could follow the train to far-away places. No one who has ever lived near railroad tracks forgets that feeling. No matter how young or old you are the whistle of the train can work its magic and awaken a desire in your heart to hop on board for an adventure. I found a whole new world walking along that lattice highway. In the middle of the day, the quarry rocks are warm and treacherous. You had to be careful not to step on a rusty nail or slash your foot on a broken bottle. This was especially true when we all walked bare-footed wherever we went. Then, there was the ever-present danger of being caught on the tracks when the train was

Train Tracks in Big Island

coming. We kids all heard stories of people who had suffered that fate. However, none of those dangers deterred us from our primary chore of gathering coal for Grandma's stove.

We scurried along the tracks picking up the pieces of precious, black gold while looking for hidden treasures that might have fallen off the train as it traveled to and from far-away places. Some days we would find just a few black nuggets large enough for our bucket. On other days, when the train passed with hitchhiking hobos on board, we got a windfall. We would toss potatoes, apples, or pears to them and the hobos would kick pockets of coal overboard for us to gather. We never tired of receiving their ill-gotten generosity. If you have ever shared what you had for lunch with an obviously hungry person, then you know the warm feeling you get by helping someone who is truly in need.

I never got a chance to go fishing with my Grandpa but, he was, as my mother recalls, a rather private person. An inquisitive youngster like me may have been more of a nuisance than a help for a serious man trying to snag a big catfish for dinner. I do recall fishing with my Uncle

Uncle Joseph Mitchell   Uncle Henry Mitchell

Joe, one of Grandpa Mitchell's four boys. Fishing was one of Uncle Joe's favorite pastimes. It was right up there with pinochle and kidding with my mom. If we're going to talk about kidding, then Uncle Henry "takes the cake." Kidding was his favorite pastime. It was followed by dancing, swearing, and whipping my Uncle Joe at pinochle.

My mother, who was the youngest girl in her family, remembers her childhood fondly. That doesn't mean she didn't have any challenges growing up. She loves her brother Joe, but can't stand her brother, Henry, because he teased her so often. Both of them have passed on, but their memories remain firmly implanted in her heart. My mother always stepped in to stop anyone who was teasing us a little too much. Now, I understand why she did that. I also understand why she had such a quick temper. How else could a skinny girl with four older brothers, survive? Her childhood experiences molded her into a confident woman with a strong will and even tougher backbone.

Grandpa Mitchell was a resourceful man. He managed to fend off starvation and, in fact, to do quite well for himself during the Depression. The Mitchells were a very fortunate family. Because they owned a farm they were able to provide for themselves during those hard times. They grew corn, peas, squash, tomatoes, collard greens, and a host of other fresh, nourishing vegetables. There was meat, but you often had to find it for yourself. Grandpa Mitchell was a steady hunter. He could track deer and flush out quail. He was patient and a deadly shot. He also trapped animals such as possum, rabbits, squirrels, and raccoons. During those difficult Depression years, people ate whatever meat they could find.

Grandpa Mitchell had farm animals, too. My mother remembers milking the cow until the day they had to sell it to pay their debts. Grandpa Mitchell raised hogs and chickens. Hogs ate scraps off of the table and almost anything else you mixed into the slop to feed them. They ate dry corn and corn cobs, stale bread and rotten cabbage leaves, raw potatoes and potato skins, turnips, carrots, and just about anything else. The chickens weren't picky eaters either. They ate corn, breadcrumbs, table scraps, and almost anything else they could find on the ground. Grandpa Mitchell kept the hogs in a pen, but the chickens were free to roam the yard. I never liked the chickens, but I didn't want to get a whipping, so I learned to avoid them. Sometimes, if you stay away from trouble, it will leave you alone.

I dodged the chickens, but I was really afraid of the rooster. He seemed to enjoy chasing me around the yard. I sometimes chucked a rock at him to get him to leave me alone, but, if I got caught, I would get a scolding or a whipping. I still hate roosters, but I got to be pretty good at "rocking" them. If you have a talent for doing something, then you practice until you get good at it, and later it becomes a handy skill to have, that's called serendipity. I got to be really good at chucking rocks, so well that I could hit anything that I aimed at. Sometimes there are things that deserve to be hit. When I took aim at a target, I rarely missed.

Life on the farm wasn't all fun and games. Each of us, from the youngest to the oldest, had daily chores to do. I fed the chickens, which I liked to do, and the hogs, which I hated. The chickens kept their distance, rarely fought amongst themselves, and showed a little courtesy when they ate. Hogs, on the other hand, were nasty, pushy pigs that looked like they were trying to stomp each other to death when they were fed. I didn't like the squirming or the snorting and I couldn't stand to hear them squeal. My dislike of the hogs was so obvious that it became a regular joke for people to squeal and watch me run.

My fear of hogs was matched only by my dislike for taking cool, well-water baths. My mother likes to tell the story about the time that I ran out of the house, around bath time one evening, to hide. When she called for me, I ran towards the cornfield and quickly ducked out of sight. I could hear footsteps coming down the corn row, so I started weaving in and out of the tall stalks trying to elude them. Finally, all was quiet. In fact it was so quiet, that I could hear the thumpity-thump of my anxious heart beating. I thought I was safe. I had lost them!

Then, I heard the squeal. My mother shouted, "Pig, pig!"

The shrillness in her voice wasn't good news. Here I was hiding among the corn rows, and a big, fat hog was coming my way. When a hog is hungry, it will eat almost anything. I heard the tall corn stalks rustling. I jumped up and ran for my life.

When I finally found my way out of the corn field, I ran as fast as I could towards the farm house shouting, "Pig, pig, pig!"

If you have ever been so frightened that you began shouting and later couldn't remember what you were saying, then you know how I felt. I had lost it. That was all that my mother needed to find me, even in the dark. When she and the others finally stopped laughing, I was dunked into the tub and scrubbed with a stinky, smelly bar of homemade, lye soap. I didn't complain that night, however. I was happy just to be rescued.

Life on the farm was full of daily surprises, like the big crawfish that lived on the bottom of our natural spring well. On a clear day you could see the water rippling over his sun-speckled back. The hues sparkled brightly with wavy shades of orange and amber interrupted by dark patches of topaz. There he lay, an armor clad submarine, motionless for hours camouflaged against the rocks on the bottom of the well. The dancing lights provided a perfect hideaway for a stealth fighter lurking among the rocks.

I remember leaning over the edge of the well with my Uncle Joe holding onto my britches, while I peered down into the depths of the water. My breath was suspended, frozen in mid-air, as I watched the crawfish circle the depths like a deep-sea gladiator. He waded into the middle of the arena with his pincers snapping, challenging all intruders. "Enter if you dare!" the ferocious crawfish seemed to be saying. You can be sure I had no intention of doing that. If you have ever fought back fear to get a close look at a ferocious tiger in the zoo, then you know the horrified look on my face that bounced back at me from my reflection in the water at the bottom of that well.

Farm life had its pleasant chores too, such as gathering coal and picking berries. I could pick my weight in raspberries in a day, and I was fearless when it came to braving the prickly limbs to reach them. It seemed a shame to me to let the juicy ones get away. Of course, the juicy ones were always just out of reach for everyone but me. I would step over a viper's den to get my hands on the sweetest berries. I developed the same kind of passion for strawberries, blueberries, blackberries, mulberries, and gooseberries. Grandma often made us a pie with some of the berries we gathered. The rest would be processed to make jelly, jams, and preserves that she stored for winter. Before we went to bed, our mother would read us a Bible story and then she would let us eat a piece of pie for dessert. Afterwards, she would tuck us into bed and let the moonlight, winking through the window, set the stage for a pleasant night's dream.

High up in the mountains on a summer night, you could hear the bull frog courting his lady and the hoot owl calling the watch every hour on the half hour. The moonlight glistened and shone the way for many a poor boy dreaming of freedom somewhere far, far away. When the moon rested, the stars took their turn twinkling overhead. The lilac and the honeysuckle was all bundled up waiting for morning. The world was at rest and the better for it because morning comes very early on the farm.

The rooster crows before the sun rises and wakes long before a dreaming boy wants to open his eyes. That is another reason why I hated roosters. They don't work like your alarm clock. You can't punch them and then go back to sleep. They don't respond to reasoning like your mom, so you can't yell that you are already up and turnover and catch a few more winks. Roosters are special. They start crowing early and they don't stop until the racket has worn you out. They dash your dreams onto the rocks of realty, turn off the snooze switch, and then blister your eardrums. I thanked God for the rising sun, so the rooster would finally stop crowing. Then, I rolled out of bed and started my day.

I haven't found anything to compare to the chill of a country morning, especially if no one has started a fire to heat the water. Fortunately, I rarely had to suffer through a cold-water morning, because someone was always up earlier to start a fire and heat our water for the day. God bless the early risers because I am definitely not one of them. I must have remembered seeing daylight and being slapped on the fanny at the beginning of my life. That experience may have destroyed any affection I might have developed for rising early. Cold water, however, doesn't spoil my day. I had plenty of occasions to get used to it. If you live in a place where cold water is

Bernie in Big Island

28

the only thing that comes out of the faucet, then you know what I am talking about. You just have to jump in, scrub fast, jump out, dry off, and then get on with your day.

Grandma was an early riser. She started the fire that warmed all of us in the morning. She also heated the water for our baths at night. She was a resourceful person who canned everything from apricots to peaches. She was a wonderful cook. She baked pound cakes that had our mouths watering. She rolled homemade biscuits that we floated on molasses and steered with fatback oars all over our plates. Grandma Mitchell was a tireless worker who toiled long after others stopped to rest. She was up before the rooster crowed and didn't go to bed until after the moon turned over to fall sleep. If you are lucky enough to have a grandmother like Grandma Mitchell, then you know how magically she makes everything look so easy and turn out so well.

I was too young to recall much about my Grandma, but I treasure every story my mother told us about her. She talked about her frequently and related stories about her children from Grandma's first marriage, my mother's half-brother, Jimmy Eubanks, and half-sister, Gladys Eubanks. Grandma Mitchell possessed those special qualities that all revered black "earth mothers" have. She was righteous, proud, intelligent, resourceful, and strong. She was a guiding light for my mother. That showed through the strength and determination that all of the Mitchells possessed. By watching my mother persevere through a half century of her own life, I have come to know my grandmother well.

I do recall my mother leaving my sister and me with Grandma Mitchell and telling us to behave. I remember playing a game of tag with my sister, Bernadine. I believed Bernadine was named after me, but my mom swore she named her after the song, *Oh Bernadette*. We were born one year and six days apart. I was lucky to be the older. If you are the older child in your family, then you too are lucky. The older child gets to do things first and benefits more than you may realize by being forced to always stay one step ahead of the other kids in the family. Like all young children we were mischievous, although I never remember Grandma Mitchell ever telling on us. My favorite prank was to crawl under the kitchen table and hide until Grandma Mitchell came into the room. Then, I would reach and tickle her leg, giggle, and crawl back out of sight. Grandma simply ignored me and kept doing her chores. This always stopped my antics. No one likes to be ignored.

On one occasion, I decided to try scaring Grandma Mitchell. When she came into the kitchen, I leapt from under the table and, surprise, I hit my head on the tabletop. Grandma was truly surprised, but not as much as I was. My head hurt and I needed all the sympathy I could get. As usual, Grandma Mitchell was sympathetic. She took me onto her lap, rubbed my aching head, and gave me a warm biscuit wrapped around a piece of fatback to make me feel better. Kindness and understanding are qualities possessed by every good "earth mother," and Grandma Mitchell showered those qualities on us. She will be remembered forever for them.

I believe my mother learned a lot from Grandma Mitchell, who carried herself with that quiet confidence that comes from believing in yourself and God. Both women were strong "earth mothers," whose lives were a testament to the strength that inner peace provides. They sincerely believed in the power of positive thinking and the miracle of prayer. They were honest to a fault and would fret for hours over the least hint of an impropriety or wrong doing towards their fellow man. They lived to serve and took pride in a job well done. They cared tirelessly for their children and comforted their men when they came home from a hard day's work.

They told wonderful fairy tales and read stories from the "good book." They made do with little or nothing and seemed to take pride in how well they managed their homes, their families, and adversity. Both were proud and resourceful and, like all "earth mothers" before them, they were truly the cornerstones of our civilization. No man enters or leaves this earth without being graced by their labor and touched by their gifts. For their many sacrifices, may God bless them one and all.

A Look Back in Time

Chapter 2: A "Moving" Childhood

Dad in the Military

When I was a child, we were always moving from one place to another. Making friends was something I looked forward to with an uneasy anticipation. My father was in the military and moving seemed to be what he did best. One might say that I dreaded it, but I would not want to describe my childhood as dreadful. I accepted the moves because they were required. I couldn't do anything about them anyway. If you had to describe some of the things you experienced during your childhood, you would probably say the same.

Dad was in the U. S. Army. We moved, like clockwork, every three years until I was more than twenty-years-old. Today, moving frequently probably seems normal, but people were far less mobile back then. If you moved frequently, you were different. Different was new, odd, curious, set apart, suspect, shunned, whispered about, left out, ignored, picked on, talked about, overlooked, not from here, alone – you know, different. Add to that being *colored* and required to move in and out of all black, all white, or mixed, but separate, neighborhoods, and you can see what it was like to grow up in a black Army family in the 1950's.

It felt like you do when you find yourself in the wrong part of town or you mistakenly get off the bus at the wrong bus stop or make a wrong turn and wind up on forbidden turf. We always were being asked, "Where are you from?" This question hid the unspoken one, "What are you doing here?" I answered that question hundreds of times, feeling each time the way it feels when you have lost your way. I became good at answering the question.

I have always been a fast talker, a quick learner, and a hell of a runner. My mom taught me to stand up for myself and to never let anyone push me around. I wasn't supposed to fight, but if anyone put their hands on me, I had her permission to "straighten them out." That may have sounded good to her, but she didn't have to do the fighting. After half a dozen "welcome to the neighborhood" fights, I decided I would rather tell a good tale or run a good mile to avoid getting into another one. There is great value in being good at deflecting and running.

My earliest memory of moving in the military was when we lived in Kansas. It was 1950 and I was five years old. My father left the military at the end of World War II but had rejoined because he couldn't find a job to support his new family. One of his earliest assignments took us to Fort Leavenworth, Kansas. It was a wonderful time for me, but that is not the way my parents remembered it.

My mother's mom, Grandma Mitchell, died while we were stationed in Kansas. My mother was able to be there with her in Virginia before she died. Later, when her favorite brother, Isaiah, died, she could not return for his funeral. My mother loved Isaiah. He was big and strong and he always stood up for her against the bullies at school. To this day, my mother claims he was in an unhappy marriage and that the circumstances of his death were never properly investigated. I don't know

Grandma Mitchell (sitting)
with Isaiah, daughter, and wife, Ester

34

whether her suspicions are correct, but I could hear the pain in her voice whenever she talked about her loss.

My father suffered similar loses during his time in the military. While he was stationed in Kansas, my father's sister, Gertrude, died. She had helped raise him after his parents passed away before he was five-years-old. My father found out about her passing a week after it happened. He was so afraid that he would not be able to

Aunt Gertrude

pay his respects to her that he left Officer Candidate's School (OCS), against the urging of his superiors. When he finally reached home, the funeral was over and his sister's apartment had been emptied. He was devastated. Upon his return to the base, he learned he had been dropped from OCS. It was a career misstep from which he would never emotionally recover.

I don't recall being told about my dad's missteps or the devastating circumstances of my mom's losses when I was younger. Those events were hidden from my sister and me. That is how most adults handled tragedy in those days; they kept it close and hid it from their children. For me, our time in Kansas was a wonderful experience. I remember staying, for a while, in a small house behind a much larger home. We were renters and I was old enough to go to kindergarten. That was a magical time for me. My teacher had a pleasant smile and a soft voice. She made all the children feel welcomed and included. There were approximately ten children in my class. We spent our time in one large room that was divided by a partition to separate the morning and afternoon activity centers. I enjoyed the daily routine. We kept busy with lots of reading, singing, drawing, coloring, and outdoor play activities.

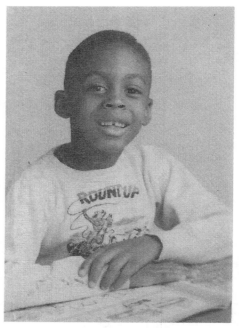

Bernard's Kindergarten School Picture

I remember one activity we had at the school. We lined up the chairs in a row and pretended to be riding a train. We had a painted replica of a train engine. It led the way while the rest of us followed in our connected chain of chairs. If you were really good, the teacher selected you to ride in the engine. I always did my best to be good, so that I would get a turn as the engineer.

It's funny the little things you remember from when you are just a young kid beginning school. That train was just the beginning of many imaginary rides from place-to-place throughout my long journey from school-to-school while my dad was in the military. I expect we all have a fond memory of school that we carry around in our heads, too. That fond memory can be very precious to hold onto when times get tough.

I was sad when we left Kansas. I missed my little school and the daily train rides. Of course, my world was terribly small at five-years-old. I understand now how little children know about the depth of the tragedies that happen around them. If you recall experiencing tragedies in your childhood that were not shielded from you, I sympathize with you. I was fortunate to be shielded. The burdens that life places on adults are often too much to be borne by children.

Our Time in Hyattsville, Maryland

When we left Kansas, we settled for a short time in an apartment complex off Addison Road in Hyattsville, Maryland. We lived in a small unit in the corner of the complex. Calling our unit small was an understatement, but the building itself looked like a castle to me. Our apartment was tucked into the crevice of the castle tower in one of the last buildings along the east row. It was only one flight up to our floor level but, for a five-year-old boy, it felt like a mile.

I thought it was a perfect place to live. We had green grass running along a labyrinth of sidewalks. Later, I would learn how important grass

Addison Road Apartment

Bernadine and Bernard
on Reed Street

and sidewalks are to people living in urban apartments. Although we lived together in a relatively small space, our family was happy to be together. The sidewalks really came in handy for playing games. We scratched hopscotch squares on them with chalk, painted in numbers from one to ten, hopped and played until the sun went down. We spun tops on the door stoops, and hid in the shrubs while playing hide-and-go-seek. For a little apartment complex, it produced a lot of wonderful childhood memories.

I don't believe we lived there very long. As I recall, we moved again just before I entered first grade. This time it wasn't a long distance move. In fact, we moved less than a mile down the hill from our apartment complex into our first home. It had a white picket fence like houses in the movies and there were other great features not available in our former apartment. It had a large backyard and a sidewalk that stretched for blocks out front. It also had a small front porch where we used to sit and listen as the evening rains played hopscotch across the oak and maple tree leaves. We had a beautiful front yard, with green grass, a brick-bordered sidewalk, and a gravel driveway. We also shared some large trees with our neighbors. The trees formed a canopy over our yard. There was one huge apple tree that reached all the way to the side of our house. Those branches would prove to be a source of eerily haunting noises during many stormy nights.

I loved our new home. It had all the wonderful things a kid needed. There was a sidewalk for roller-skating and bike riding. There were giant apple and maple trees for picking a juicy snack or climbing to the roof of the house. There was a large back yard where we played tag, wrestled, and hid Easter eggs. We had a screened-in front porch with a great view of Reed Street, our front yard, and our neighbors. With all of these really nice features, you would have believed the house was perfect. I think it was for everyone but me.

There were four of us in the family when we moved to Reed Street, my mother and father, my sister Bernadine, and me. The problem with that combination was the small number of bedrooms in our new house. There were two bedrooms downstairs and, space for additional bedrooms upstairs in the attic. My mother and father took one room, and my sister got the other one downstairs. As my mother explained it to me, my room was going to be upstairs in the attic. She didn't want my sister to spend her nights in the attic, so I had the upper rooms all to myself. My mother consoled me by telling me I was her big boy and I would understand it had to be that way.

I admit I felt abandoned by the family's decision to banish me to the attic. I tried to maintain a straight face, but I expect that my mother and my sister both knew that the arrangement wasn't my favorite. As the months went by, I came to dread going upstairs by myself. I would give all kinds of excuses to drag out the night before finally sulking and begrudgingly climbing the stairway to the "cave." I had to duck my head to get to my section of the room. My father had setup a bed for me next to the middle partition in the attic. It was the tallest section so I was able to stand when I got to my bed. A small nightstand sat next to the bed. I used the top drawer to store all my favorite things: a smooth shiny rock I found at the creek, my favorite marble and, my whistle, which I believed I would need if something happened to me in the attic, and a picture of me as a baby standing in the middle of the highway in Big Island, Virginia, looking lost and bewildered.

Every morning, my mother would send my sister to call me to come down for breakfast. Bernadine would stand at the bottom of the stairs and yell at me until I poked my head around the corner of the stairway and threw something at her. It was our regular routine. My mother would scold me for picking on my sister and I would pretend to be sorry. I know I should have been more understanding, but I just couldn't hide my envy of my sister and the rest of the family who lived together downstairs.

It wasn't long after we moved into the new house that I began to experience the horror that was my life in the attic. The first fall storm hit our house hard with terrible lightning, howling wind, and drenching rain. The huge trees outside swayed and the tree limbs crashed against the side of the house. I jumped straight up in my bed wondering whether or not the far window was going to come crashing in. The lightening flashed in the sky outside. It curled around the tree limbs and ran up the branches as if it were searching for me. The rain lashed at the windowsill and the lightening peered inside as I held my breath. Mere moments seemed like forever. I nearly passed out as I waited for the crashing thunder that followed the lightening. My terror of those moments increased as the intensity of the storm wore on. I couldn't go back to sleep. I didn't have anywhere to hide from the lightening, or the thunder, or my fear of the branches crashing against my window. I was stuck in the attic alone and no one would have heard me if I cried.

The next morning, I shared my horrible experience with my family. I expected them to sympathize with me and tell me I would be all right. I was wrong. My father dismissed my fears by telling me to put them behind me and face my challenges like a man. My mother pretended not to understand reinforcing my father's dismissal. My sister laughed at me and called me names until my mother told her to be quiet. There was a full court press to shut down my complaining. I had to accept the finality of my situation. I felt ashamed and abandoned. I lowered my head and let out a small sigh before getting up from the table and grabbing my book bag for school. I said good-bye without even looking back. I tried not to see my sister running to catch up with me as I trudged up the hill on my way to school.

I wish I could say that the criticism that I got from my family changed my point of view and resolved my fears about the attic. It didn't. The episode had the opposite effect. I became more isolated and frightened. I developed a host of elaborate diversions to hide my fears because no one close to me was going to help me to deal with them. I left a lamp on in my room. When my father complained, I hid it under a shirt. I began covering my head with blankets and only coming up for air the next morning when the sunlight entered the room. I started counting sheep to distract myself, so I could fall asleep. I tried everything I could think of to gain some control. Nothing seemed to work and I carried the weight of my abandonment with me everywhere I went for many, many years afterwards.

The family next door was much larger than ours. They had nine children. The father, Mr. Houston, was a minister and his wife, Mrs. Houston, was a gifted hairdresser. They had eight girls and one boy. My mom spent hours talking with Mrs. Houston. Occasionally, she would go to the beauty shop to get her hair done and on some occasions, she would only have to go next door to get a quick hair makeover. They became very good friends. A few of the girls were fun to play with, especially for Bernadine.

Our family was very small compared to our neighbor's. I felt overwhelmed by all of the girls. Then something happened to improve the odds. My mother had another baby, a boy. She named him Mercer Wellington Lee, after Bobby Mercer and Duke Ellington. He was born in Garfield Memorial Hospital in Southeast Washington in August of 1953. When Mom brought him home, I knew I would never get out of the attic but I looked forward to sharing it with a little brother. That didn't happen. They made room for him downstairs.

As time went on, a new family named the Gilkesons, moved down the street from us. My dad and Mr. Gilkeson worked together on the post. Mr. Gilkeson could fix almost anything with his hands. He used his skills to run a number of after-hour businesses that helped to support his family. He repaired washing machines, refrigerators, televisions, and other electrical appliances during his time off. His repair shop was so popular that his yard looked like a perpetual flea market. He had a curious way of talking, almost as if he were reciting pages from an encyclopedia.

My dad admired him for his knowledge, confidence, and resourcefulness. He also enjoyed his company. In time, my mother became good friends with his wife, as did we with their three children.

The neighborhood was full of children to play with. We had a lively time on summer afternoons. We made skateboards with old roller-skates and scooted up and down the sidewalk in

Mercer Wellington Lee

front of the houses. We played tag and hide-and-go-seek while our parents relaxed on the porch. One day, my dad bought me a mechanical airplane made of balsa wood. It had an odd device that looked like a slingshot that you used to launch it high into the sky. I didn't listen when I was warned to wait until we could go to an open field to fly it. I launched it as high as I could in front of our house and then I watched as it sailed over our roof into the bright, blue sky. The usually sulky wind whipped up briefly and, instead of coming down, my beautiful plane just kept climbing. Higher and higher it climbed until I could barely see it through the trees as it sailed over the rooftops. After a wonderful maiden flight, my mechanical airplane sailed out of sight. I looked all over the neighborhood for it, but it was gone. I miss it to this day. My dad never bought me another one like it.

There was a steep hill at the end of the block that we would climb with our bicycles. When we got to the top, we would turn and come rolling down the hill as fast as we could with a playmate sitting on the handlebars. I know my sister trusted me because she volunteered to be one of my handlebar riders. I realize now that our ride down the hill was really dangerous. It was as reckless a stunt as you could imagine. For starters, there were potholes in the pavement and no one wore any headgear. There was an intersection at the bottom of the hill with a stop sign on our side of the road, but we never paid attention to it. Any car coming around the curve in that area would have been blind-sided by a kid riding a bicycle through the stop sign.

When I was young, the need for caution just didn't cross my mind. I definitely didn't let it get in the way of our having fun. I realize now that only God protects the young from catastrophes when they take foolish chances with their lives. Don't forget to thank Him when He spares yours.

Our summer days weren't just filled with fun. We also had chores to do. Once a week, my mom would send me to get a loaf of day-old-bread from the Wonder Bread Bakery. I would ride my bike up the hill until I reached the section across from Fairmount Heights High School. Then, I would jump off my bike and walk it up the steepest part of the hill until I reached the Addison Road intersection. From there, the bakery was easy to find. You just had to follow your nose.

When I finally reached the bakery door, I would stand there, close my eyes, and let my mind drift away. When my nose captured the aroma of the wonderful bakery scents coming from the pastry on the shelves, and the bread in the oven, that was the most rewarding part of the trip. I would get a loaf of day-old bread and a package of the freshest dinner rolls that I could find. Before I headed back down the hill towards home, however, I had to stop at the ice cream parlor next door and buy my mom a pint of peach ice cream. Peach was her favorite flavor, and she waited all week to have some. In truth, she would have nearly all of it; she rarely gave us more than a spoonful. It was a delicacy that she reserved for herself and no amount of begging on our part was ever good enough to persuade her.

One day, I was coasting down the hill with my bag of goodies, when a couple of local dogs came running after me. I lifted my feet into the air, and kept on coasting. I was able to outrun them, but I really hated the way dogs chased me when I was on my bike. I would do almost anything to avoid them. Sometimes I would turn onto a side street and then double back when the dogs were gone. Other times, I would sling rocks at them or swing a stick to get them off of me. After my trip to the store, I couldn't defend myself easily without dropping my packages. Putting my feet up was the best that I could do.

The raised feet maneuver usually worked, except one day when it didn't. This time the bike slipped when I executed the maneuver and I spilled my goodies. When I tried to catch them, the bike tumbled. I fell, scratched my leg, and bent my bicycle handlebars. Fortunately, no one saw me. I recovered quickly and rode on. When I got home, I had to explain to everyone why my pants were torn and the bread was squashed. My dad was not impressed with my explanation. He instructed me to go to bed early as a punishment. I felt my dad's response was unfair. My knee hurt and I dreaded not having anything to eat. It was a long night, but I swore I would get those dogs sooner or later. My chance came sooner.

The next day I was skating in front of the house and sort of showing off for the girls next door. Out of nowhere, our neighbor's big, burly, sandy-colored chow came scrambling across the street snarling at me. This dog never stopped barking when we were outside playing. This was not the first time he had slipped his noose and chased me but, this time, he caught me completely by surprise. I was startled so I scrambled in an effort to get away from him. I bore down and increased my speed until I appeared to lose him. Then, without warning, he clipped my legs. I tripped and fell right in front of my house, where all the kids could see me. I hollered in pain as my whole body was dashed to the pavement. The dog became frightened when I yelled and ran back to its front yard.

My sister and the girls who had been watching all came running. When she heard me holler, my mother came hurrying out of the house after them. There I was, with all of them staring at me, while I was sprawled on the sidewalk in front of the house. My mother asked me what had happened.

I told her, "The dog bit me!"

I had a scratch on my side from falling the day before. The slide on the sidewalk had opened it up again, so it was bleeding profusely. My mother called my dad and they discussed what to do next. I heard them mention the words "dog bite," and I knew this was going to cost me a trip to the doctor's office. I was right.

Dad put me in the car, and together they drove me to the Fort Meade Army Medical Facility. I got checked out, but they didn't need to do any stitching. The medic cleansed my wound and gave my mother some salve to apply to it, so it would heal faster. Afterwards, he had a brief conversation with both of my parents and then told them they could take me home. I don't think they believed my dog bite story, but I didn't care. My parents had shown more concern and consideration for me over the dog bite incident, than they had ever shown in the many months I had been suffering in the attic.

The next day my dad went over to talk with the dog's owner who seemed pretty upset. The owner tried to claim that he kept the dog tied up, and couldn't be responsible if the kids teased it, until it broke loose. My dad wasn't buying his story. He told our neighbor that he would have the dog shot if it chased any of his children again. I guess coming from an active army soldier, those words had a menacing ring to them. From that day on, the dog was tethered on a long chain. It barked but it never ran into the street to chase any of us again.

My Memories of Grade School

When I was in the first grade, we walked to school. Parents today are much too fearful now to allow their kids to walk anywhere. This was an earlier time and our parents trusted us to get to school on our own safely. We had approximately a mile to walk each way, so we definitely needed to leave on time. Our school was a one level, red brick building with windows all around. It sat on the corner at the intersection of three busy streets, which made for a rather treacherous crossing if you got there too late for a crossing guard to escort you.

We lived at the bottom of a long, steep hill off of North Englewood Drive. It proved to be a tough climb when we were going to school in the morning and a really fun descent when we returned from school in the afternoon. The streets were lined with single-family homes. Each home had a small picket fence, composed of wood, bricks, rocks or some other yard markers, to delineate the property lines. The small driveways were filled with used cars and new taxicabs. Driving a taxicab in the Metropolitan D.C. area was one of the few jobs a Negro could do to supplement his income. Our dad drove a taxi at night and on the weekends for years. I expect that it was one of the ways he was able to afford to pay for our home on Reed Street.

My sister and I left the house each morning in a hurry fearful that we would not be on time for school. Both of us carried a brown paper bag with our lunch in it, a small book bag with pencils, paper, and notebooks, and something for show-and-tell on Fridays. We weren't alone walking to school. Fifteen to twenty kids took the same route. Most of them lived near us and we enjoyed talking as we walked with the other neighborhood kids. If we were lucky, we could get a ride to the top of the hill with our dad, who would drop us off and make a right turn onto Addison Road to head to work. From the top of the hill, we trekked the next half a mile along Addison Road until we reached Fairmount Heights Elementary School.

I was in first grade. My sister Bernadine was one year behind me in kindergarten. The first week at school one kid in my class just seemed to enjoy picking on me. He bumped me on the playground, pulled my book bag off my shoulder on the way to school, or punched me in the arm for no reason. At the end of the week, he and two other boys followed Bernadine, a few of our friends, and me as we walked home from school. When we crossed the intersection and headed down the sidewalk towards home, a small rock came whizzing by my head. I turned to see who had thrown it, but no one stepped forward to claim the dirty deed. A short time later, a second rock hit my pants leg and skipped off the sidewalk onto the street. This time I didn't turn around, I knew who it was. Seconds later, I felt a smack in the back of my head. I reached my hand back to touch the spot and blood trickled down through my fingers. I was stunned. I felt faint, and suddenly dropped to my knees on the sidewalk with my head shielded in my hands.

The next few seconds were a blur. I remember seeing my sister staring at me and then looking directly over my shoulder at the culprit. She dropped her book bag and lit out after him without saying a single word. He ran, but she ran faster. When Bernadine finally caught him, she jumped onto his back and beat him across the head until he fell to the ground. She didn't stop there. She proceeded to whip his head again and again until he began to cry for help. A friend of hers obliged him by calmly talking my sister down from her frantic state and helping her to her feet. The boy lay there whimpering, not understanding what he had done to deserve such a beating.

Bernadine walked back over to me and asked, "Can we go home now?"

My friend helped me get up and together we walked the rest of the way home. I had to get my mother to rinse my shirt for me so the bloodstains wouldn't set in. She cleansed my wounded head and placed a small, cotton bandage over my bruise. When she asked me what had happened, I pretended that I hadn't seen the incident because I didn't want my sister to get into trouble for fighting. The next day at school, the boy came up to me and apologized. He said he wanted to be my friend and then begged me to keep my sister from bothering him after school. I accepted his apology; we clasped pinky fingers to seal our agreement. I never had to worry about being bullied by him, or anyone else, at Fairmount Heights Elementary School again.

A Look Back in Time

Chapter 3: Our First Move to Georgia

Getting Used to Clay Country

I was entering the fifth grade when we moved to Georgia. We were living near Fort Gordon in a small housing development that was only half-completed. The homes were nicely built. There were an ample number of bedrooms and this provided me with a welcome haven in our new neighborhood. We lived off post in the beginning, so I got a chance to meet many of the local kids and their families. Most of them were friendly and fun to be around. I don't remember having much trouble getting settled into the neighborhood.

The second week there, two brothers, one who was my age and one slightly older, befriended me. They seemed to know all the fun places to hide around the neighborhood. We spent time searching for "buried treasure" in and around the unfinished houses. Of course, our parents warned us about going over there. We got into trouble more than a few times for it. It was, however, a never-ending source of fun and surprises, so we sneaked off to play among the unfinished houses as often as we could.

This was a time of reckless adventure. We had such fun sliding down the side of the sand and clay-filled pits dug out around the area. It was most fun after it rained because we could jump into the water or wade across the shallow ponds in our bare feet. Hardly anyone wore shoes in the summer, so bare feet, short pants that had been cut off from old trousers with a pair of scissors, and no shirt were all we needed to be dressed to have some fun. As the summer wore on, the tadpoles hatched in the clay pits. We scooped them up with our hands into a pail, carried them home, and waited for them to grow into frogs.

If you were an enterprising kid like I was, you could make some money collecting clay chunks from the clay pits. In many areas, Georgia clay was prized for its dry, chalky look and savored by local women who believed it was a good source of calcium. They were especially fond of eating clay if they were expecting a baby. My friends and I would collect a bucket full, and then sell pieces of it to local women who thanked us for our efforts with two shiny, new nickels. That was enough money for two jaw breakers, two large cookies, and two small packs of bubble gum. Needless to say, we loved our clay pits.

Our scavenger hunts at the clay pits were cut short one day when one of our friends nearly drowned. He wanted to jump into the water badly because it was really hot that day. However, the night before, the rain had flooded the pits and left more than five feet of fresh, clear water. The clay pits looked so inviting in all that heat that the boy didn't wait to see how deep it was. He jumped in from high above the pit and immediately sank to the bottom. The murky bottom was even worse than the clear water. It acted like quicksand and grabbed his legs. It refused to let him go. The more he fought, the murkier the water became and then he went under.

When he didn't surface right away, we nearly panicked. We didn't know what had happened to him, but we knew it wasn't good. We scrambled to the edge of the pit and tried to stretch out to reach him. The water was too deep and the pit was too wide. I said a silent prayer, and heard the words, "He will provide." That was when one of the older boys spotted a tree limb, which we dragged to the edge of the pit and thrust into the water. The drowning kid grabbed it and we pulled to get him out. He was covered with muck and had a scared, wide-eyed look on his face. We never told anyone about the incident, but, afterwards, we stayed away from the pits when it rained.

We had some help keeping ourselves out of the pits. Soon afterwards, stories began to surface about strange, flesh eating animals that were supposed to be hiding in the pits. There were even pictures in the papers of footprints in the sand, which supposedly belonged to one of the "monsters." Of course we didn't believe any of the stories. We scoured the pit surfaces for more than a week trying to find one of those footprints. I know we must have walked back and forth across one area of the pits over a dozen times in the same day. No matter how carefully we searched, nothing ever showed up.

Finally, a kid came back late one night with his hair sticking straight up on his head, eyes wide open, and a "scared out of your mind look" on his face, babbling about nearly being grabbed by one of those pit monsters. After that, we stopped going there. That was enough to get us to find other places to play besides the pits. On the bright side, after those stories came out about the monsters, the price of clay chunks skyrocketed to twenty-five cents apiece! It was good money, but I wasn't going to get caught by anyone or anything trying to make some of it. If you have ever had a close call with death, then you know what I learned. The next time we might not be so lucky. That was all I needed to know.

Weird Willie

We lived on a street with a lot of other children our age whose fathers and/or mothers worked at the military post. It was a great setup. On most days, we spent all of our time outside playing games. We played hide-and-go-seek, steal the bacon, red rover, or some other form of a "run and try not to get tagged" game. Playing with all the neighborhood kids, from sunup to sundown, day after day, was the joy of my life. The games kept us occupied and taught us how to get along with each other. Sure, we had our squabbles but, for the most part, the kids were fair. I don't recall anyone getting too upset about winning or losing. It was just fun to join in with everyone, pick a game, and play.

There was one kid who seemed to always be goofing off or playing around. He would hide behind trees and peer at us. He would run away if you called him and then stand at a distance and stare at the rest of us. We called him Weird Willie. He was a straggly looking kid with nappy hair. He very often wore baggy clothes. I believe he had an older sister, but I don't remember her playing games with us. His aunt was nice; she smiled at us whenever she came outside to call for Willie to come home.

I awoke early one morning to find the sun was already up and shining brightly. I didn't want to eat my oatmeal, so I grabbed a couple of apples and skipped outside before my mother could make me. The early morning sun had begun to sear the grass. The vividly bright, wild flowers waved gently in the summer breeze while a noisy group of sparrows fought over a discarded piece of bread. I sat down on the stoop and began eating one of the apples I had saved from the day before. It had a small brown spot on one side, but I knew how to eat around that. It wasn't bad for an early morning snack and it tasted a lot better than oatmeal.

To my surprise, I saw Willie peeking from behind the big oak tree in his front yard. He seemed to be studying me from a distance. I pretended not to notice him, as he slid from behind one oak tree, only to disappear behind another one. This game of "slide and hide" went on for a while; there were quite a few large trees in our front yards. Slowly and cautiously, Willie inched closer, until he was only a few yards from our front porch. Finally, he took one last step, paused and then very carefully leaned one arm against the porch railing.

He seemed to be unsure of himself, and I wondered if he had always been so cautious and afraid. Spontaneously, I opened my hand with an apple resting inside my palm and shifted my head to the side. Willie noticed the friendly gesture right away. He smiled, and then began working his way around the porch. Then, he stopped suddenly and listened with his head turned slightly up in the air. I started to say hello, but thought better of it. I kept my lips held tightly together.

Willie inched shyly along the railing and stopped just a few feet from where I sat. He opened his hand and cocked his head again slightly to the side. I watched him as he stared at the apple and tried not to look at me. I extended my hand. Willie plucked the apple right out of it and ran back to behind the oak tree. There was a lonely silence. I am almost certain Willie thought I was going to run after him to retrieve my apple. I might have done it too if I hadn't been so stunned by what I had just observed.

Very cautiously, Willie peered from behind the tree. I could hear his breathing. He sounded excited, if not scared. I sat perfectly still for what seemed like an eternity. When Willie finally realized I wasn't chasing him, he seemed to relax. Then he stepped from behind the tree, peered at the apple and smiled. The silence was broken when he took a big bite out of the apple and began chewing noisily. My breakfast snack was gone. I waved at Willie, got up and went back inside to eat my oatmeal.

Later that day, all of the neighborhood kids were outside playing. When Willie came out, he kept his distance, but I could tell he wanted to play too. The kids began a game of hide-and-go-seek. The tall oak tree, in the middle of the yard, was designated as the safety zone. It wasn't long before kids were running around chasing each other, hollering and screaming, and racing to the safety of the tree. Willie watched as we played and, before long, he was really into the game. He ran from his front porch to the tree and back again. He seemed to be chasing someone, but no one was in sight.

A few of the kids stopped to look, made a couple of snide remarks and then returned to playing.

Willie seemed to notice the attention and stepped up his game. He flailed his arms in a wavy motion and ran headlong into the tree. He was stunned by the contact, stumbled backwards, and sat on the ground holding his head. The kids looked stunned too, then pointed at him and began laughing. Willie took the gestures as positive reinforcement and slowly got to his feet. Before I could grasp what was going to happen next, Willie took off again running towards the tree.

When I realized what he was going to do, I knew I had to beat him to it. I ducked my head and sprinted as fast as I could, trying desperately to reach the spot between Willie and the tree. I just made it in time; we collided and landed in a heap. All the kids began laughing. They laughed even louder, as we struggled to get up. I was stunned, embarrassed, and furious. What were they thinking? We could have been seriously hurt! Why were they encouraging this weak-minded kid to bash his brains out? What fun was there in such nonsense?

I scrambled to my feet, threw my hands up in the air, and yelled, "Stop!"

All the kids stared at me with surprised looks on their faces. Even Willie gazed up from the ground with a curious look on his face. At that moment, I didn't care. The silliness had gone far enough.

"It's not funny," I said. "He could have really hurt himself. Is that what you want?"

All the kids stared at me; and then, one by one, they hung their heads in shame. Willie seemed confused. He looked at me and then he looked at the other kids. He didn't seem to understand what was happening, but then he did an amazing thing. He pushed himself up off the ground, stood tall, and walked over to me. All the kids stared at him, wondering what he was going to do next. I wondered too.

Then to my surprise, Willie stood squarely in front of me, and put out both his hands in two solid fists; then, he looked around the yard from kid to kid. Nobody moved. Then Willie turned to me, lifted me off the ground and gave me a big hug. There was a hushed silence, as all the kids stared in amazement. This shy, overly reserved, boy had made a very bold statement. Somehow I had connected with him, and he understood. The kids could laugh at him, but he wasn't going to tolerate them laughing at me. I had made a new friend. If you have ever felt vindicated, when you have taken an unpopular position in support of your principles, then you know how proud I was at that moment for taking a stand in the yard.

Good News, Good News

There wasn't a lot of mixing between the races in Georgia in 1955. In fact, segregation was the norm for children and adults in the entire South. Sure, we spoke to each other, but separate and unequal were the law of the land. That is what makes the next story so unbelievable.

Early one Saturday morning, we heard singing outside of our house. I looked out of the window and saw four white people walking down our dusty, dirty road wearing bright, 'Sunday-Go-To-Meeting' clothes. One young man had a guitar, a young woman held a bright colored tambourine, and a somewhat older gentlemen carried a large, brown Bible, which he was waving high above his head. A pleasant looking woman in a straw hat led the procession. The spectacle was a sight to see. They appeared to be marching in a parade, but I didn't see a band or a line of circus wagons.

A minute later, there was a firm, determined knock on our door. My mother opened the door to a short, rather plump lady with a rolled up straw hat who smiled broadly at us as we stared at her.

"Hello," she said. "My name is Ms. Emily. I am the good news lady come to invite you to our revival meeting tomorrow evening."

My mother smiled back at Ms. Emily and invited her to step inside. To my surprise, she graciously accepted. Once inside, she gazed at the mantle and immediately spotted the family pictures. When Ms. Emily asked about them, my mother answered politely and offered to show them to her. The entire exchange took no more than a minute, but Ms. Emily had impressed my mom with her interest in our family.

My mom jumped at the opportunity to entertain a house guest. They struck up a conversation that lasted far longer than any I had ever seen my mother hold with a stranger. It was as if they had been long lost friends, catching up on bygone memories from each other's world.

Finally Ms. Emily said, "We have a lot of people to tell about the good news, so I must be getting along. We want you to tell all of your friends to let their children come to the green and white house at the end of the block to hear the missionary deliver the good news message."

My mom thanked her for stopping by to tell us about the meeting. She didn't commit to attending, but said she would consider it. After the lady left, my mother called her friend next door to ask about the visitors. Our neighbor said she had met them a year earlier. She said they were traveling missionaries and that she planned to let her kids attend their Good News Bible School at the William's house for the next four weeks. My mom thanked her, and then sat us down to talk about what we had all seen and heard. We were excited to find out what they were talking about. What was the good news?

The next afternoon, a few men gathered in the open field at the end of the block. All the neighborhood kids gathered to watch as the men began to work. Within a few hours, they had raised a large, white tent and placed a few chairs, spaced liberally apart, under it. Then two of the men walked by us carrying a small crate. They placed the crate on the ground in the front of the tent. The setup must have been complete, because the men all came together in a small group, said a few words, and then began to leave. As they left, one of the men walked over to us and said, "Expect to see all of you at tonight's revival. Now go on home."

Early that evening, my mother, with my sister and me in tow, walked down to the end of the block to attend the revival. Mother sat in one of the chairs while we sat on the dusty ground. One by one, our neighbors filled the tent. When the spaces were all taken, the latecomers sat around the perimeter. Polite chatter filled the air as neighbors greeted each other and waited for the revival to begin. Without warning there was a hushed silence and quietly everyone around us rose to their feet. We turned to look at our mother. We were surprised to see that she was already standing, so we stood, too. She was looking straight ahead. We looked too but couldn't see anything. Then, without a word, a tall wiry-looking man with a large Bible under his arm walked around the tent and stood on top of the crate.

"Welcome, everyone," he said. "We are delighted to have you join us this evening for our Good News Revival."

The crowd murmured for a second and then burst out in a long, loud applause. As the applause subsided, Ms. Emily appeared next to the minister. She wore a white, linen dress and white gloves. She even wore white shoes that matched the rest of her ensemble. In her hand, she carried a brown hymnal like the ones in your church pew. She opened to a page, lifted her chin upwards, and began to sing.

"Oh, we'll all go to meet Him by-and-by.

Oh, we'll all go to meet Him by-and-by.

Oh, we'll all go to meet Him, oh we'll all go to meet Him,

Oh we'll all go to met Him by-and-by!"

The audience loved it. Soon everyone was singing, clapping, and enjoying themselves. My sister and I joined in, singing right along with our mother. When she finished the first song, Ms. Emily began another one and the chorus rose as we all sang along with her. The round of singing seemed to go on for quite a while. When everyone had joined in singing at least one song they knew, Ms. Emily paused, lowered her voice and bowed her head. Silence fell over the crowd. Slowly, fainter than a whisper, Ms. Emily lifted her voice until we could all hear the incantations of "Amazing Grace."

My mother had taught us that song. We had heard it every Sunday morning at church. The kids even sang it in our Sunday Bible School classes. As the chorus rose and we all joined in, I noticed a solemn, calmness settle in over the crowd. Men and women sang in unison with a somber resolve and deliberate purpose. Unlike the opening joyfulness, the tone of this song was different. No one seemed to mind that the mood had changed. My sister stood motionless staring at our mother. As I turned, I noticed the tears streaming down Mother's face.

"Amazing grace, how sweet the sound, that saved a wretch like me…"

The words trailed off into the balmy air. I watched my sister and my mother enthralled in the singing, unaware or not caring at all, as the tears streamed down their faces. If you have ever sat in the back of a church and listened to the chorus of solemn voices raised in unison praising the Lord, then you know how I felt watching my mother and my sister touched by the spirit bringing the good news.

Finally, Ms. Emily stopped singing. Then, she looked around at the crowd and back at the minister. The minister raised the Bible in his hand and asked everyone to bow their heads as he prayed. I wanted to see what he was going to do next, so I raised mine. My mother squeezed my left hand and I quickly put my head down.

When the prayer was over, the minister told everyone to be seated. Then, Ms. Emily stepped forward, welcomed us all, and introduced Pastor McClendon. Pastor McClendon thanked everyone for coming and immediately began serving up the good news. He read from the Bible and explained the meanings to all of us as we listened to him. Some of the older men in the crowd said "Amen!" as he accentuated passages of his sermon. The ladies waved their fans to shake up the balmy air and keep away the late evening mosquitoes. The pastor preached on for what seemed like a day and a half.

Then, at the end of a roaring crescendo, he shook the Bible in the air, and proclaimed, "We are all God's children and He wants you to know He loves you!"

A loud chorus of, "Amen! Amen! Amen!" followed. We had just heard the Good News.

For the next four weeks, my sister and I spent every Thursday evening at the Williams'. The missionaries didn't waste any time teaching us to sing the Good News Song.

"On time, on time to good news school today,

On time, on time you must not stay away..."

We read from the good book and learned to recite Bible verses, which we shared with our family and friends. The more we learned about the love of God, the less different we felt in our good news school. It didn't seem to bother the white missionaries that we were black. After a while, it didn't seem to bother me that they were white. They told us that God loves all the little children. They didn't say red, yellow, black, and white. I expect that version came later, but they did make us feel welcome and that was unusual for both the place and times.

Maybe that was the lesson. Although we were in a segregated state and in a separate community just for people of color, it didn't matter to the white missionaries and it didn't matter to God. If you have ever wondered why people of color are able to accept the Good News story of salvation, even from someone who doesn't look like them, perhaps as a child they experienced uncommon love and shared a mutual respect with messengers bringing the Good News.

First Day Ever at the Pool

I managed to make two really good friends in a short period of time. I was like that. Since we moved so often, I had to work fast to get acclimated to each new neighborhood. My new friends were Freddie and Walter. Freddie was older. He seemed to know what he was doing and the other kids usually followed his lead. Walter was closer to my age. He was a bit on the heavy side, but we got along just fine. Walter had a way of making you feel comfortable when he was around. He was always eager to answer my questions and I liked that. He helped me get to know the other kids a lot quicker than I would have on my own.

Freddie was always asking us if we wanted to go swimming at the community pool. He was willing to take us if we said yes. I couldn't swim and chose not to take him up on his offer. He didn't seem to mind at first but, after a while, he started teasing me about it. I tried my best to ignore him and that worked for the first few months. It wasn't until the dog days of summer really hit us that the idea of getting into a cool swimming pool seemed like a really good one.

I asked Walter about the kids at the pool. He didn't seem to mind telling me about all of the fun they seemed to be having playing in the water. He didn't swim either, but he could float, and he usually stayed near the shallow end where he could manage all right. Swimming was a subject I preferred to avoid discussing. On top of that, going to the pool for the first time was an outing I was somewhat afraid to pursue. In spite of the nagging feeling in my stomach, I pressed on. Walter's admission to limited swimming skills encouraged me.

"So what do they do at the pool?" I asked.

"Oh. They play a lot of games," Walter offered. "They even toss balls around in the water. Sometimes I join in but, most of the time, I just watch."

The honest comment Walter made about watching the other kids play fit him perfectly. He was definitely not a risk taker. After hearing his admission, I began to feel even better about the invitation to join the guys at the pool. After I inquired whether there was a lifeguard on duty all of the time and Walter assured me there was, I began to warm to the idea. Walter described how the lifeguard usually sits in a big chair and blows his whistle if the kids start horsing around too much. I didn't quite understand what Walter meant by the term horsing around, so I asked him to explain it.

Walter leaped at the opportunity to explain how they rode on each other's backs and then tried to pull the other guy down off of his horse. That didn't sound like something I would be anxious to get into but seeing the broad smile on Walter's face made it clear that he thought it was fun. I wondered if the guys always had that much fun in the water. I peppered Walter with a series of questions about his antics at the swimming pool.

Walter answered my questions eagerly. I believe he could tell I was warming to the idea of going swimming with them. Walter finally told me that the best thing about swimming for him was what they did when they finished. He said that they all get together and go to Charlie's Grill for hot dogs!

It sounded too good to be true. That's when I felt that nagging feeling in my stomach again. I wondered if the lifeguards really knew what they were doing. I wanted to ask how often they rescued people. Walter sensed my hesitation. I could see his mind searching for something to say that would convince me to go. That was when he began telling me about the lifeguards keeping everything in check. He even claimed that sometimes if the guys go too far horsing around, the lifeguard will blow his whistle really loudly. If they don't stop then, he might throw all of them out of the pool. Walter smiled when he said that, as if he were reliving an episode he had been involved in himself.

"Have you ever been thrown out of the pool?" I asked. Walter didn't reply right away, but when he finally did he assured me that he always tried to keep his distance from those kinds of shenanigans. I liked the way Walter described his approach to avoiding the horseplay. I believed I could do a lot worse than going to the pool for the first time with a friend like Walter. It was that resolution which caused me to change my mind and decide to say alright the next time that Freddie asked me to join them at the pool.

It was a normal sunny day in August and the wind had decided to take a vacation. The hot, humid air seemed to just hang there, a few feet above our heads, waiting for a breeze to come along. It could have waited all summer because we were not feeling it. The heat sapped our strength and left all of us sweating with our tongues hanging out. It was so bad even the ice cream man took a break and stayed home.

Walter and I were sitting on the porch trying to keep cool when Freddie appeared. He immediately began complaining that he was burning up and asked if we wanted to go to the pool. Walter looked disinterested. After all, it was a long walk to get to the section of town where the pool was located. You had to pass the corner store at the bottom of the hill, walk uphill to the local gas station, cross the street in front of the post office, pass the library, go through the main square, and then walk through the school yard before you got to the pool. After a few minutes of haggling, however, Walter gave in and decided he would go with Freddie to the pool.

"Are you in Nathaniel?" Freddie asked. Nathaniel was what Freddie called me when he wanted to get under my skin. It was my middle name. I rarely heard it used by itself and the way he used it always annoyed me. I wasn't looking forward to the long walk, but a dip in the water seemed to be a really good idea given the sweltering heat wave we were under. I told them I would see if my mother would let me go and promised to meet them back there in fifteen minutes. Freddie couldn't help needling me a little more. He warned me not to be late or Walter and he would leave without me. I assured both of them that I would be right back. I didn't want them leaving me and then coming back telling me what a great time they had.

I hurried home to ask my mother the loaded question. She knew I couldn't swim; neither could she. It had been a sore subject with her for a while. It seems her brothers dunked her in the pond once and she never forgave them for it. I hoped she would be in a good mood because, this time, I really wanted to go. I found my mother in the kitchen. She was peeling potatoes for supper. That was a job I liked to do when she let me. I would have offered to help her finish peeling them, but I knew I would be late if I did.

"Mom, can I go to the swimming pool with the guys? I asked.

She turned around slowly and gave me a long look. I could tell by her hesitation that she was wondering what guys I was talking about. I quickly filled in the gaps by telling her Freddie and Walter had invited me to join them for a swim at the pool. She took a long pause and then turned back around to finish peeling the potatoes. I could tell my mother was thinking about it. She was weighing all the possibilities. She answered in a measured voice.

"I expect you to be home for dinner," she said. "Be careful and don't be horsing around, you hear?"

I answered, "Yes, ma'am." Then, I turned quickly and ran out of the door to catch up with the guys. I let the words sink in that she had said not to horse around. They would come back to haunt me later. I was half-way to Walter's house when I realized I had forgotten to put on my swimming trunks. Quickly, I turned and ran back to the house only to find my mother holding them in her hands waiting for me. She smiled and I smiled back at her. I could always count on my mother to know what to do in any circumstance. She was a true earth mother, and earth mothers rarely let you down. I believe she thought I would forget my ears if they weren't attached to either side of my face. I yelled good-bye and then ran as fast as I could to catch up to the guys.

They hadn't gone very far before I spotted them. They seemed amused that I was panting as I scrambled to catch up with them. Freddie gave me a 'you look ridiculous' look as I slowed down, bent over and grabbed my stomach, trying to catch my breath. When I complained to the guys for leaving me behind, neither Freddie nor Walter responded; instead, both of them kept walking, ignoring me altogether. I tried to convince the guys that I hadn't been that late. Freddie just stared straight ahead while Walter peeked at me and smiled.

"Gotcha," Freddie said. They both started laughing at me. I laughed too. It was a mean joke, but they were my friends. Freddie pushed me on one shoulder and Walter responded by pushing me back on the other. I responded with a yell and that just edged them on. Walter squeezed in and then so did Freddie. Soon I felt like a baloney sandwich someone had sat on at the park. I pleaded with the guys to let up, but Freddie just laughed and Walter hooted. I finally managed to break free. Then, we all locked arms and strolled down the middle of the street with not a care in the world.

It was a long walk to get to the section of town where the pool was located. We had left around midday, so it was hot. Walter began sweating and he wiped the perspiration off his face with the back of his hand. We had barely gotten to the top of the hill, when I spotted the corner store below. It was a welcome sight to all of us. The fan would be blowing inside and they had cool drinks to sell. We gleefully skipped our way down the hill in a hurry to get to the store and out of the sun.

The wonderful smells of baked bread, fresh strawberries, pineapples, peaches, and persimmons whiffed heavily through the air as we scrambled into the store. The heavy screen door slammed noisily behind us and the tepid breeze from the store fan washed across our faces. If you have ever spent an afternoon riding on a bus with no air conditioning then you know how good we felt when those air currents from the circulating fan met our faces.

Freddy walked up to the store counter and began talking with the cute girl who worked there on weekdays during the summer. Her name was Gloria. She was sporting a sassy ponytail. I don't believe she noticed how much Freddie liked her, but he really hoped she would. Gloria was a few grades above us all. I think she was in high school. She had a cute way of leaning closer to ask a question. She would pop her big wad of bubble gum noisily from time to time. Freddie pointed to the cooler and asked Gloria if they had any cold root beer. She shook her head slightly as her way of saying yes, and he strolled over to the upright cooler to take a look.

Walter fell into a trance once we entered the store. He headed straight for the circulating fan and hadn't left the spot. I followed Freddie over to take a look at the sodas in the cooler. The shiny white cooler top opened and Freddie dipped his long arm into the churning water. He felt around for a second and then lifted a root beer out of the water and high into the air. The cold water droplets from the bottle streamed down Freddie's arm like a speeding bobsled on a trial run. When I asked Freddie if they had any orange soda, he assured me that they did. He smiled when he pointed to the churning water and described the ice-cold, Nehi orange sodas in the bottom of the cooler.

I made the mistake of asking Freddie to get it for me, and he shoved a hand in my face and told me to get it myself. I reached down into the cold, gurgling water and searched frantically to find my orange soda. The water was really cold and I couldn't see anything but the tops of the bottles. It took me a while, and a few wrong guesses, to finally land a Nehi orange soda. My fingers were tingling, when I finally brought it up. The water droplets splashed onto my bare feet, and the water felt awfully good as the droplets oozed between my toes.

"Are you going to buy that soda or just stand there and look at it?" Gloria chimed.

I was thoroughly embarrassed as I scrounged through my pants pocket to find my nickel. When I finally handed it to her, she gave me a funny look. I wanted to ask if something was wrong, but I was too afraid to open my mouth.

Then Gloria asked, "Did you dress yourself?"

I responded with a puzzled look.

She continued, "You put your shirt on backwards."

The guys laughed. I was so embarrassed that I nearly dropped my orange soda. Gloria laughed, too.

Freddie looked like he was ashamed to be seen with me. He looked over at Gloria and she smiled at him. I was always in a hurry and often looked like a mess, but I hadn't intended to be an embarrassment for Freddie. Gloria seemed to sense my dilemma and dropped her eyes to avoid further embarrassing me. After that, she always took time to talk with Freddie whenever we came into the store. I think I was Freddie's icebreaker. Walter bought himself a strawberry pop and some juicy fruit candies. We said good-bye and headed out toward the pool again.

We crossed the street in front of the local gas station. The old, sour faced hound dog that lived there looked up as we passed, but he was too lazy to bark at us. He lay quietly soaking up the little bit of shade on the corner of the station next to the tall spruce. We never knew why anyone would want to keep a dog around that was so lazy. I don't think we saw him run, jump, or even roll over a single time. Word had it that he used to be a great hunting dog in his day. He could tree a possum in no time. He even won a local contest for the station owner for the most quail rousted, shot, and bagged in a single

Saturday afternoon. If you have an old dog lying around your neighborhood, you might want to find out what he used to be good for.

Walter was getting tired. He no longer kept up with us. The further we went, the further behind he fell. Freddie yelled at him a couple of times, but I encouraged him to keep going. We weren't that far from the pool. We crossed at the corner and then walked pass the local post office. A couple of blocks later, we were at the local library where Freddie's aunt cleaned the bookshelves after hours. Aunt Wilda was a large, pleasant woman who wore speckled eyeglasses. She was also a Sunday school teacher at the Baptist church on Freeman Avenue. Freddie sometimes stopped at the library to say hello, but today he was in a hurry to get into the cool water at the pool.

The bronze statue of a confederate soldier stood in the middle of the town square. It was a little rusted from the weather, but it stood as tall as any horse and rider I had ever seen. The scabbard and blade strapped to the soldier's side shone brightly in the afternoon sun. His pancake flop hat was tilted to the side and he stared straight ahead into the future. Little did he know how much change he would see in his lifetime.

We reached the schoolyard and Walter slipped into the seat on one of the swings to stop and catch his breath. Freddie frowned at Walter for a second, but then shrugged. He leaned against one of the large maple trees and tried to catch a little shade himself. I sat on one of the kids' rocking horses and nearly burned the skin off of my leg.

"Owww, it's hot!" I cried.

"No joke," Freddie laughed. "Why don't you try sitting on your swimming trunks?"

I whimpered and quickly I slipped them under me. The soft silk felt a lot better than the hot metal seat of the rocking horse. I eased into the seat and leaned back against the supports. The faint summer clouds were all aglow with reds, yellows, and azure blues as the sun sprinkled its magical rays across the sky. A bunch of turkey buzzards swirled overhead. Each one seemed to be trying to outdo the other by catching sudden wind updrafts, carrying them higher and higher. The playground was empty, quiet and peaceful. The day was almost perfect. I should have known it wouldn't last. The whole experience was over in a few minutes. Freddie waved his arms in the air and bobbed his head to one side. We trudged behind him on to our final destination at the pool.

As we turned the corner on Booker T. Washington Boulevard, we could hear the growing commotion ahead of us long before we could see the pool. It was a combination of screams, shouts, shrieks, and uncontrolled laughter. The sounds mimicked an all night party, except these were sober young people, not a crowd of raucous, drunk adults. I began to get an uneasy feeling deep down in my stomach. The more I tried to ignore it, the more pronounced it became.

When Walter asked me if I was going to be all right, I answered softly under my breath. I willed myself to just stay calm and follow Walter's lead. He'd been to the pool before and I knew he wouldn't let me down. Freddie got excited when he realized we were finally close enough to see the pool. The water looked so good!

"I'm going to make the biggest splash you have ever seen," Walter blurted out. "I bet all our friends are here. I can't wait to dunk 'um!"

The jubilation of my two friends was more than I could bear. While they were looking forward to splashing and dunking in the water, I was frightened beyond anyone's imagination.

The next half an hour was a complete blur. My entire body trembled. I felt myself swirling around like the birds. I began to feel sick in my stomach and faint in my head. I lurched, stumbled, and then crashed into Walter. Unaware of the depth of my trauma, Walter turned abruptly and pushed me back. That's when I realized I had been walking with my eyes closed.

I forced myself to open them only to gaze in shock at the most unforgettable sight in my life. There in front of me, less than fifty yards away, was a sea of screaming black and brown faces, jumping up and down in the water and shouting at the top of their lungs. My mind visualized a huge hornet's nest. I had disturbed it and now every one of the hornets was buzzing and gyrating wildly, jumping up in the air and looking around trying to find me.

Walter urged me to come on and complained that I was making them late. With that admonishment, he turned and took off at a gallop towards the pool. I was frozen in my tracks. It was all I could do to drag one foot behind the other until I reached the fence. When Walter looked back, he saw me clinging to the fence staring in amazement at all the commotion. I don't know how, but he sensed something was wrong. He looked at the screaming kids in the pool and back at me. Without saying a word, he reversed his direction and didn't stop until he was standing beside me next to the fence. He looked at me, and then he looked down at his feet. He didn't say a word.

Freddie took off running towards the gate leaving Walter and me standing near the fence. Soon, we saw him emerge from the shower covered with shiny droplets of water. He plunged into the pool and disappeared. For a moment, my worst fears had been realized. Then, Freddie reappeared from the depths of the water near the other end of the pool and let out a huge yell. He was all right. I was so relieved. I sunk down next to the fence to regain my composure.

Walter asked if I wanted him to stay there with me. Then, he rested his fat left hand on my shoulder. I told him to go ahead and swim with his friends.

"I'll be all right. I was just going to sit there and watch," I said.

Walter shrugged and studied me for a moment. I could see the recognition in his eyes. He knew exactly what I was feeling. He seemed to understand. I guess he hadn't forgotten that he had felt the same way about a new experience not so long ago.

Walter gave me a slight pat on the head and then handed me one of his juicy fruit candies from the store. He told me that it would keep my energy level up until he came back. Then, he turned and ran towards the gate to the pool. I crouched into a shaded area near the fence and watched Freddie and Walter enjoying themselves swimming and splashing in the water. Seeing them having so much fun actually calmed my stomach. Before I realized it, I was no longer in a trauma.

A half an hour later, Freddie came over to the fence and asked me if I wanted to come in. I told him that I wasn't ready yet and thanked him for asking. My heart must not have been in it because he stooped to get a good look at me. I couldn't see his eyes because mine were full of tears. I don't know what turned them on, but I couldn't turn them off. Freddie sighed.

"Wait here," Freddie ordered. "I'm going to get Walter and I'll be right back."

I lifted my right hand to let him know I heard him and then dropped my head back down into my lap. Freddie walked off, entered the gate, and then disappeared into the pool house. A few minutes later, Walter opened the gate to exit the pool. He trudged silently behind Freddie, with his head hung down, looking at his bare feet.

When he reached me, he smiled and said, "Come on, Nathaniel. We're going home."

The Boy Scouts "Teach Me a Lesson"

My friends Freddie and Walter were not the only influences in my life during my stay in Georgia. I was young and rather impressionable. I lacked much of the worldly experience that others kids seemed to possess, but that didn't keep me from trying to fit in. I watched the boys wrestle and shadow box. I tried my hand at both, but I couldn't get the hang of either. Then, one summer a really cool kid arrived on our block. He was a few years older than most of us and he had a swagger that you couldn't miss.

Rubin was a special guy. His dad was a Marine in the Special Forces and he carried himself like he knew it. His hair was curly for a colored boy and he had light hazel-colored eyes. He was moderate in height and sported huge, over developed biceps on both arms. His silky smooth eyebrows spread liberally across his face, veering slightly up then down. He had a chiseled nose and a rock-solid chin that had the nerve to be dimpled. His smile was infectious, at least for all the girls. They swooned over him like he was a luscious, banana sundae. Maybe it was the sweet smelling cologne he wore or the hush puppy shoes. Whatever it was, I wanted it. I doubt that he ever knew, but Rubin was definitely my idol.

From the moment I saw him and heard the girls gossiping about him behind his back, I wanted to trade places. He was the envy of all the guys. His soft-spoken, gentle demeanor caught us all off guard. We had no come back for his confident swagger or his style. He was in a league all his own. We followed him from corner to corner, like a starry-eyed bunch of groupies. The girls formed a solid ring around him. We guys trailed behind them trying not to look too obvious. It didn't matter to Rubin. He seemed to be in his own world just enjoying walking and sharing laughs with his entourage.

Soon after Rubin appeared, I began a nightly ritual of rotating my arms and doing push-ups to strengthen my biceps. I didn't know if it would work, but I did know I wanted to look more like Rubin and less like me. I kept the whole routine to myself, not telling a soul. My mom noticed my eagerness to turn in early and wondered if I was all right. I assured her I was fine, and quickly went to my room to take up my exercise routine. This went on for a few months, and then the summer was over, and Rubin headed back with his family to Camp Pendleton. I expected I would miss him, so I promised myself I would keep up the exercise routine in his memory. That summer experience, which increased my awareness of my physical shortcomings, also started me on my way to self-improvement. It would be one of many awakenings that had a lasting effect on my life.

After Rubin left, the summer seemed somewhat uneventful. The guys lay around and talked about what they were going to do when they grew up. One kid was going to be a jockey and ride in the derby. Another kid wanted to buy a farm and plant corn, beans, and collards. When we asked him what he was going to do with all those vegetables, he said he was going to eat them. It didn't seem like any career path I wanted to follow. When the fellows finally got around to asking me what I wanted to be, I told them an officer in the Army.

"So you want to be a big shot in the Army, huh?" Freddie chuckled. "I bet you've never even been on a camp out."

That got me a little riled up, but I tried to stay calm. When Freddie asked if I had any idea of what kind of soldier I was going to be, I snapped, "Sure I do, but I'm not going to tell you about it."

I didn't expect what came next. Freddie told me he and Walter were going to the boy scouts that night. He dared me to come with them. I asked him about what time they were leaving and Freddie indicated that they were going around six-thirty. He suggested that I meet them at the corner near the big oak tree and added that I should bring a gym bag and some rope.

"Alright," I replied. Then, with some hesitation, asked "What is the rope for?"

"I knew it," Freddie laughed.

He was sure I had probably never tied a square knot before, but he knew that I had better be ready to learn. I left Freddie and the guys standing on the corner. With that last remark ringing in my ears, I headed home. My mother was busy drying the dishes, and she looked up suddenly. She was surprised to see me come in so early.

She asked me if everything was all right, and I assured her it was. I told her I had just come in to look for some things so I would be ready for the scouts later that evening. She looked a little surprised, but I believe she felt the scouts might be a good place for a young man to learn a few things. She asked me what kind of things I might need her to help me find.

I told her not to bother because I could handle it myself. I hustled off to my room to do a round of push-ups. I finished my workout and then began looking for some rope. I found a three-foot section of clothes line, which I thought would be perfect for tying knots. I put it in my blue gym bag, with a small towel and a few pieces of licorice. Then I hurried to the kitchen to tell my mother that I was off to the scouts meeting and would be home around 8:30. Mom didn't look up until I mentioned the time we were returning. When she asked me why the meeting was so late in the evening, I really couldn't give her a good answer. I told her I thought it was because Freddie's dad was going to take us after work, and they had to wait until he ate his dinner.

I was making it all up on the fly, and Mom seemed to suspect something wasn't right. I know she wanted to ask me if I had talked with Freddie's dad, and if he had said it was all right for me to ride with them. I tried to head off the question by adding that Freddie asked me to come, and he thinks that I could learn a lot about scouting, and it could help prepare me to become an officer in the Army. My mom looked like I had just slapped her in the face. She didn't say anything right away, but she paused to ponder my words. It was the first time she had ever heard me verbalize a career choice for my future, and I suspect it wasn't the one she had in mind for me.

Finally, she spoke. She would talk with Freddie's mom and see if she believed it would be all right for me to go with her boys to scouting. I waited by the door. It didn't take long for Mom to complete her call. Apparently, Freddie's mom said it was OK, because my mom gave me a big hug, told me to be careful, and to come straight home after the meeting.

I sprang off the porch and hurried across the yard to meet the fellows at the corner. I waited so long that I thought I had gotten the time mixed up. Finally, Freddie's dad pulled up a half an hour later. I thanked him for letting me go and climbed into the back seat with Walter. I suspected we were late, but I didn't want to make any waves so I didn't say anything about it.

We crossed the main highway, rolled over the railroad tracks, and raced towards the old Little League baseball field. The local baseball team used it as a clubhouse and the boy scouts met there when the team was away. I had seen the fellows in their snappy, blue uniforms and often wondered what they did as scouts. I guess I was finally going to find out. Freddie thanked his dad for giving us a ride. We all jumped out of the car and ran towards the clubhouse.

Our entrance must have caused a commotion because everyone turned to look at us. The Scoutmaster was a stout, stocky man who greeted us with a bristling scowl on his face. He looked at Freddie and then over at me as if he were about to toss me out on my ears.

"Who's this," the Scoutmaster barked. Freddie hung his head sheepishly and told him my name was Bernard. The Scoutmaster scowled and asked Freddie what I was doing in his clubhouse? When Freddie realized he didn't have a good answer for that one, he didn't say anything at all. The Scoutmaster looked at Walter, and asked him if he knew me well. Walter responded by telling him that I wanted to become a scout and grow up to join the Army. That response seemed to soften the look on the Scoutmaster's face. He smirked, rubbed his chin, and told us to get in line with all the other boys. Then he shouted, "That means you too, Bernard!"

I jumped to do what he said. Walter and Freddie followed close on my heels. The rest of the evening was a blur. The Scoutmaster separated the boys into two groups and then he told the ones in line with me to wait over by the door. There were seven of us, including Freddie, Walter and me. Several of the boys began shaking, and I wondered what they were afraid of. I didn't have to wonder very long.

The Scoutmaster hollered for us to take off our shirts, as he separated the other boys into two three-foot wide lines stretching across the room. I looked at Walter, but he just hung his head as he pulled at his shirt that was stuck around his elbow. I thought I saw the beginnings of a few small tears, but I hoped I was imagining it. Freddie pulled his t-shirt over his head and then helped Walter remove his. No one said a word as we stood there naked from the waist up.

"You boys are late," the Scoutmaster barked, "and now you're going to have to pay the penalty." He turned towards the other boys in the line and shouted, "What's our motto boys'?"

They all answered that it was to always be on time sir! He barked at them again and got the same answer a lot louder. It was then I realized what was about to happen. Each of the boys took off his belt and wrapped the buckle around his wrist.

The Scoutmaster pointed to the first boy in front of me and said, "Get your sorry, black a...s through the line!"

With that order, the kid covered his face, and began shuffling his feet through the gauntlet of belts lashing his back and slashing around his head.

I froze in my tracks. This couldn't be happening. This was The Boy Scouts, not a prison camp. What was wrong with these people? Why had the Scoutmaster gotten these boys so riled up that they would try to hurt us over being a few minutes late? Before I could answer my own questions, Freddie bumped into me and whispered for me to get going so we could get it over with. I sprang forward and the lashes began stinging my body. I could feel every one of them. They felt like a razor blade slicing large swatches of meat off of my bones. Then, I felt a thunk and realized someone had hit me with a belt buckle squarely on my head. I cursed under my breath and was relieved to know that, through all the slashing, no one had actually heard me.

I pressed on until the end and then leaned against the far wall to catch my breath. The sweat started pouring off of me and the salty water streamed into my welts, stung my arms, singed my back and caused

79

swelling in the soft tissue around my eyelids. Freddie stood beside me, while Walter slumped on his shoulder. Freddie leaned over to whisper something to Walter and then straightened up right away. Freddie turned slightly as the Scoutmaster barked, "Do it again."

This time Freddie led the line. He looked back over his shoulders at us and gave a faint nod. We understood what he wanted but it didn't make it any easier to do. The Scoutmaster seemed angry because we took longer than he wanted to get started, so he ordered all of the guys in the line to unbuckle. I didn't know what that meant, but I was sure I wouldn't like it. Freddie surged forward with his arms shielding his face. Walter followed, pressing as close to his brother as he could. I was next in line followed by the four other boys who were all moaning now under the deluge.

It seemed to take forever to get through the line so I was grateful when I saw we were near the end. I shouldn't have looked up. A kid hit me across my face and the buckle slashed the corner of my eye. I felt the blood trickle down as I staggered and reached for Walter to steady myself. Walter didn't look back as I leaned against him and struggled to get to the end of the gauntlet. I don't know how I made it. I don't recall who handed me the tissue, but I held it close to my face and tried to steady myself. Everything was swirling now. I felt faint and watched as my body was slowly lifted off the floor. They sat me down in a corner where another small, wiry-looking man, who I learned later was a medical technician in the Army, checked my vital signs. Once he gave the OK sign to the Scoutmaster, everyone backed away and left me alone.

They must have decided to go on with the meeting. I don't know. I dozed off and can't remember a thing that happened after that. Finally, Freddie shook me and I awoke to a light being shined in my face. I squinted to see who was holding the light, and I saw the Scoutmaster standing over me. It was time to go. He motioned for a few of the fellows to help me to my feet. I got up slowly and stretched and squared my shoulders. I looked straight ahead and walked, on my own, towards the exit door at the far end of the room. Freddie appeared beside me. Walter wasn't far behind. Together, we left the building and crossed the street to wait for Walter's dad to pick us up. While we waited, no one said a word. When Walter's dad arrived, I climbed into the back seat and pretended to be asleep. Freddie made small talk as his dad drove us home. Walter helped me get out of the car and walked with me to the house. He sighed once, but he didn't speak to me until we were at the front porch.

"Sorry," Walter said, not looking up to see how I was taking it. "I guess scouting can be hard sometimes. I should have warned you."

I told him it was alright. He took his and I took mine, so I guess we both passed the test. Being a soldier wouldn't be easy either, but at least I believed if I were captured, I could survive. With those stoic thoughts swimming in my head, I climbed the steps, opened the door and disappeared into my sanctuary, where no one was waiting to teach me a lesson.

Chapter 4: Moving Onto the Post

Clearing Quarters

I remember the weekend we all celebrated Dad's promotion and the benefits that would come with it. He had finished another round of military school classes and was given a new title and privileges. Our dad had qualified for on post housing for himself and for his family. We learned that we would be moving the very next weekend.

Our mom was elated. She pranced around the house like a proud peacock. You would have thought she had earned that promotion, not my dad. Her happiness was infectious. We all took part and pranced around the room with her. The entire weekend was one long party. Mom and Dad invited all of their friends over to the house to celebrate. They bought hamburgers and cooked out on the grill. They set up card tables and the adults smacked pinochle cards on tabletops past midnight.

We kids had a good time, too. With little or no supervision, we were free to spend the night any way we chose. We formed teams and played lots of games. We played Red Rover, Red Rover, running back and forth and crashing into the other team's arms until they felt like they would collapse. We played Steal the Bacon, a game where you had to snatch a handkerchief off the ground and run to safety. To be fair, we switched players to even the sides and made sure the younger kids competed against each other. The object of the games was to have fun, not necessarily beat the other team. The older kids kept everything in line, so nobody ever got too upset about the outcome.

As night fell, we switched to playing shadow games. We borrowed a flash light and made huge shadows against the side of the house. Kids cheered as their friends imitated images of elephants, horses and bears. The most popular and easiest image to make was a floppy-eared rabbit.

After making shadow images, we played hide-and-go-seek. The kids were very comfortable now with Willie being the home free judge. He would sit at the base of the tree and call out "free" whenever a kid managed to touch the tree before being tagged. The honor was so special to him that he would squeal if anyone got caught. That would let us all know not to try to come home yet.

When it finally got too dark to play in the yard, we all sat down on and near the porch and listened to big kids talk, usually about the girls.

"You know she like you," one of the boys would say.

"No, she doesn't," the other one would answer, "but I heard you tried to talk to her. So what's up with that?"

This conversation went on for some time as each one of the boys tried to outdo the other with his version of the truth. Of course, the girls were talking about the boys in their little corner, too. One of the girls would say that one of the boys thinks he's so cute and her friend would add that she thought so too. Then they would go back and forth with comments like how he likes one of them so much and if you like him so much, why don't you tell him.

Someone would add that they had heard one of the boys say he liked a girl at the candy store. After that exchange, all the girls would giggle and the boys would strain their ears to hear what all the commotion was about. The more the girls giggled, the more curious the boys became. It was a perfect evening of he says, she says fun and games. My sister hung out with the girls. I would hear bits and pieces of the giggle-provoking conversations from her later. The perfect night could have lasted longer but, eventually, it came to an end. The parents and their children left for their homes, and we went inside to get a good night's sleep for the next day's activities. If you have lived in a military house when it's time to move, then you know exactly what I'm talking about. It's the ritual of "clearing quarters."

Every child in the house has assigned chores on a regular weekend but, just before a move, the "to do" lists gets so much longer. Instead of scrubbing and waxing the kitchen floor, I now had to scrub, wax and buff the bedrooms, hall, kitchen and front room. My sister had to clean all of the dishes and help Mom wrap them in newspaper and pack them into boxes for the move. That exercise always took a lot longer to complete than you might think. My mom, who is given to sweet bouts of nostalgia, would take her time and spin yarns about all of the special china pieces she wrapped prior to tucking them into a box one-at-a-time for shipping. I always thought my sister encouraged her, so she would take longer to finish the job. That left me as the one Dad assigned all of the extra tasks before we moved.

The hardest chore to complete was cleaning the stove. We would scrub all of the gas eyelets and grill covers until they were shiny and bright. If you have ever cleaned a greasy barbecue grill, then you know what we had to do to get years of grease off of those stove top parts. That task seemed to always find its way to my list. No matter how many floors I did, or how many bathrooms I cleaned, the stove was mine to do. As time passed, I learned to do it without much complaining. Eventually, I became very proud of my role as the lead member of the stove cleaning team. Of all the items on the quarters cleaning list, failure to properly clean the kitchen stove was the one most likely to cause a family to fail to clear quarters. You never wanted to have that failure on your dad's record, and I worked very hard to be sure I wasn't the one to place it there.

When the day came to clear quarters, we all waited outside as the inspection team went through our former home with a fine-tooth comb. All items sighted as "needing further attention" were referred to my dad. We were fortunate; no major items were checked as deficient. We cleared quarters. Now that we were homeless, we needed a place to stay for the night. My dad found us one at a small motel near the south end of town.

Mom had packed ham sandwiches for dinner. The sandwiches were slices of brown sugar ham on home baked rolls. Mom had baked leavened bread (rolls) for Sunday dinner and then used the dough that was left over to make cinnamon rolls for our dessert. We shared the remaining portions of macaroni and cheese with our ham sandwiches. None of these items needed to be refrigerated or heated for us to enjoy. Mom was just good at what she did and we trusted her to know exactly what to do to care for all of us during the move. True to the "Earth Mother" she was, she guided us through the process, again and again, with ease and grace. We benefited very much from her sensible, country knowledge, which she used to feed and care for us all. After a grueling day clearing quarters, my dad finally collapsed on the bed and we sat on the floor with Mom playing a card game, I declare War!

Meeting the New Neighbors

Monday morning was a special day for all of us. We rose early and piled into the family car for the trip to our new home. It was a forty-five minute drive and the chatter in the car was lively.

"When will I get to see Freddie and Walter again?" I asked. "I'm going to miss them a lot."

This wasn't the first time we had moved, but this was the first time I had made two good friends. The thought of leaving them hurt. My mother tried to play her conciliatory role by reminding me that we would see them at church. That didn't help much. My sister looked unsympathetic; she was tired of all my whining. After all, she hadn't made many friends since we moved the last time and she sure wasn't going to miss mine.

"Are there any girls where we are going?" my sister asked.

She was beginning to warm up to the idea of meeting someone new. My dad leaned backwards and smiled at her. Then, my mother assured my sister that there would be some girls she could play with when we got to our new home. My sister began humming a little tune softly at the thought of having girls her own age to play with. For the first time in quite a while, she looked contented. I guess that's what happens when you find there's going to be someone who will understand you for a change.

We finally arrived at the entrance to the army post. A modern day sentry in full military armor, complete with hat, gun, boots, and all, guarded the entrance to the gate. The guard motioned for us to stop and Dad reached under the sun visor to retrieve his military credentials. He handed them to the Military Policeman (MP) and waited to be cleared for entry. The MP checked a list of names on his clipboard before poking his head into the car to check us out and get a head count.

The MP was clean-shaven and dressed as neatly as any soldier I had ever seen. His khakis uniform was starched and the brass on his lapels was shiny and bright. His hair was cut short and edged so finely that his hairline faded into his scalp. He wore dark sunshades and a trooper's hat with a spit-shined hat brim that narrowly hid his eyebrows. When he handed my dad's credentials back to him, I imagined his fingernails were cut to the quick and clean as a whistle, but I couldn't tell because he wore white gloves. Dad thanked him and, without saying a word, the MP waived us through.

The long, winding road to our destination was coming to a close. The trees lined the entry way and neatly cut branches waved at us as we passed by. It was a perfect day and the windows to the car were down. We could smell the honeysuckle spilling over the bushes that lined the road. We passed the transportation depot or motor pool, where all the jeeps, trucks and heavy hauling equipment were kept. We crossed over the underpass, and got a marvelous glimpse of the neatly arranged rows of whitewashed barracks that lined the roadway beyond.

We could see the parade field where my dad would assemble for early morning inspections. Far beyond the horizon were similar fields of neatly dressed young men, who were up before dawn, ready and waiting to be evaluated, drilled, and trained. As I grew older, I would hear the burgle sound in the morning and jump out of bed myself to begin my day, just like my dad. It was a tradition that would follow me, years later, all the way to military camp in Pennsylvania. The rigor of army life was ingrained in me early. I would carry those lessons with me for the rest of my life.

It wasn't long after we began winding our way along that spacious, tree-lined highway, that we saw the entryway for a section of stately looking residences. These grand palaces, as we would come to call them, were reserved for the Post Commander and members of his elite staff. These were residences for the Army Officers who gave the orders and planned the strategies for battle. My dad took a long look at the main entrance to the officer's quarters and a momentary sadness came over his face. It lingered just a short while. He raised his head and looked upward and sighed. My mom reached across the front seat and touched his hand gently. It was all she could do to console him. The entire episode lasted less than a few seconds, but I knew it was a significant flashback to a chapter in their lives. It would be years before I would learn the secret of my dad's sorrow.

"I want you to promise me something, Buddy," my dad blurted out. "Are you listening to me?"

I sat up straight and prepared to answer him as truthfully as I could.

"I want you to promise me that you will become an officer in the U. S. Army when you grow up to be a man. I don't want you to settle. I want you to be the very best. Can you promise me that?"

I had no comeback except to take the challenge. I knew it was a special request because my dad had asked me in front of the entire family. I assured him that I would do my best to honor his request. I promised to make him proud of me and I promised to be the best officer ever. Upon hearing my response, my dad's entire body seemed to rest easier in the car seat, as if a heavy burden had been lifted from his shoulders. He had passed "the Torch" to me. His eyes fastened on the road ahead.

We approached the Post Exchange (PX) where all the newest comic books could be purchased. It was in a large complex of parking spaces situated right next to the commissary, where Mom and Dad would shop on Saturdays for the groceries we needed for Sunday dinner. As we continued down the divided roadway, I remember seeing a school crossing sign. It read, Fort Gordon Elementary School. The sight caused me to perk up and get excited about the prospects of meeting new friends. The crossing led into a set of red brick buildings adorned on each side by large athletic fields where I imagined kids would be running around and playing games when school started. This would be the first school we attended on the post. I would learn later that my imagination was a little ahead of its time.

My dad slowed down and read another entrance sign for the enlisted men's housing section. The entryway broadened and then split onto a roadway that became a one-way street. We saw a row of neatly stacked two-story, whitewashed, barracks style houses. Each housing unit was numbered above the door and each building was identified by a green and white painted sign out front. Dad pulled next to building 2401, slowed, and stopped abruptly.

"We're here," he said proudly.

We all cheered and spilled out of the car to see our new home. Dad motioned for us to go around to the side door to unit 2401 B. It was a huge door with an inlaid frame painted green. I would learn that the Army loved the color green even more than it loved mashed potatoes.

Dad reached into his pocket and pulled out a packet with the door key. He opened the packet slowly, gave the key a twist, and tried the door. Nothing happened. He tried it again, and then paused to think things over. Before we could ask what was wrong, Dad bounded up the steps and knocked on the door upstairs. No one answered. He knocked again, still no answer. He inserted the key and, of course, the door opened. So much for the Army's effectiveness and efficiency, even the military can make mistakes.

This left us with somewhat of a dilemma. We had a key to a housing unit that opened a different unit than we had been assigned. In the Army it is more important to follow orders than to be smart and solve mysteries, so Dad knew what he had to do. He left us sitting at the bottom of the steps while he went to see the Quartermaster Team about the mix-up in his housing unit assignment. This was before the days of cell phones so we were stuck without any way to know when he might return. Mom approached the whole episode with relative calmness. She asked me to get our basket of food out of the car trunk and to bring a cushion for her to sit on. Soon, we were settled under one of the shade trees enjoying our lunch.

Bernadine seemed anxious because she hadn't seen any girls in the complex. In fact we hadn't seen anyone at all. It was early in the day and rather pleasant outside. We wondered where all the kids might be. It didn't take long to find the answer to that question.

I saw him first as he peered out the window on the bottom floor. Then, abruptly the curtains at the window closed and I could hear someone talking inside. It sounded like a young girl, but I couldn't tell from the distance. My sister heard it too. She recognized a girl's voice and shouted to our mother that there was a girl in there.

Just as abruptly as the curtain had opened, it closed, and a young boy slid through a slightly cracked kitchen door and stood in front of the downstairs unit near the sidewalk. He seemed to beam with delight when he saw me. I guess he had expected some new neighbors and we were finally here. I spotted him standing there and did what any kid would do. I waved. To my surprise, he waved back and showed one tooth missing when he smiled. My mother nodded her head in my direction and I didn't need any more encouragement. I was off in a sprint to meet our new neighbor. I reached him in record time, slowed to a brisk walk, and stopped just at the curb to the sidewalk. The boy bounded over it and gave me a big hug. I didn't realize how large a kid he was but that hug completely took the wind right out of me.

"I'm Anthony," he blurted out smiling broadly. "Who are you?"

"My name is Bernard, but you can call me Buddy."

"O.K. Buddy," he beamed, "you can call me Tony."

Just then, a young girl exited the kitchen doorway. She was short and stocky with a long ponytail hanging down her back. She looked a little older than her brother, but I couldn't tell for sure. My sister saw her before I did and she began to point towards the building. I turned slowly and the girl stopped, eying me cautiously. My sister, who had followed close behind me, saw the girl's hesitation. She spoke up quickly to assure her new friend that I wasn't going to bother her. I thanked her sarcastically for knowing how to make a guy feel welcome. With that exchange of words, Tony laughed and so did his sister, Julia. The ice had been broken. We had met the neighbors. The new kids were no longer strangers.

Tony and Julia's mom, whose last name was Camarillo, emerged in the doorway and invited us all into the house to meet the family. Tony's grandmother, who was visiting with them before school started, greeted us in the dining room. She seemed to be very old and very nice. Mrs. Camarillo offered our mother a glass of ice tea. Our mother hesitated, and then seeing the hurt look in Mrs. Camarillo's eyes accepted her offer graciously. Then, turning towards my sister and me, Mom asked whether we could all have a glass of cold water.

Mrs. Camarillo looked pleased as she hurried to serve her new guests. Tony wanted to take me to his room to show me his comic book collection. I asked Mom if it was alright for me to go with him and she said it was. My sister disappeared, as well, with her newfound friend. Julia was anxious to show my sister her latest crochet patterns. My sister told me later how thrilled Julia was to share the stories behind the patterns.

The time went quickly and we hardly noticed when Dad returned with the correct unit information. It didn't take him long to find us. He could hear Mom's laughter from outside on the sidewalk. Mom thanked Mrs. Camarillo and her family for their gracious hospitality and we headed upstairs to our new home. When Dad opened the door this time, he seemed relieved. We walked into the spacious kitchen and dinette area, just off the back porch. The unit had a huge living room and small study, which I could see Mom eying as we entered the area. There was one large, and two small bedrooms at the other end of the house. Bernadine would have her own room. When she saw the bedrooms, she shrieked with joy. We all celebrated with her. It was a new beginning for our family. If you have ever been welcomed to a new neighborhood and felt lucky to be accepted so soon, then you know how we felt after a long moving day, on a bright summer afternoon in Georgia in 1955.

Chapter 5: Marbles Anyone?

It didn't take me long to get adjusted to my new home. I learned the names of all of my neighbors the second day we were there. The Coles, in Unit 1, had two gray Siamese cats. In addition to Tony's family, the Camarillo's below us, there were the Richardson's in Unit 2. They had a teenage son named Danny who smoked cigarettes. Danny was often missing in action, so he could not be found out. The kids would keep their distance when Danny was out and about, because he was known for losing his temper. I didn't see anything wrong with him, but I kept my distance, too. Besides, I already had met Tony and believed he and I could become good friends.

It wasn't long after we arrived that my hunch about Tony proved to be true. He came knocking at my door very early a couple of days later. He seemed really excited about something. I peeked at him through the screen. He really wanted to come in. I told him to wait a minute. I would put on some clothes. Then, I would meet him under the shade tree. Tony seemed a little put off, but I was in too big a hurry to explain it to him. How can you tell a new friend that your mother doesn't like you opening her door to just anyone, especially an uninvited visitor so early in the morning?

In fact, our mother would have been a little upset if she knew how familiar Tony seemed to have been acting after only one short afternoon. Our family wasn't stuck up, but we did have rules and expectations of common courtesy. In particular, we kids were not allowed to ever go to a neighbor's house unless we had been invited, our mother knew their mom, and she had assured our mother that we were not intruding on their privacy. Getting permission to visit someone in their home meant we had to do more than just knocking on their door and saying hello.

I dressed in a hurry and ran outside. I found Tony near the corner of our building. He was bent over looking down and appeared to be scratching something on the ground. I approached in a hurry and he seemed surprised to see me. I wanted to know what was up, so I blurted out the question although I was a little bit winded. Tony didn't respond, so I peeked over his shoulder at the figure he had drawn on the ground. It looked like a circle about thirty-six inches in diameter. When I inquired about what he was doing, Tony looked up and explained he was getting ready to setup for the game. When I asked him what game he was talking about, and who would be playing, he informed me that the game was championship marbles, and all the guys would be there soon to play.

I wondered what guys he was talking about because I hadn't seen anyone other than Tony since I had arrived. Tony assured me that the whole gang would be coming; they all wanted to play on the day after payday. I didn't understand why payday was special to the game. I also wondered what the connection was for a group of guys getting together to play marbles? Apparently, Tony hadn't thought about that question before, so he just waved me off with a hunch of his shoulders. I would find out later that the main reason all the guys got together after payday was to show off their newest additions to their marble collections. The same tradition would be repeated later for comic book collections, miniature matchbox cars, effervescent rocks, coins, and bottle cap collections.

I watched as Tony carefully placed a small finger point in the middle of the circle, and then stepped back to admire his handy work. He wanted to know what I thought about the setup. I said that it looked all right, knowing that it would all depend upon what size marbles they would be using. If everyone had regular marbles, then a four-foot circle was good enough. If they were using peewees, then a smaller circle might work better. If, however, they were using one-inch "boulders" for shooters, then a five-foot circle would be fairer. I didn't offer Tony any of this advice. I was new and didn't believe I should be butting my nose in and challenging the local house rules so early.

Tony dropped back to his knees and began to spread his cache of marbles on the ground. He had some real beauties. There were colorful peewees, shiny crystal clear cat's eyes, and a few multicolored boulders. I spotted one particularly nice looking cat's eye. Tony watched me as I stared at it momentarily.

"You like that one?" he asked.

"It looks like a crystal, yellow light inside a shiny cat's eye," I said.

Tony smiled and replied with pride, "I won it in a competition a few weeks ago. I had to win it back two times before I finally pocketed it for good. Jimmy has some of the nicest marbles anyone on the block has ever seen!"

I asked him who Jimmy was. I wanted to know a little more about some of these marble-playing guys. Tony told me that Jimmy was one of the guys he invited to come over and play marbles because Jimmy always has the best set of new marbles in his stash the day after payday. Tony believed Jimmy's mom bought them for him as a reward for keeping up with his schoolwork.

Tony explained that Jimmy got really excited about every new batch he saw. Jimmy was able to rattle off facts about all the variations in the marbles they stocked at the local department stores. He had stopped going to the local Post Exchange 'PX' to buy marbles. He claimed they cheated him with a batch of low quality marbles that they got from China. Jimmy claimed that the PX didn't have the best discounts on the better quality ones anyway. Tony didn't know if he was right, but he did know that Jimmy had a beauty of a collection wherever he got them from.

I guess Tony could tell I was really interested. He looked directly at me and caught me staring at his prize marble. Tony eyed me for a moment, and then he did a rather unexpected thing. He opened his hand and offered me his yellow, crystal clear, cat's eye marble. I hesitated just briefly. Then I reached out and took it. Tony assured me I could have it. It definitely was a beauty, but I didn't have anything to give him in return. That was when Tony told me not to worry about that, hesitating slightly as if he was rethinking his offer. He assured me I could make it up to him later. I told him that was really nice of him and promised him that I wouldn't forget where I got it.

"I know it's going to be my lucky piece," I told Tony. With that gesture, I cupped the cat's eye in my hand, turned, and sprinted towards the house so I could show my mom what Tony had given me. I yelled to Tony that I would be right back. Tony just looked at me and shook his head, seemingly unaware of how precious a gift he had given me.

My mother was inside making breakfast and she looked up when I came running in. When I entered the kitchen, she admonished me for slamming the screen door. I promised her I wouldn't do it again. I don't know why kids promise things like that, we all know we won't remember the next time we are excited and want to show something off. My mother asked me to show her what I had in my hand, not waiting for me to unveil my new find. I blurted out that Tony had given me his prized, crystal clear, yellow cat's eye marble. My mother seemed concerned and asked to see it. I was unaware of how tightly I had been holding my new gift until I felt the blood drain back into my fingers when I opened my hand to show her the beautiful cat's eye.

"You can't keep that," Mom said. "What is his mom going to say about you taking his prize marble?"

I was crestfallen. I knew my mother was right, but I really wanted to keep the cat's eye. I didn't understand what she was trying to tell me, but I would learn that lesson later on in the day. I pleaded with Mom to change her mind. I was feeling very misunderstood at that moment. I told her that Tony said I could keep it as a gift. I promised her I would be able to pay him back later. I explained I really wanted to keep it. My mother didn't look up right away. When she did, she eyed me sharply. Her words were penetrating and direct. She ordered me to return Tony's prize marble to him and not to question her decision.

Without saying another word, I turned and walked slowly out of the house to return Tony's prized cat's eye marble. Tony was still standing near the corner of the building eying his handy work. When he saw me coming, he smiled and motioned towards the ring. He asked me again if I thought he had done a good job designing the ring. I answered that he had, without actually bothering to pay very much attention to what he was trying to show me. When I finally made the effort to really look, I thought he had done a pretty good job of it. I assured him that he would do all right firing shots across a ring as true as that one. Tony said thanks and added that he would try to remember that in the heat of the contest.

I was glad to have made him feel good about his chances of winning, but I didn't want to tell him that my mom was making me return his gift. When he finally asked me what had my mother thought of the gift, I fell silent. This put him off guard for a moment, but he recovered quickly. This time he asked again pointedly, shifted from his right foot to lean back, and perched with his weight on his left so he could get a better look at me and the ring. Left- handed guys do that sort of thing from time-to-time. I believe they think it gives them an edge over us *righties.* I acknowledged that I had heard him by nodding my head, but I still didn't want to tell him what my mother had said. I just told him that I was sorry.

"Sorry for what?" Tony asked bending a little towards his left knee and looking up at me with a puzzled glance.

This time I responded immediately, "My mom said I would have to give it back. So here!"

I placed the crystal, yellow cat's eye marble in his hand, dropped my head, turned quickly and walked away. Tony just stood there and stared at me. I don't know what he was thinking, but I bet he was feeling a whole lot better than I was at the moment.

I spent the rest of the morning in the house helping my mother open and unpack boxes from the move. The morning went quickly and, after a short lunch break, I asked my mother if I could go outside and play with the boys. I must have been a good helper because she said that I could.

When I stepped outside into the midday sunlight the sun flashed into my eyes, and I couldn't see a thing. When my eyes adjusted to the brightness, I saw a gang of boys gathered around the corner of our building. They seemed to be engaged in some sought of group activity. I approached slowly as not to disturb them. I didn't recognize any of the guys, so I began looking for Tony.

"Good shot," said a boy in a green tank top. The guys all nodded their heads in agreement. There must have been eight or nine of them. They were all gathered around the ring that Tony had drawn earlier. Then, I saw Tony. He was kneeling at the edge of the ring with his favorite shooter tucked and ready to go. There were two marbles left in the ring, and Tony seemed ready to pick off both of them. He cocked his head to one side and eyed his next shot. A solid, azure blue marble sat close to the edge of the ring. Tony knuckled down, took aim, and fired. His shooter glanced off the side of the marble, and swerved out of bounds.

"Uhhh!" sputtered the boy who had just complimented Tony a minute before.

Tony dropped his head and turned to eye the other contestant who was now crouched very close to the ring. He looked about the same age as we were, but a lock of his curly, blond hair was nearly covering his eyes. He was studying the ring, the two targets, and his unexpected opportunity. If he played it right, he could close out the game and be declared the winner. In order for that to happen, he needed to punch the blue marble, near the edge, out of the ring, and then stick. If he could pull it off, the last shot would be easy. The kid with the curly hair took aim, cocked his head to the side, and fired. His beautiful, crystal green, cat's eye crashed into the azure blue marble, and it went flying out of the ring. Unlike Tony's shooter on the previous shot, the crystal green cat's eye stuck in the ring. We all watched it as it spun around and finally came to a stop. I glanced at Tony, and I could see he was not enjoying the game nearly as much as the blond-haired kid.

The last marble inside the ring was ripe for the plucking and Tony's opponent intended to do exactly that. The prize marble left in the ring was Tony's crystal, yellow cat's eye. Tony would explain later how he had been pressured into anteing it up in order to match the prized fire red, flash cat's eye that the blond-haired kid dropped in to start the game. There was nothing that Tony could do to save his prize marble. The blond-haired kid took aim. In an instant, it was struck and blasted out of the ring. One of the boys retrieved the prize.

The blond-haired kid placed it into his purple pouch, tipped his baseball hat, and said, "Great game Tony!" See you tomorrow for another round, O.K.?"

"Sure, Jimmy," Tony answered reluctantly. Then he let out a hollow sigh, turned, and began to wipe his eyes with his sleeve.

The blond-haired kid motioned to a couple of the guys. They murmured something to each other and then joined him. Together, they walked away towards the building across the street from ours. I could hear the laughter coming from the group as they jostled with one another. Somehow I knew I would see them sooner than later, especially the blond-haired kid named Jimmy.

Tony didn't say a word. He looked sick. I didn't know what to tell him, after all, it was my fault he still had the crystal, yellow cat's eye in his pouch. If I had kept it when he gave it to me, he wouldn't have been feeling so low after losing it. I tried to make light of the whole thing by poking fun at the tall kid with the high water pants. I laughed and then blurted out that the tall kid must have bought his pants at the hog feed store. Tony nodded to let me know he heard me, but didn't raise his head or reply. Instead, he walked slowly back towards the building staircase and leaned against the railing. He sighed loudly, and then he murmured something that I didn't understand. I asked him to explain. He whined that he was sorry that he wouldn't see his prize marble again. When I asked him why, he shrugged and told me that Jimmy always puts the prize marbles he wins from the guys in his trophy cup.

"What trophy cup?" I asked glad to have something other than his lost marble to talk about.

Tony explained that Jimmy had a trophy cup that he won throwing rings at a round peg at the carnival. He told me Jimmy always put his prize cat-eyes marbles in it, and then sat it on the window so we could all see what he'd won from each of the guys. Tony continued talking so softly that I could hardly hear him. He told me that Jimmy had about a half dozen of his prize marbles in the trophy cup. Then came the zinger, Tony lamented that he sure wished he hadn't put his crystal, yellow cat's eye in the ring. Before I could stop myself, I asked him why he had done that. That probably wasn't the smartest question to ask given the circumstances.

Tony responded that Jimmy had told all the guys that he was going to give them a chance to win one of his favorites if they would all put up one of their own. Tony hadn't wanted to be left out, so he dropped in his yellow cat's eye. He waved his hands in the air to let me know that I, and everyone else, knew the rest of the story. I nodded silently to acknowledge that I understood. Tony had been snookered, and I had let him down. It was my fault that his prize marble was lost.

Tony shrugged. I reached over to pat him on the shoulder, but he put up both his hands. I guess he wasn't feeling very much like being a pal. I folded my arms as a reflex and waited to see what he wanted to do next. He sighed again, turned and opened his screen door, and then disappeared inside. I stood there for a long while thinking about how I would make it up to him. It didn't take me very long to come up with a plan.

I rushed into the house and sped past my mother who was cleaning out the cabinets before unpacking the dishes. She saw that I was in a hurry and, of course, inquired about my haste. Not wanting to put her off or sound too suspicious, I shouted back over my shoulder that I needed to find my tin box with my things in it. With those few words out of my mouth, I ran towards my bedroom. She took the opening for a chance to task me with some work adding that we hadn't unpacked any of the things for the bedrooms yet, but I could help her do that now. That was just like my mother. She could always find something she wanted me to do at the very moment I was on a mission. When I pleaded with her to help me find my tin box, she obliged and said that she knew I wouldn't mind helping her unpack some of the boxes over by the sofa while we looked for my tin box. I agreed and then added that it was important because it had my marble collection in it. Then, I trudged over to the couch and began tearing the tape off one of the boxes.

It wasn't long before we were unpacking the mementos and figurines to go into mother's china cabinet. Then we unpacked the washcloths, sheets, and towels for the linen closet. Finally, we unpacked a large carton with some of my baseball equipment in it. I just knew my tin box had to be in there somewhere. I fumbled around near the bottom and touched a familiar latch on the side of my tin box. I couldn't get it out, of course, until I had nearly emptied the entire carton. My mother looked at me curiously as I rummaged through my old trophies, baseball gear, and comic books, until I had removed enough stuff to pull out the tin box. Tucked inside a gray sweat sock, I found my stash of prized marbles.

I turned the sock inside out and poured the contents onto the bedroom floor. I don't know why I did that; the marbles rolled everywhere. I had to get down on the floor and scoop them up with both hands to keep them from disappearing under the bed. They were all there. I had a set of white crystal cat's eyes, four lime green and white solids, three blue crystal cat's eyes, several peewees, my 'old faithful' one-inch steely, two prized tiger eyes, a half-inch blue speckled snowflake solid, and a precious crystal clear, speckled red, white, and blue boulder.

That evening, I went looking for the blond-haired kid. I found him in the middle of a game on the corner of his building. The guys were all engrossed in the game, so I took the time to check out my surroundings. The buildings were all the same, except this unit included a front entrance with a long sidewalk leading up to it. My building had a short sidewalk and then a few steps leading up to the front entrance. I guess that was because it was at the corner. I looked into a few of the windows to see if I could spot the trophy cup that Tony had told me about. It didn't take me long. It was sitting on the windowsill looking like a big jar of candy. I couldn't tell whether Tony's crystal, yellow cat's eye marble was in there or not. I could tell by the number of marbles in the trophy cup, that a lot of kids had lost their favorite ones to Jimmy.

I finished surveying the territory and eased up next to one of the kids watching the game. It was almost over and it looked like Jimmy was about ready to run the tables again. He was hunched over the center of a large circle taking aim at the few marbles left in the ring. He was using a crystal clear, red streaked boulder to clear his targets. It proved to be a lethal weapon. A couple of shots later, Jimmy had cleaned the ring. The kid he just defeated shook his head and put his hands up in an "'I give up" sought of gesture. All the other kids nodded their heads in agreement and Jimmy looked pleased to have won again.

The silence was broken when a big kid pointed at me and asked, "What are you looking at?"

Always quick to respond to a challenge, I looked right at him and shot a question back, "Who's asking?

The big kid replied, "Billy Thurmond."

"I'm Bernard, but my friends call me Buddy."

The big kid responded that he wasn't my friend. He asked me why I was there and where Tony was. The response got under my skin. I shot a mean look his way as I told him that I didn't know where Tony was and that it wasn't my day to watch him. I could tell that answer didn't set well with the big kid but, before he could step forward to teach me some manners, a couple of guys slipped between us.

"Hey," Jimmy said, "I know this guy. I saw him at the game this morning."

I was thankful for the acknowledgment because I didn't really want to get into a fight in my first week in the neighborhood. Jimmy turned towards Billy Thurmond and then looked at me. He then explained that he thought Tony was going to join him for another round of winner takes all. That was my opening. I told Jimmy that I believed Tony would be coming later but, for right now, I wouldn't mind getting in on a little of that action if he was still offering.

Jimmy couldn't resist the challenge. He nodded and parted the guys by waving his arms. He stood a few feet away waiting for me to show my marbles. I reached into my sock and felt around for one of my blue cat's eyes. When I found one, I slipped it out, lifted my head and looked at it through the afternoon sunlight. As the rays burst through the crystal, it shone like a sparkling, blue diamond.

"Nice," Jimmy said, "but I already got one of those. What else do you have in your sock?"

I hesitated for a moment and one of the guys said, "I bet that he don't have nothing in that sock."

That comment produced an outburst of laughter that I was more than happy to hear. I looked around and, to my surprise it looked like all the guys standing there were in on it. I took advantage of the pause afterwards to hold up my prize crystal white, sparkling cat's eye at eye level firmly between my thumb and forefinger. I could see Jimmy's eyes light up the moment he saw it. Everyone let out a round of "ooohhs and aaahhs."

The contest was on. Jimmy began laying down the rules. After explaining who would go first, Jimmy spat out his favorite phrase, "It's for keepsies."

The guys standing around us nodded their heads in agreement as Jimmy pushed a lock of his blond hair back off of his eyes.

"Keepsies it is," I agreed with a smile on my face and dropped the sparkling, crystal white, cat's eye into the ring. Jimmy took out one of his green, crystal cat's eyes and held it up for all the bystanders and me to see. I shrugged. Then, I lied and told him that I already had one. This didn't seem to faze Jimmy at all. He responded with a second purple cat's eye and upped the ante. I was impressed with the variety in his bag, but I didn't let on.

Instead, I asked nonchalantly, "Is that the best that you can do?"

"No," Jimmy replied, "but I don't believe you can match any of the prize marbles in my set."

Now we were talking. I rested my right arm in the palm of my left hand and supported my chin with my thumb and forefinger, like the statue of *The Thinker.* I then put up my prize boulder and challenged him to match it with his shooter and the crystal, yellow cat's eye he had won from Tony earlier that morning. A pale shadow came over Jimmy's face. He was studying me, but couldn't seem to decide what he wanted to do next. The big kid gave him a nudge and said, "You can take him, Jimmy."

Jimmy reached into his pouch, pulled out Tony's cat's eye, and dropped it into the center of the ring. I reached into my sock and pulled out my prize boulder and dropped it into the center of the ring. As I stepped back, I watched the guys look in awe. There in the middle of the circle lay a crystal clear, speckled red, white and blue boulder. It was stunning. Red, white and blue - you can't get any more American than that.

A red-haired boy let out a big, "Gosh."

I know he wanted to ask me where I had gotten such an unusual boulder. I let his curiosity hang out there in space. I wasn't going to do any bragging until I had beaten Jimmy and won Tony's yellow cat's eye back. After a brief pause for the shock to settle in, I shuffled my feet to show my impatience and looked directly at Jimmy. Jimmy saw me gazing at him, but he couldn't resist staring at the prize I had dropped into the ring.

"Let's do it," Jimmy said. With that comment, he dropped his crystal clear, red streaked boulder into the ring, retrieved another shooter out of his pouch and kneeled down to lag. The big kid dragged his shoe across a sandy spot in the yard. We watched as Jimmy took aim. Held tightly between his thumb and forefinger was a crystal clear, blue speckled cat's eye. It actually sparkled in the afternoon sunlight. Then in a flash, it was tumbling towards the line. The whole crowd held their breath as Jimmy's shooter came to rest a couple of inches away from the line. Pretty good I thought, and then it was my turn.

I walked slowly to the lag point and surveyed the terrain. The big kid had picked a good spot. There were no rocks, shards of glass or small twigs to get in the way. It looked like smooth sailing from where I stood. A few kids whispered back and forth behind me. I let the chatter sail right over my head without blinking an eye. This was too important a game for me to get distracted. I took a knee and retrieved my shooter from my pocket. I heard the gasp as the fellows got a look at 'old faithful.' I had named my steely shooter that after it won me seven games in a row the month before we moved.

"No fair!" the big kid yelled, "No steely shooters allowed."

I refreshed his memory by going over the rules that Jimmy had laid down. That rule wasn't in there. The look on the big kid's face turned sour. I shot a quick look around to see what the odds would be if things began to get ugly. No one moved. I waited for the big kid to advance. He hesitated for a second and then looked at Jimmy. I looked at Jimmy, too, and gave him a shoulder hunch that said, so are we playing or what? I could tell he was conflicted. He wanted to prove how good he was, but he didn't want to cross the big kid. I took advantage of the moment to turn to the big kid and remind him that it was Jimmy's call. That seemed to break Jimmy's trance. He waved his arms to back everyone off and muttered something that sounded like he agreed. I shook my head to indicate it was settled.

I turned towards the lag line, took a knee, aimed, and propelled my shooter within an inch of the line. That produced another gasp, and I figured by now everyone knew I was a serious contender. I could tell Jimmy knew it, too. He looked straight up in the air and muttered something that I couldn't understand, but I bet it wasn't nice. I took the obligatory walk around the ring to get a bearing on my line of attack. Tony's cat's eye had landed right next to my sparkling boulder. The other two marbles were more dispersed. I cleared a small spot next to the ring, knuckled down and took aim at my crystal white, sparkling cat's eye.

"No leaning," the big kid said.

It was his way of letting me know he was still watching me. I shifted to my left side, closed my left eye, and focused my right eye squarely on the white cat's eye in the ring. Old faithful sprang from my thumb, rolled directly towards the target, hit solidly, and then stuck in the ring. The white cat's eye sailed out the other side of the ring, and then rolled to a stop. I picked it up and dropped it into my sock. No one made a sound. That was all right with me, because I really needed to concentrate. The shot had left me with a dilemma. I found myself beside my prize boulder with no clear shot of Tony's prize cat's eye. Jimmy must have sensed my predicament because he cleared his throat and then winked at the big kid. I really needed to concentrate now, and I blocked out everything around me so I could focus on my next shot. At that moment, I was so into the game, I didn't see Tony when he joined the crowd.

"Are you going to shoot, or what?" Jimmy chided me. I guess I had that coming, but it rattled me more than I wanted to admit. To add to the confusion, the big red-haired kid muttered something about me stalling and then moved in closer to get a better look. I knelt next to my shooter, knuckled down and took aim. The marble sprang out of my hand, and smashed head on into Jimmy's boulder. It jarred it enough to push it slowly out of the ring. Even before I could pick up my new prize, I realized the impact had caused my shooter to veer to the right, and roll onto the line making up the ring. My turn was over!

The red-haired kid shouted that I was out, and all the others began to chime in. Their champion had been saved by the ring. Sour looking faces turned to joy, as if it was the most wonderful news any of them had received in years. I dropped my head slightly, and looked up to see Jimmy walking confidently up to the ring. He passed me without even looking my way, and then walked very deliberately around the ring looking for the best angle to attack. I began to get that sick feeling you get in your stomach when you know you are about to be creamed. All

I could think of was how disappointed Tony was going to be to know I tried to win his shooter back and failed.

Finally, Jimmy took a knee next to the ring. He cocked his head to the right and perched his shooter squarely into the crook of his index finger. I could see from the angle he was taking that he intended to punch out my red, white and blue crystal clear, sparkling boulder first. I knew he wanted it from the moment he saw me holding it up in the light. My stomach turned over again and I was feeling a little faint. Jimmy was just one shot away from bringing me down. If he sank this shot, my day wasn't going to end well at all.

Jimmy must have sensed my anxiety. He paused to peek at me just for a moment. Then, he cocked his head, squeezed his shooter and watched as it sprang forward towards the prize. The collision echoed from the ring in the yard across all the hills I had ever climbed. I just knew my stars-and-strips was a' goner. The suspense was terrible, but I couldn't turn away as Jimmy's marble just kept on spinning. The prize boulder veered towards the edge of the ring, and then gravity took over. Jimmy had underestimated the mass of the boulder; and his shot, which grazed it, left a little too much ring to cover. The boulder gradually came to a stop right at my feet, and rested a half-inch inside the ring. I stared at it for a moment not really understanding the good fortune that had befallen me. Jimmy was out. The crowd fell silent and then from a deep, deep cavern inside surfaced a mountain of sighs. They were overwhelming. They went on and on inside my head.

The cleanup was easy. My shot bounced my shooter off the boulder, which ricocheted and rolled out of the ring. The angle I used was just tight enough to allow my shooter to roll gently towards the center of the ring. When the dust cleared and my shooter had stopped rotating, Tony's crystal, yellow cat's eye was on the outside of the ring and headed for my sock.

"Foul," cried Jimmy. "You stepped on the ring!"

"I did not!"

Jimmy looked perturbed as some of the fellows backing his side chimed in. The scene was getting ugly again and I wasn't sure what their next move would be. I stood slowly and backed up to clear some space, but the crowd had formed a solid circle around me. The red-haired kid called me a cheater and claimed I had fouled. His face was beet red and his eyes had narrowed to form to two angry slits. The next few moments were a blur. Then, the big kid pushed Jimmy into the circle with me.

"You aren't gonna let him get away with that are you, Jimmy?" scowled the big kid standing firmly behind him.

Jimmy looked confused. I could tell that he really wasn't ready to throw down, but given the pressure anything was possible. I braced myself for the inevitable charge. The big kid shoved Jimmy hard and he flew face-forward towards my chest. I stepped aside and watched him tumble head first towards the ground. He fell awkwardly and hit his face on the red-haired kid's shoe. Blood squirted out of his nose and a horrible look came over his face. He wiped his nose, saw the blood on his hands, and panicked. Before anyone could calm him down, Jimmy was running towards his house screaming at the top of his lungs. We all looked at each other trying to determine what had happened to cause such a commotion.

We didn't have very long to wait. Jimmy emerged from the house with his mom marching in lockstep beside him. She looked angry and she was definitely on a mission. All eyes were on me, and I felt like a stranger in no man's land. It wasn't my fault that Jimmy had fallen. Why were they all looking at me? Jimmy's mom pointed a finger my way, and asked him if I was the one? Jimmy answered her with what seemed to be a yes, in a voice so low that we could barely hear him. His mom walked over to me, stopped, and gave me a mean stare. Then she looked me straight in the eyes and accused me of taking her son's marbles. I tried to explain, as politely as I could, that I had won them fair and square. Apparently, that wasn't what she wanted to hear.

"Give them to me," Jimmy's mom said, "and don't you ever do anything like that again. Do you understand?"

I had no answer. I was being confronted by an adult and was confused. Why was I the villain when I had played the game the way we always played it? My heart sank and my head drooped. I reached into my sock to retrieve Jimmy's marbles, when I heard footsteps behind me. Then, I heard a soft voice ask, "Are you all right, Buddy?" Buddy was what my mother called me when she was trying to get my attention.

I turned to face her and saw my new friend, Tony, standing next to her looking winded. I assured my mother that I was all right and silently thanked God feeling really blessed to finally have someone there who cared about me. I told her that Jimmy and I had a misunderstanding, but it was going to be O.K.

My mother wanted to know what kind of misunderstanding I was talking about. She asked me to explain, while directing her gaze at Jimmy's mom who was standing a few feet away from us. That was when Jimmy's mom interrupted and accused me of taking her son's marbles. She explained to my mother that she had told me to give them back. My mother seemed startled at her words, so she repeated them for effect. I could see she was getting a little agitated and I really wanted to end the whole incident without any more finger pointing. Before I could say another word, my mother turned to face Jimmy's mom and walked briskly in her direction. She stopped a half step short of her, looked her right in the face, then leaned and whispered something in her left ear. The two women looked at each other and then walked silently towards the front of the building.

We all stood there looking puzzled as they exchanged words. Suddenly, my mother turned towards us and motioned for me to join them. That knot which had been hovering in my stomach got a whole lot tighter. I tried to imagine what the two mothers might ask me. I believed I had already told them everything they needed to know. I hadn't taken Jimmy's marbles. I had won them fair and square. When I reached the two ladies, my mother motioned for me to stand in front of her, and she placed both her hands on my shoulders. I felt the weight of two fifty-pound cement bags about to bury me beneath the pile. My mother spoke first.

"This is Mrs. Wilkerson. She wants to ask you a few questions."

"Hello, Mrs. Wilkerson," I tried to say as politely as I could, but it didn't come out that way. My voice squeaked like someone was squeezing the life out of me. Jimmy's mom looked me in the eyes. She was studying me to see if she could trust me to tell her the truth. When she finally spoke, she asked me to show her Jimmy's marbles. I took Jimmy's crystal clear, red streaked boulder out of my sock and placed it in her hands. When she saw it, she looked shocked. Then she asked me to explain how I came to hold Jimmy's prize boulder.

At first, I was lost for words. I didn't know how I would be able to explain owning such a prize as that. I glanced up at my mother and saw the calmness in her eyes. She nodded her head for me to answer the question. I told Mrs. Wilkerson that Jimmy had put it up in the contest and that I had won it fair and square in the game. Jimmy's mom looked curious. Then she asked me why would Jimmy do such a thing as that?

I answered her by holding up my crystal clear, red, white and blue, star-spangled boulder.

"My, my," Jimmy's mom exclaimed. She looked impressed and, to my surprise, she complimented me on having such a fine looking specimen. I acknowledged her compliment by smiling, and then she asked me where I had gotten it. I told Mrs. Wilkerson that my mother had bought it for me as a birthday present.

Then, Mrs. Wilkerson turned to my mother and said, "Helen, you'll have to show me where I can buy one of those for Jimmy. I know he would just love to have one."

I was shocked. She had called my mother by her first name, just like you would an old and trusted friend. The next thing Mrs. Wilkerson did was just as startling. She asked if she could hold my prize boulder. Then, she motioned for Jimmy to join us. He responded promptly to her signaling to him. When he joined us, he actually looked relieved to be away from the crowd. Jimmy's mom began by telling him that she understood he had played for some pretty high stakes and then she held up his prize boulder. Jimmy looked embarrassed when his mom confirmed that the crystal clear, red streaked boulder that belonged to him had been in my possession. When his mom asked him how he had lost it, Jimmy just shrugged his shoulders and looked away.

"Was this what you were expecting to get for it?" Mrs. Wilkerson queried.

She held up the star-spangled banner boulder. It shone brightly in the sunlight. Jimmy just hung his head and didn't respond. At that moment, I felt sorry for him. It must have really been embarrassing to know your mother realized you had gambled big and lost. Then, Mrs. Wilkerson surprised me; she admonished Jimmy for fighting. Jimmy looked hurt.

I don't know why I spoke up, but I blurted out that we hadn't been fighting. Jimmy's mom looked in my direction and then back at him. That's when Jimmy nodded his head slowly to affirm what I had said. For the first time that day, I saw my mother smile.

"I think you should give Jimmy his prize marble back," my mother said.

That sounded like a very good idea to me. I held out my hand. Mrs. Wilkerson placed Jimmy's boulder squarely in my palm. Without hesitating, I turned and gave it to Jimmy. His face beamed, like he had never been so happy to see something so precious in his life. My mother thanked Mrs. Wilkerson for her cooperation. Then she accepted my prize boulder, turned, and handed it to me. My mother thanked Mrs. Wilkerson again. I gave Jimmy a nod. Then my mother and I turned together and walked slowly back towards the house.

I had been unaware of Tony's presence until then. He had been standing there all the time watching us as the drama unfolded. I told my mother I would be home in a minute. She told me it was all right that she understood. I walked over to Tony and asked him to open his hand. When he did, I deposited his prize yellow, cat's eye marble squarely in the middle of his outstretched palm. He looked startled, but I reassured him that now it was his. I explained how I had won it fair and square in the game, and that it was a special gift from me to him. Tony smiled broadly. Then, he took his sparkling, yellow cat's eye marble and stuffed it into his pants pocket. The two of us walked back to the house together in silence. We had been tested and our friendship had survived. There was no need for conversation; we had both experienced enough drama for one day.

Chapter 6: Attending a New School

Morning at the Bus Stop

Summer time was great. We played outside every single day. Bernadine and I got to know all of the kids and actually made a few new friends. As the summer came to an end, we were all looking forward to going back to school. Since we were new to the neighborhood, we really didn't know what to expect. I was entering the fifth grade and my sister was going into the forth.

Our mother was very supportive, and she prepared us well for our first day of school. Before we went to bed, she helped us lay out the clothes we were going to wear. I planned to wear a pair of denim jeans, a green and white checkered shirt, and a new pair of Buster Brown shoes that Mom had bought for me at the Post Exchange (PX). My sister chose a colorful blue dress, black and white shoes, and a book bag with butterflies on it. We were as ready as you could get for our first day at school. Our mother made sure we got a good night's sleep. She cooked cinnamon rolls from leftover dough used to bake Dad's favorite Sunday rolls. Then, she coaxed us into bed early by giving each of us a cinnamon roll as a treat.

We took turns reading a bedtime story while Mom looked on. Then, we brushed our teeth, said our prayers, and climbed into bed. It was going to be a long day tomorrow for two kids who were used to getting up late. We had to be at the bus stop by 6:30 a.m. and that meant getting up around 5:30 a.m. in the morning. Of course, we wanted to fall asleep right away, but the anticipation of the first day of school made it hard to do. I guess we could have counted sheep, but I remember counting frogs instead. The frogs kept jumping over each other and croaking softly until I finally fell asleep.

Mother woke us up right on time. We could always count on her to do that. She grew up in the country and didn't need an alarm clock to wake herself up. It was a God-given gift that never let her down. When she woke us, we could smell sausage cooking on the kitchen stove. That was enough incentive to get us going. I scrambled to grab my toothbrush and comb and tried to beat my sister into the bathroom. As usual, I lost that one. Fifteen minutes later, she was out and I finally got my turn. I brushed my teeth as quickly as I could and brushed over my hair almost as quickly.

My mother gave us both a keen once over when we entered the kitchen. I just knew she was going to find something wrong with my outfit. I was surprised when she complimented me on how I looked and didn't correct anything. My sister got a new ribbon tied into her hair. She seemed so proud of how she looked. I guess she had earned it since she sat for hours on Saturday with mother pressing her hair with a hot comb. It was a routine that would be repeated, week after week, for many years in our home. Pressing hair was an art that women of color believed they needed to endure to look their best. It would be years before black women wore African styled hair as a source of pride. My sister paid a dear price for the practice. I watched her squirm to avoid the heat and occasionally holler when the hot comb accidentally singed the skin on the back of her neck. Today, when I see a young boy squirming while getting his hair cut, I wonder how he would have felt if he had to have his hair pressed like my sister did.

There was excitement in the air; there always was given the anticipation of meeting new friends on the first day of school. I wondered what Tony would be wearing on his first day of school. I guess I would see when we met at the bus stop. A slow aching feeling began creeping up into my stomach. I tried to get it to go away, but it crept back in and hung on tight. It was the anticipation of being accepted or rejected by a new group of kids. I had felt it many times before. We had moved at least three times since kindergarten and I had always been able to adjust quickly to my new environment. I was sure I would be able to do it again. That didn't stop me, however, from worrying about what it would be like this time.

My mother's voice interrupted my daydreaming. She asked my sister and me to take our seats so we could get ready to eat our breakfast. I hadn't noticed Dad sitting there, but he seemed pleased with how I looked on this first day of school too.

"Don't forget to come straight home after school," Dad said, "and remember you are the oldest, so you take care of your sister. Understand?"

I answered my dad as I always did when he reminded me to man up and take care of my sister but, that morning, my usually strong affirmative voice seemed a little stronger than usual. Meeting the new guys and recovering Tony's marble must have boosted my confidence. Dad looked pleased with my response. My mother looked proud of both of her children that morning. Mother served dishes of my favorite breakfast foods, fried apples with sausages, biscuits, and marmalade jam. Dad drank black coffee and Mom sipped hot tea. Our day was beginning like a regular Monday morning.

My sister was nervous about beginning the year in a new school. I was sure she would feel better after meeting some of the other children at school. I tried to calm some of her fears by smiling at her, but it didn't work. She gave me a smirk and wanted to know what I thought was so amusing so early in the morning. I thought about returning her sarcasm with a comment about her nappy head, but it looked nice pressed and she looked frightened. My mother stepped in with a calming voice and told my sister how nice she looked in her blue floral skirt. My sister thanked her for the compliment and seemed to relax just a little. Unfortunately, it was too late for that. Dad rose to get his jacket, placed his hat with the shiny brim on his head, and turned to say goodbye. Our mother gave him a hug, and motioned for us to do the same. We jumped at the opportunity. Soon we were all embraced in a firm group hug that seemed to last forever.

My dad told us all that he would see us when he got home. Then, he turned, exited the kitchen, and headed out for the first day of his week at work. Our mother lingered briefly to watch him head down the stairs and walk towards the car. Dad looked so good in his pressed khakis uniform. His service medals shined brightly in the early morning sunlight. I would learn much later that our mother saw him as her shining knight who left every day to go out to fight the dragons for his family. I saw him as the strong, black man who I too would one day grow up to be.

I took those thoughts with me to the bus stop. I could see the guys and girls waiting at the far corner for the bus. I motioned to my sister to hurry up so we could join them. She seemed a little reluctant to follow me, but I really didn't understand why. We walked the half block to the far corner of our row of buildings. When we got there, I looked for Tony, but I didn't see him right away. Bernadine saw her new friend, Julia, but she seemed a little reticent to speak to her. I was oblivious to the entire exchange until one of the neighborhood boys spoke up, and asked me what we were doing standing at their bus stop? For a moment, I didn't know how to respond. It never occurred to me that there was more than one bus stop in our subdivision. At that moment, I realized that I didn't even know the name of the school we would be attending. I had thought we would just get on the bus and show up at the school. Besides, wasn't that what a school bus was supposed to do? The boy who had spoken to us looked puzzled, too. I would learn very soon why.

My sister pulled my arm and whispered in my ear. She told me that we were supposed to be at the other bus stop near the corner of our house. Why I hadn't known that was a mystery to me. I would find out later that her friend, Julia, had explained it to her the day before. Of course, my sister wasn't going to take the lead and try to change my mind when I struck out in the wrong direction, so I was facing the embarrassment now for both of us. I nodded faintly, took her hand, and walked briskly back towards our apartment building. I heard a few snickers as we walked away, but I was too focused on getting us onto the right bus to pay any attention to them.

It was good that I hadn't waited another minute. When I looked up the school bus was waiting at our corner. As I glanced behind me, I noticed the bus at the other corner was pulling away. When I turned back to look at our bus, it was pulling away too. I nearly panicked. No one wants to miss the bus on the first day of school. How would I explain it to Mom and Dad? I was supposed to be in charge, and I had blown it! That sick feeling I had earlier began to rise up in my throat. I tried to yell to get the bus driver to stop, but it seemed that I was too late. I grabbed my sister's arm and we both ran towards the bus stop. Devine providence must have been on our side because a kid looking out of the back window waved at us and, a few seconds later, the bus driver pulled over to the side of the road.

When we got to the bus we were panting. Fortunately, we were one of the first stops along the route and only a few kids were on the bus ahead of us. I thanked the bus driver for waiting for us and he smiled. My sister slid into a seat behind the bus driver and I followed her lead. The bus driver leaned back to ask us if we were going to Booker T. Washington Elementary School? I knew who Booker T. Washington was, but I didn't know he had a school. My sister sensed my hesitation and answered for me. After she spoke to the driver, he nodded his head, turned, and steered the bus back onto the roadway on our route.

We sat quietly watching as the buildings whizzed by. Before long we had exited the post, and made our way onto the interstate highway. For the first time in our lives, we were riding on a bus heading towards a school that we had never seen. For the first time in our lives, we were traveling outside of the military base where we lived, without our mother or father in the driver's seat. For the first time in our lives, we were on our way to a new school in the south in the fifties, and we had no idea of what to expect when we got there.

My nervousness turned my stomach sour. I was aware of the ache I always seemed to get when I was under stress. I couldn't let my sister know I was afraid. I was supposed to be strong to protect her. I wondered who would be strong for me. It was times like those when I would turn inward and look for strength in my faith. My sister and I had been raised in the Baptist Church. We were Christians and we believed that God would protect us if we only asked him to. I wasn't shy about asking. I dropped my head and said a prayer to do just that. I didn't care who saw me at the moment. I needed a sign that would help me get through this day and I needed it from a power greater than myself. I felt that I was walking blindly into the dark and I wasn't intending to go it alone.

My sister squeezed my hand as I said a silent Amen. I looked up and we were turning off the highway heading down a dirt road. There were cornfields all around us. I noticed the dust trailing our bus as we sped towards our destination, wherever that was going to be. I turned towards my sister and gave her a curious look. She turned her head to the side and looked back at me. I sensed that she wanted me to understand that she didn't know anymore about this trip than I did. We squeezed each other's hand just a little harder. We were going to be all right.

The bus slowed and made a short right turn. Kids on the bus began to whisper. I could see a large building across the way in the middle of a cornfield. It looked magnificent. We were arriving at our new school. Everyone around us seemed to be as surprised at seeing it as we were. My heart began to race. I glanced at my sister and she seemed lost in a trance. I knew she was just as awed as I was at our first sighting of Booker T. Washington Elementary School. Whatever the rest of the day would bring, it could never match our bus stop adventure. We had finally arrived at our new school. We were safe, and our new school was magnificent!

Story Time Anyone?

I had been at our new school, the Palace in the Cornfield, for a few months before my teacher, Mrs. Lamb asked me to watch the class while she went to the main office for a parent's conference. I am not certain why I was selected, but it may have had something to do with a story I told earlier in the year. Mrs. Lamb and the kids in our Arts and Crafts class were always looking for new ways to express ourselves. We painted a mural of a rolling English countryside. We made castanets out of corn flake box tops and walnut shells. We built a landscape for a model train set with twigs, fir clippings, and small stones. We really were creative.

I hadn't distinguished myself at all until the day we separated into groups and made up stories to present to the class. My group was all over the place with the themes they wanted to cover. I watched as each member described his idea and then tried to convince the others to accept it for the group. Finally, when our time for creative discussion was over, and we had to deliver the goods, no one wanted to step forward to represent us. I don't know why I volunteered, unless it was because everyone was looking at me. As I stepped to the front of the class, all the students giggled and began whispering to themselves. I walked slowly to the middle of the room. I turned my back on the class to gather my thoughts. The entire class fell silent.

I turned abruptly to face my peers and scanned the classroom quickly to get an idea of the mood. Everyone was watching me intently waiting to see what I would do next. I reached down towards my toes, pretended to pick up something from the floor, and gazed at my outstretched fingers as if I were holding something in my hands.

Then, I said out loud for everyone to hear, "I wonder what's in the box?"

It was a game I had learned to play with myself. I would makeup stories about faraway places and imagine that I was able to bring back the things I saw there in a box.

"I don't see anything!" blurted out one of the kids in the front row.

I looked straight at him and smiled. I then informed him that I hadn't opened it yet so, of course, he didn't see anything. The other members of the class erupted in laughter. I was off on a tear. I pretended to open the top cover on the box and then jumped backwards in surprise. That brought a sudden "ooh" from the class as everyone strained their necks to see what I had been frightened by. I told them it was a mongoose, as if I knew what that was. One boy wanted to know where did the mongoose come from. That was my opening to change the scene.

I put my pointer finger up to my lips, to quiet the class, and then whispered that the mongoose in the box came from the jungle. I saw the eyes of my classmates open wide and then freeze on the box in my hands. When I had them all looking at the box, I ducked down as if I had heard a sudden sound behind me. The kids in the back of the class stood up and leaned forward trying to get a look at me huddled near the floor.

I then told everyone to close their eyes and to not make a sound. When I was sure their eyes were closed, I began to make very faint animal call imitations. I made the sound of a cockatoo and then a shrieking monkey. I made the sound of a howling wind, and a growling leopard. No one uttered a word as I went from one animal sound to the next. When I looked up everyone was watching me intently, including my teacher, Mrs. Lamb.

After a good ten minutes of jungle story excitement, Mrs. Lamb thanked me and asked me to take my seat. My classmates gave me a rousing round of applause. From that day on, they would ask for me to tell another story whenever we had the time. Word of my newly discovered talent spread and soon I was being asked to watch other classes for a few minutes while the teachers went to the main office. That was fine with me. When you are the new kid in town, you would rather be known for something good than not to be known at all.

A few months after I started school, we had a school assembly. It was planned as a treat for the quarterly visit by our parents. Mrs. Lamb asked me if I would like to tell a story as a representative of our class. I told her that I would and she sent a letter home to my mother letting her know that I was going to be featured during the assembly. My mother was very proud of me. She marked the date on the kitchen calendar showing when she would be coming to see me perform. I was pleased that she was going to be there and looked forward to the assembly.

When the day came for me to perform, I was ready. I had practiced my animal imitations and even picked up a few new ones from the guys on my block. I had my theme set in my head and was confident I would be a smash. As I sat there in the first row, I noticed a few teachers and the assistant principal eying me. Before my story telling success, I would have taken their interest in me as a negative. Now I was certain they too were waiting to see what I had to say. Their curiosity emboldened me even more.

I guess I got so wrapped up in the coming excitement, I failed to realize the MC had called my name. I believe the introduction included my grade, my teacher's name, and a lead-in to my presentation. In my haze, I totally missed it all.

"You're up, Bernard!" a voice from behind me said. Now get up there and make us proud."

As I turned to see who had called my name, I caught a glimpse of a full audience sitting behind me. I couldn't see my mom, but I knew she was there. I could feel the adrenaline rushing to my head. I was so startled that I jumped up abruptly and nearly fell on my face. Fortunately, only a few of the members in the audience could actually see me, so the damage was contained to a minimum. As I strode to the staircase and ascended, I wrestled with my nerves to get a grip so I could begin my story. I was in luck. My class saw me take the stage and the applause began. I could feel their arms of approval wrapped around me. That was all I needed to begin. I stood with my back to the audience for a few seconds and the auditorium fell silent.

I began my story with an introduction of my main character who was looking for something on the ground. He appeared to carry a spyglass in his hand and was peering down at the stage searching for something small and hidden on the ground. As I crossed the stage, I could hear a few kids ask each other what I was looking for. That was my cue. I reached down and grabbed for something at my feet. I pretended to pick it up and then cupped my hands to take a look at it. I could picture my classmates leaning forward to try to get a look at it, too. Then, I began to make a small noise like a bullfrog. The laughter began. I continued to parrot a bullfrog, until I was sure everyone had gotten the clue. Then,

I abruptly jumped backwards and opened my hands pretending that the bullfrog had suddenly jumped out. The crowd roared with laughter. I threw up my hands and walked to center stage.

Thus began my soliloquy. I introduced myself as a bold explorer who was searching for a rare bird and asked the kids in the audience if they would like to go along with me on the hunt? They begin to yell yes. I waved my hands to quiet the bunch and began my tale. I explained how I came to know about this rare bird. I pretended to open a large book and pointed to the bird's picture. Of course, there was no book and no picture, but that didn't keep the kids in the audience from leaning forward to try to get a look at them. I described the bird in detail. I spread my hands apart to indicate how tall he was. I pretended to smooth his feathers while I described the silky, layered plumage I was searching for.

Next, I pretended to pick up an object and looked through it into the audience. I peered out into space and let the audience experience being watched. Then, when I was sure I had their attention, I let out a shrill bird call. One kid in the second row was so startled that he fell out of his chair. I couldn't have asked for a better prop. The audience laughed as he climbed back into his seat and I peered at him through my pretend telescope. When the audience began to grow restless, I knew it was time to take my story to a new venue. I recalled the times that I was trying to hold the attention of my class while the teacher was out of the room. I immediately went to my old standby routine.

"It was dark in the jungle." I uttered with a slow, deliberate, and ominous tone. Then, I gave the call of a macaw. You could hear a pin drop in the crowd. I began walking slowly around the stage, slightly bent over peering through my imaginary telescope looking for the rare bird. I uttered another strange sound, turned to the audience, and whispered that we had just encountered an elephant. I followed it with a monkey, a lion, and a tiger. I don't know if you could tell the tiger from the lion, but they both seemed to intrigue the kids in the audience. I was on my way to produce my next jungle guest when I caught the eye of one of the teachers back stage. She seemed to be trying to communicate something to me. I guess I didn't want to understand what she was trying to tell me, because I smiled and kept walking across the stage.   This routine went on for a few minutes, before I realized the teacher was whispering something to me from across the stage. I leaned forward to see if I could understand what she was saying, but that brought a round of laughter from the audience, and I couldn't resist doing it again.

This routine went on for a few minutes more, and I totally lost track of the time. Now I was scrambling to find a way to wrap up my story before my teacher snatched me off of the stage. It seemed like a short period of time to me, but later my mother would persuade me otherwise. I finally ended my story by catching the rare bird, and putting it in a cage. I carried my imaginary bird to the center of the stage, and then showed it to all the kids on both sides of the isle. I pretended to whistle at the bird, and it whistled back. I had learned to do that trick with my jaws closed, so it actually looked like the sound was coming from somewhere other than me. The kids loved it and the applause grew louder.

As the level of applause continued to grow, I realized that it wasn't just for me. The teacher who had been trying to get my attention had come onto the stage. When I looked up, there she was. Before I could say another word, she thanked the audience for coming and thanked me for telling my story. I took a big bow and exited the stage. The thundering applause was overwhelming. I loved every minute of it!

On the way home, my mother couldn't stop laughing at my surprised look when I saw the teacher come on stage to get me. My mother asked me if I knew how long I had been talking. She wanted to know if I realized that the assembly's closing bell had rung. I told her that I hadn't heard it, but I believed I had gone over my time.

"Yes, you did," my mother acknowledged. "Yes you did...and by a long shot!"

It would not be the last time I had an opportunity to be on stage. It would not be the last time I underestimated the time of a performance. It had been a magical moment. I would remember it so clearly afterwards, each time I stepped on stage.

A Narrow Escape

My escapade on the school stage proved to be a blessing for me. The kids in my class were awed at what I had done. They couldn't imagine going up there themselves and telling a story in front of the entire school. Of course, a few of them were jealous, but I pretended not to notice that. The school year rolled along and I was having fun learning in the palace. We called it that because the main building was massive. It stretched as far as the eye could see in all directions. It appeared that someone had decided to build it large enough to hold every kid in the county. I didn't understand why because only colored kids went there.

Colored was the word used to describe Negroes or black people in 1955. It was a term used by whites and blacks in the United States and abroad. Often when a white person wanted to acknowledge a distinguished person of color, they would say he or she was a credit to the Negro race. Overtime, the terms used to address people of color changed from colored to Afro-American to black to African-American. If you look at a copy of a United States census form today, you will find a set of race categories that still use some of those terms.

The term colored was important in those days, particularly in states that practiced segregation of the races. In those states, colored kids were not permitted to attend schools with whites. To enforce the segregation rules, counties built separate school facilities for whites and coloreds. The larger the school, the more coloreds could be bused there to maintain the social separation of the races. That was why my sister and I had been at the wrong bus stop. We had never lived in an integrated environment before where we were forced to separate to go to school. Our neighborhood in Maryland had been segregated and we hadn't even noticed!

Shortly after the school year began, I found myself in a predicament. I stayed out too long for an afternoon school recess and found myself in the principal's office. It really wasn't my fault, but that didn't seem to matter to the teacher who turned me in. I had been playing in the big cornfield; that was where we played when we went outside for a break. Unfortunately, due to circumstances beyond my control, I failed to get back into the building before the second recess bell rang. The penalty for getting back late was a trip to the principal's office and a paddling for not obeying the rules. As I sat there in the lobby of the principal's office, I tried to stay calm. It wasn't my fault. I should not have been there. I wish I had just left the ball in the field. I wouldn't have been locked out of the building. Now, I was going to be paddled. It took all of the fun out of a really swell day.

I had always enjoyed going outside. I liked the fresh air and the sunshine. I loved to run and dodge balls as the kids tried to hit us. I also enjoyed playing in our favorite game of kick ball. We used a large, rubber ball that would sail high in the air when we kicked it. I loved to run the bases and dared anyone to hit me with the ball before I scored a run. It was a game I could have played all day. Unfortunately, the afternoon break was only twenty-five minutes long. That usually meant that one team would get a chance to be up and the other team would get caught in the middle of their turn when the bell rang. There was always a lot of complaining about stopping before all the players could take their turn kicking the ball. Often a team would try to finish their turn and be late getting back from recess. That was what happened that day.

I tried to be a good citizen. I even pleaded with my team members to stop the game and get back inside the building before the second recess bell rang. Beanie Treadwell didn't want to hear it. He was on the other team and they hadn't completed their turn at kicking the ball. The members on my team weren't sympathetic to Beanie's complaint. They kept saying that we had won and he needed to give up. I really wouldn't have cared about the disagreement, but I needed to return the ball before going back to class. I had been entrusted with a kick ball, and I would be held accountable if I failed to return it.

Beanie kept holding the ball and threatening to throw it off into the high weeds, if he didn't get his chance to kick. Nothing I said to him would change his mind. Finally, after all of the other kids had gone, Beanie turned and kicked the ball far into the air into the high weeds. I swore at him, which I shouldn't have done, and then scrambled to go get the ball. I could hear the second recess bell ringing loudly as I returned with the ball in my arms.

I tried the side door where we had exited only to find it had been locked. I nearly panicked. I knew the penalty for returning late from recess. I had heard other kids in my class talk about the huge board the principal used to paddle them with. Each time a kid returned from a trip to the principal's office, the story about the size of the board got bigger. I had never been to the principal's office, so I had no frame of reference for what was to happen next. I was going to find out. I saw a teacher waving to me from the building at the other end of the school. She seemed agitated. I ran in her direction as fast as I could.

When I got close to her, she barked out a command. She told me to get into the building and go straight to the principal's office. I didn't know exactly where the office was, but I was sure she would help me find it. I felt myself trembling slightly as I marched behind her on my way to the office. The stories I had heard about the size of the paddle and the screams coming from the victims started running through my head. I began to feel sick. It was all I could do to hold myself together. I hadn't done anything wrong and I hoped someone would listen to me before they began paddling.

As we turned the corner, I saw a large wood frame door looming ahead of us. It seemed to be bigger than the other doors we passed. I knew it had to be the principal's office. I was not going to be spared. When we entered the office, the teacher pointed to a corner and told me to go take a seat. I summoned the courage to speak. I muttered a few words trying to explain what had happened.

The teacher didn't even look at me. She just pointed and said, "Go sit down!"

I was crushed. I knew this wasn't going to end well. I dropped my head and trudged over to the corner. I must not have been looking where I was going, because a kid who told me to get off his feet startled me. As I looked up I saw Beanie sitting next to an empty chair. He had been caught coming in late, too. I could have been really mad at him, but I wasn't. I was so disheartened by my own dilemma that I just lifted my foot, shrugged my shoulders, and sat down hard. Beanie gave me a sly look. I could tell he wasn't quite sure of what to say.

Finally, he leaned over close to me and whispered, "I guess we got caught, huh."

I didn't respond to him. I was too wrapped up in my own troubles to spend time going over recent history.

Then, we heard whap …whap… whap followed by a shrill scream. There was no mistaking the circumstances. Someone was being paddled and they weren't all that happy about it. Beanie squirmed in his seat. I sat up straight, and then I almost fell head over heels to the floor. This couldn't be happening to me. What would I tell my mother? How would I explain my paddling to my sister?

Beanie looked scared. He had been to the principal's office before. If he was afraid to get a paddling, what did that mean for me? I buckled over and began to rock back and forth in my seat.

I recited the twenty-third psalm; "The Lord is my shepherd I shall not want…"

When I came to the part about walking through the valley of the shadows of death, a big lump froze in my throat. I couldn't breathe. I thought I was going to pass out. A teacher calling my name startled me. I looked up to see Mrs. Lamb motioning me to get up and follow her. It was like a dream. I walked towards her without making a sound. I was unaware that I was tiptoeing by the other kids waiting in line to be paddled.

Mrs. Lamb smiled at the secretary as we passed and thanked her for the note. A secretary whom I did not even know saved me. Apparently, she had seen me the day before in the school assembly and recognized me when I entered the office. I don't know why she called Mrs. Lamb, but I was so grateful to her for her kindness. She had seen something in me that told her I was not a troublemaker. She had taken it upon herself to rescue me from my impending disaster. I will be forever grateful to her for what she did.

Mrs. Lamb didn't ask me to explain why I was in the principal's office. Instead, she escorted me to my next class and explained to the teacher that I was late because I had gone with her on an errand. I slipped quietly into my desk and avoided the stares that I received from my classmates. I was never late getting back to the building after recess again. I don't know whether Beanie was paddled or not. It really didn't matter to me. I had narrowly missed being paddled for a stupid stunt by a fellow classmate. I knew I had dodged a bullet, and I swore to be more careful next time.

I met my sister after school at our bus stop. We rode home together and I shared with her my close call in the principal's office. She seemed amazed that I had escaped without being paddled.

"That will teach you to stay out too long with those stupid boys," she said. "They won't even let us girls play kick ball when we go out for recess."

I had never noticed that the girls were excluded from our games until my sister pointed it out. We spent the rest of the time riding home in silence looking out the window. It was a balmy fall afternoon and we were glad they let us put the windows down on the bus. No one worried about us sticking our arms out of the windows; we were too disciplined to do something stupid like that. When we got home, the bus stopped at our usual spot on the corner. We said goodbye to our classmates and jumped off the bus to head home with our friends. The second bus had just pulled into its spot at the far corner of the block. The white kids exited the bus and began walking in all directions towards their homes. Tony and Julia ran towards us. Whites and coloreds walked home together.

Chocolate Frozen Custard

The year was 1955 and most public facilities in the United States were still segregated. Although the famous civil rights victories of the 1960's would follow, in 1955 separate but equal was still the predominate law of the land. Whites and Negroes still had a lot of differences to resolve before either group could accept the idea of color not being the defining measurement of a person's worth. It was in that environment that the unthinkable occurred. The Tasty Freeze Frozen Custard stand, which stood at the top of the hill a mile from our house, introduced a new flavor, chocolate!

Chocolate was a huge success. Every person I talked to wanted to get a cone just to see how good it was. They may have had their reasons for wanting to try the new flavor, but I had my own. In a world where colored and chocolate were synonymous to Negroes, we were stunned to find such an outward display of public acceptance for the new flavor. Somehow it seemed odd to me that chocolate skin wasn't welcome, but chocolate custard was. I just had to see what was so magical about this new flavor custard.

News of the chocolate custard spread quickly. All my friends were talking about it. The white kids on our block couldn't seem to get enough; some of them had been back several times already. My pockets weren't so fat, but I had saved enough change by the end of the week to buy a small cone. I was so excited when I came home after school; I forgot to scrub the kitchen floor before going outside to play. When my mother realized what I had done, she grounded me. That meant I couldn't leave the house and definitely couldn't leave the area to get my frozen custard.

I dragged myself back into the house, and finished scrubbing the floor just before dinnertime. I knew we were going to eat soon, but I wanted to get a frozen custard cone so badly that I pretended to forget.

When I asked my mother to let me go outside for just a few minutes before dinner, she agreed, but cautioned me to stay within shouting distance. I was long gone before those words of warning could settle in. I jumped onto my bicycle and sped towards the hill. I would normally take the hill slowly, meandering from one side to the next, but I was so pumped that I stood high on my pedals and charged straight up the hill.

At the top of the first mound, I got my second wind and pushed on. When I reached the crest of the hill, I smiled. The frozen custard stand was in sight. A few minutes more and I would be rounding the corner heading straight for the stand. I should have known there would be a line at the stand. It took me nearly fifteen minutes to get within seeing distance to read the sign listing all the flavors. There it was at the bottom right of the second list, New: Chocolate Custard!

It was all I could do to contain myself. I was finally going to get to try this new flavor. When I got to the front of the line, I had nearly forgotten what I was going to ask for. I recovered just in time because the guy behind me was beginning to get impatient.

"I would like to have a cone of chocolate," I said.

The words dragged out of my mouth sounding like they were coming from somewhere on the other side of the hill. The ice cream vendor couldn't understand what I was saying, so he asked me to repeat it. Before I could answer him, the guy behind me spoke.

"He wants a cone of chocolate custard, and I wish you would give it to him so I can get mine."

The vendor shook his head, reached for a cone, and began filling it with a smooth, chocolate stream of frozen custard. When he had finished, I gave him my money and wrapped the napkin around the cone to keep it from dripping all over me. I stepped aside quickly and let the impatient guy behind me move to the front of the line. I pretended I didn't see the disgusted look on his face because I was too busy licking my custard. The first lick tasted so good that I almost dropped the cone while celebrating. After a few more licks, I just knew I had to share my newly found marvel with the whole family. I climbed on my bicycle and sped off on my way home. That's when the rain began to fall. It was a thin mist that slowly covered the roadway making it somewhat treacherous for traveling on a bike. In spite of the mist and the danger of falling, I pressed on.

I started down the hill, breezed past the first curve, went over the hump, and headed towards the next level. The mist was coming down harder now. The spray was blinding my eyes. I knew I was in a precarious position riding on a slick road with one hand carrying an ice cream cone. In addition to the messy conditions, the evening lights had just come on. It had taken longer for me to get my treat than I had anticipated. It was getting dark, and my mother was going to miss me for sure.

As I turned the corner at the bottom of the hill, I entered the cobblestone roadway, which curved around the outskirts of our apartment complex. There was a bright light shining in my eyes from the corner post that marked the beginning of the street. For the briefest of moments I couldn't see a thing. Then, I heard the horn blow and wheels screech. I looked right into the jaws of death. I was headed straight for a military personnel carrier three sizes bigger than a Ford F150. I hit the brakes, braced myself, and waited for the truck to wipe me out.

The bicycle slipped to one side on the wet pavement and together we careened towards the front wheels of the truck. The whole scene was unreal. The street lamp shone brightly directly above the spot where it appeared the bike and truck impact would occur. I could see the mist floating wildly in the air as the light beam appeared to scatter its droplets. My frozen custard cone flew out of my hand, sailed into the air, and landed squarely against my chest. The bicycle handlebars twisted and the tires pointed skyward as we hurtled towards the truck.

The next few seconds were a blur. The bicycle tires hit the truck tires and the bike stopped just short of rolling under the truck. My left knee scrapped the pavement, and my left thigh provided a cushion for the impact. The gigantic truck came to a stop just short of rolling over me. I lay on the pavement under the truck with my eyes closed and a frightened look frozen on my face. The truck driver scrambled out of his truck and dropped immediately to the pavement to examine the damage. I appeared to be unconscious, but in my head I was praying frantically in an unknown tongue. God had spared my life. I had survived with only a few bad scratches.

The soldier took my arm and pulled me from under the truck. He sat me on the curb, and then went back to retrieve my bicycle. The handlebars were twisted and my rear tire was bent severely, where the truck tires had impacted it. I thanked the soldier for rescuing me and told him I was sorry for being so careless. He asked me my name. When he recognized whose kid I was, he smiled.

"Sarge is really going to be surprised when I tell him what happened tonight," he said.

Then, he popped his lighter and tried in vain to light his cigar. He finally gave up and told me to get on home.

"Don't be riding in the rain the next time I come through."

I thanked him again for saving me and slowly walked my bicycle back towards our house.

My leg hurt, my knee hurt, and my ego was crushed. I parked my bicycle in the rear of the building and managed to drag myself up the stairs to the back door. When my mother saw me she stood frozen in place. I didn't know what to say, so I just reached out for her with both arms. I would like to remember how strong I was at that moment, but the shock of the whole incident had beaten me down. I became emotional. The whole story tumbled out of my mouth in a torrent. I confessed to leaving the grounds and described how I almost got killed sliding under the truck.

I could see the disbelief on my mother's face. I had disobeyed her and she had nearly lost me. I had worried her nearly to death when I didn't come home after she called for me. Then, as the rainy mist began, she had become even more concerned for my welfare. As her fear rose, she tried not to panic. I was somewhere out there in the dark, in the rain, on my bicycle and definitely in danger. She confided that her heart had nearly stopped around the exact moment I had crashed into the truck. It frightened her so that she went to a corner of the house and prayed. It was a story I would hear many times during my life. The spiritual connection my mother had with each of her children was legendary and scarily uncanny.

Needless to say, the entire family celebrated my surviving a near death experience. I was grounded for a month and I found myself without a bicycle and walking for a long time afterwards. I know I should have died that evening. I had made all the wrong choices. I had disregarded all the good advice I received from those who cared about me. I can only say how thankful I was afterwards to still be alive. If you find yourself disregarding the helpful advice of those who care about you, you may want to seriously rethink your decisions. My outcome doesn't have to track with yours. Someone else may have to tell your story.

Chapter 7: The Poetry Reading Contest

I don't recall how I came to be singled out to compete in the annual poetry reading contest, but I do remember one of the good church sisters submitting my name. It really wasn't unusual for me to be reciting poetry, since I seemed to avail myself of every opportunity to speak in public in the front of a crowd. I was a junior member of the Baptist Training Union at our church. Once each month I would read a scripture or recite a verse. In fact, one of the games we played on Sunday evenings was to recite Bible verses. We sat in a circle reciting verses until everyone exhausted their knowledge.

Once I had been selected to compete, however, I ran with it. The contest was going to be held in three weeks and the winners would receive prizes. We were told that the poetry selection could be humorous or serious and should be three minutes in length. This was a church sponsored contest so the subject matter should be in good taste. Candidates would be judged on style, clarity, delivery, originality, and reception by the audience. My mother was thrilled that I had been chosen to participate. She always seemed to enjoy these opportunities to be creative. She spent an afternoon pouring through old books looking for something nice for me to read. I had already memorized "The Night before Christmas," but we decided that wouldn't be very original.

That week at school, I was given a small book of illustrated poems from the library. Ms. Waters, our school's librarian, was very helpful. She had set the little green book aside especially for such an occasion as this. She presented it to me the second time I came looking for some more poetry material. I thanked her politely and sat down to skim through the pages. I just knew something good was inside. I was right. A funny caricature caught my eye. It was a fish in a brown tuxedo with tails. I laughed out loud and then muffled my voice and began reading the lines.

> A fish took a notion, to come from the ocean,
> And take in the sights of the town.
> So he bought him a hat and a bright red cravat,
> And a one-legged trouser of brown,
> He did…a one-legged trouser of brown.

It was fascinating and instantly caught my imagination. I could just see myself walking onto the stage wearing a top hat and tails. It would be a riot!

It wasn't long before I had all the lines memorized and began practicing my delivery daily in front of my mother's mirror. There is something about seeing your own image reflected inside of a mirror. I started laughing and couldn't stop. My sister wasn't much help either. She saw me practicing and began screaming and falling on the floor with laughter. I really don't know what was so funny about that fish, but every time she heard the phrase "one legged trouser," she would holler with laughter and fall on the floor all over again.

My mother was more helpful. She spent the three weeks coaching me on diction, posture, presentation, eye contact, and poetic flair – all the things I would need to know to perform well. I believe it was her sincere interest in poetry that actually sparked my own. It nearly rivaled my father's interest in sports. My mother was very fond of telling me about her childhood school experiences. She was especially fond of her recitation and reading experiences. She related stories about how she felt very proud of being selected often to read for the other students out loud in her classes.

When I finally thought that I had all of the lines down pat, I gave a recital for my class at school. It went really well. Everyone seemed to like it. The encouragement I received gave me all the confidence I needed to face the judges. Finally, the big day arrived and we all piled into the family car for the trip into Augusta, Georgia, for round one of the competition. I was scheduled to go on stage at 7:30 PM. We arrived in plenty of time for my performance. My costume consisted of a brown suit and a nice bow tie that I borrowed from the neighbors.

Upon entering the small church addition, I spotted a row of contestants already seated up front. The room was filled with kids and their parents who had come to see them perform and to be entertained. A soundly built, stately looking woman in a small white hat was directing people as they came in. She spotted me right away. Her left eyebrow appeared to rise slightly as she motioned for me to come up and join the other contestants who were all sitting in a row of chairs facing the audience.

"I'm Mrs. Higgins, and your name is…?" she asked.

"Bernard," I answered politely. "Bernard N. Lee, Jr."

I always added the junior to please my father. Mrs. Higgins did not seem to be pleased or amused. She did manage to smooth out her tersely knitted, tight lips to give me a lukewarm smile. After welcoming me, she noted that I must be representing Shiloh Baptist Church. She then referenced my Sunday school teacher, Mrs. Walls, and shared with me some nice things Mrs. Walls had told her about me.

I thanked her for sharing the compliments. Mrs. Walls was one of those good sisters, who said something nice about everyone. Mrs. Higgins then turned towards my parents and told them they were welcome to sit in the back. Afterwards, she led me to the front of the room and showed me to my seat. As we walked, she turned her head slightly and informed me that we would get started as soon as Mrs. Annabelle got there. Mrs. Annabelle, I would come to find out later, was the Chairwoman of the Women's Circle, which was hosting the Poetry Reading Contest. She was late, and everyone was waiting for her to arrive. I would also find out later that her daughter, Lillie, a quiet brunette, with a long ponytail and soft brown eyes, had sat next to me.

When Mrs. Annabelle arrived, she whispered a few words to Mrs. Higgins and then motioned for the lights to be dimmed. Introductions followed with a welcome for the parents and guests and an acknowledgment of the sponsors. Next, the judges were introduced. They included two elderly ladies, one fashionably dressed man, and Mrs. Annabelle, who apologized for being late.

A minister rose to give the opening prayer. Then, Mrs. Annabelle read the rules of the contest. Contestants who survived the opening round competition would be invited back the following week to compete for the championship.

Each contestant was introduced, escorted to the center of the small stage, and timed as they took their turn to recite. I realized immediately that my preparation was going to pay off. The first three contestants read their selections. When it came to be my turn, I eased out of my chair and walked briskly to the center of the room. I was given the time limit and told that I could proceed. As I looked out into the faceless crowd, I felt a calm come over me. The amber spotlight shown so brightly, that I couldn't see any faces, not even those of the guests in the first row.

I introduced my poem remembering to give both the title and the name of the author. Then, I paused to take a deep breath and glanced over at the other contestants. Lillie had a smirk on her face. I stepped back from the podium and began delivering my presentation. It didn't take long to get into the flow of it. Before I knew it, the fish was walking and so was I, to the delight of the audience. The applause was absolutely resounding; it sounded like I was a winner. As I sat down next to Lillie, she glanced my way. She wore a slight smile on her face and a glow of admiration in her eyes. Lillie was introduced next.

"I think I shall never see a poem as lovely as a tree."

Those beautiful words were coming from an equally beautiful girl. The competition was on! Winning wasn't going to be easy. The applause for Lillie's recital was equally deafening; the crowd was there in force to support their hometown girl. Lillie took a bow and elegantly walked back to her seat. Annabelle had clapped the loudest. We were told the finalists would be announced as soon as the judges could decide. The judges disappeared into a back room to tabulate the voting, which seemed to take forever. The four finalists were asked to stand and face the audience. My dad was beaming and my mom was in tears. Lillie and I were selected for the finals. My mom hugged me. When I turned to congratulate Lillie, she was gone.

The next two weeks were used for final preparations. The mental workout was just as taxing as the previous weeks had been. As word spread of my selection for the finals, I began to receive well wishes and compliments from proud church members and local friends. I took my mom's advice on always trying for originality and sat down to write a few verses of my own to add to the poem.

> His suit fit so queerly, that everyone nearly,
>> Went following onto the street,
> But the best of it all, was how handsome and tall,
>> He walked when he didn't have feet,
> He did...he walked when he didn't have feet.

Now I must confess that, I surely would guess that,
    A fish trying walking would fail,
But with little advice, he walked perfectly nice,
    On the very tip toes of his tail,
He did…on the very tiptoes of his tail.

With his bright red cravat, his silky black hat,
    And his pants of rich darkish brown,
He fast twirled his cane, in a fashion so plain,
    And strutted right on through the town,
He did…he strutted right on through the town!

When Friday night came I was ready for the showdown. My mother informed me that we were going to ride with the Rawlings, a family that lived a block away. We had known the Rawlings since my father was stationed in Fort Benning, Georgia, a few tours earlier. Mrs. Rawlings was a rather self-absorbed lady with an air about herself that slightly irritated my mother and me. Mr. Rawlings and my father worked on the base together. They occasionally played cards at our house when it was our turn to host the card party.

Friday evening, when we drove to their apartment, my father went in to let them know we were ready to go. He came back out almost immediately and announced that they were not ready. He suggested that we return home, wait a while, and then try again. We stopped back by our place, and went inside. Thank God for the break, I had just enough time to go to the bathroom. A short time later, we piled back into our car and went over to the Rawlings. We waited and waited. Finally they came out. After a brief discussion about who should drive, my father agreed to ride with them, and we all piled into their car. Mr. Rawlings drove and my father sat in the front seat with him. I was squeezed into the back seat between my mother and Mrs. Rawlings. If you have ever been sandwiched between two people in a revolving door, then you know exactly how pressed I felt.

We were leaving later than we had planned, but we still had a chance to make it there on time. Then it happened. We were a few miles from the house when Mrs. Rawlings began complaining about not having worn her favorite mink stole. The more she complained, the more she convinced herself we needed to return home to get it. Finally, her husband relented. He turned around and went back to get her fur. I realized later that thoughtless move would prove to be fatal. I rode all the way to the church with two dead minks staring me in the face. Needless to say, when we finally arrived at the church, all the doors were closed and the parking lot was full. We were late. Mrs. Annabelle looked very perturbed as she guarded the door. We hurried up to the church. Once inside, Mrs. Annabelle raised an eyebrow and pointed me in the direction of my seat up front.

Lillie's presentation was excellent. She ended with a curtsy that was quite elegant. I smiled and she returned the favor with a big grin and a sigh of relief. The two other contestants had completed their presentations before I arrived, so it was my turn at the podium. As I approached the front, Mrs. Annabelle pointed to the clock. I nodded and faced the audience.

"A fish took a notion to come from the ocean..."

The words flowed from my heart in a sing, song rhythm that would have made a songbird proud. I captured all of the imagination I could and wove it into a colorful and vivid account of a walking anomaly in tails. I politely tipped my hat, tapped my cane, and gestured to my bow tie as I spun my tale. The audience loved it. Then, when everyone thought I had finished, I tossed aside my written text, stepped down closer to the audience and delivered my two original verses. There was a hush, and for a few minutes, absolute silence. The fish talked, walked, strutted and bowed to the amazement of the crowd. When I finally concluded my performance, the audience erupted in applause. As I returned to my seat, I could hear the buzz in my ears, as everyone seemed to whisper their approval.

It took the judges quite a while to decide who had won. Then, they finally returned from their deliberations. Mrs. Annabelle strode to the front, took the microphone, and opened a small, folded sheet of paper. She carefully eyed the audience, and then slowly read the list of prizes for first, second and third place.

"And now for third prize," she barked, "we have tickets to a Saturday matinée at the local theater... worth exactly twenty-five cents on post, and seventy-five cents downtown."

Third prize went to a bespeckled, young man who had read a version of John Weldon Johnson's, "The Creation." The work he chose was substantial, but he talked so low, when he delivered it, that hardly anyone could hear him. The second prize was awarded to me. I could hear a gasp when the results were announced. Mrs. Annabelle, sensing a negative response to the committee's selection, cleared her throat and addressed the audience.

"I believe I should tell you that Mr. Lee's presentation was outstanding. However, he failed to arrive on time and you know we must all teach our young people to be on time. So, we gave his first place award to the runner-up to teach him a lesson."

I was embarrassed beyond measure. It was bad enough that I had failed to win the contest, but I believed I had also dishonored my family and friends. I lowered my head in defeat. I only raised it slowly to hear Lillie's name announced as the contest winner. My prize was three pairs of argyle socks. Lillie received a twenty-five dollar savings bond, which would be worth fifty dollars when it matured. I glanced at her. She lowered her head in a small gesture of sympathy towards me. Then, she smiled ever so slightly. She liked my fish and I liked her. I realized then that some contests weren't necessarily about winning. I had won a heart and lost a contest. The ride home was forgettable.

Chapter 8: The Move to Fort Bliss, Texas (6th Grade)

Crossing the Desert to School

I could have gotten used to living in Georgia. The summers were bright and sunny and the winters were mild. I had made a few good friends and my sock of marbles was overflowing. Things were beginning to look promising. Then, we got the news. Our dad was being transferred to another post to begin a new career path in the Army. He had been selected to attend a special school where soldiers were being trained to operate and maintain the first nuclear-capable, surface-to-surface rocket system. It was a major career step for him. He would later be given the honor of being the first Negro to teach other soldiers how to operate and maintain the electrical system for the rocket, which was nicknamed The Honest John. It was an honor I barely understood at the time, but I would realize later in life how very special his selection had been.

We moved into a housing complex of ranch style townhouses on the post in Fort Bliss, Texas. There was a huge parade field across the street from our new home where we flew kites and played touch football. The complex had a brand new sidewalk, which circled the block. It served as our track for roller skating races. It was so cool. It stretched so far that you couldn't see the end of it. When the track finally curved and disappeared around the corner of the buildings, you had to look between the buildings on the backside to see which team was winning.

In Texas, we went to school on the post with all of the military kids that were our age. It was the first time my sister and I had ever attended a school with white kids. I was unaware at the time, but in 1954 the United States Supreme Court had ruled that public schools should be desegregated. The name of the case was 'Brown v. Board of Education.'

In the case, the team representing Brown, a Negro, had argued that the existing system of separate but equal public school systems for white children and colored children was unequal and unfair. The court agreed and the United States Army was one of the first government agencies to follow the court's directive to desegregate its schools.

The elementary school we attended was half a mile from our house. It was an easy walk if you consider walking across a desert easy. Texas was a lot hotter in the summer than Georgia and the area where we lived was right in the middle of a sandy desert. That fact might have been imposing for an adult, but it was pure fun for us kids. The desert had large dunes that we could jump off of into the warm sand. It had cactus plants that rose high above our heads. In the spring, they bloomed with colorful flowers and in the afternoon they cast long shadows across the sands. Whenever we passed a cactus, we had to be careful or we would catch a needle or two. The desert also had lots of tumbleweeds, dried prickly, plants that resembled spheres. When the wind caught the tumbleweeds, they rolled through the desert like a herd of thorny bowling balls.

To us kids, the desert was a magical place. It was alive with prairie dogs, roadrunners, horned toads, and very colorful lizards. It also had a snake or two, but we tried not to worry about that. On the cool afternoons, we would walk across the sand dunes with our bare feet warming slowly underneath us. We searched for arrowheads and other lost artifacts in the sand. We stripped tree limbs and used cord to make bows and arrows. Then we went hunting for roadrunners. I don't recall us ever catching one.

I do recall us catching a horned toad lizard and bringing it back home to show our friends. None of our mothers would allow us to bring one into the house, so we would hide them in our pants pockets. One of the whippings I received was for the horned toad that chased my sister from room to room when it got loose. My mother was angry with me for frightening her, but I thought it was worth it. My sister looked so funny running wildly back-and-forth throughout the house. It was not the only whipping I earned. I got a similar reward for placing a six-inch tarantula spider on the kitchen table.

My sister and I made friends easily at our new home. We shared stories about the places we lived before we came to Texas and we enjoyed having other kids share similar stories of their own. We played tag, red-rover red rover, and marbles almost daily. We held roller skating contests with tag teams of two each. Sometimes we raced the girls against the boys. Other times we mixed it up and held tag teams of boys and girls. I always picked my sister for my partner if we ran mixed races. I don't know why, but girls are faster than boys at some ages, and my sister was faster than any boy I knew for her age until we were in high school.

The summer went quickly. Fall came and it was time for school to begin. I was in the sixth grade and Bernadine was in the fifth. The first day of school we loaded up our book bags, and headed across the desert. It took about ten minutes to navigate the path we had scouted for ourselves earlier through the desert to our school. We arrived on time and found our classes. I recall my class had about five rows of seats arranged seven across. My teacher was an average size brunette. She wore a cotton print dress with flowers on it. She had a pleasant smile and a business-like manner that quickly calmed the class. She welcomed us to sixth grade and asked each of us to stand, say the "Pledge of Allegiance to the Flag," and introduce ourselves to the class.

When we had finished that exercise, the teacher began going over the class rules. We were shown where the exit doors were in case of a fire. Then, we were asked if anyone had ever been through an 'air raid drill.' A few kids raised their hands. I wasn't one of them. I had never heard of an 'air raid drill.' The teacher explained what we were to do and told us that we would be practicing the drill later in the week. I didn't pay much attention to what she was saying, because I was daydreaming about airplanes. When the teacher asked me to stand and repeat the instruction for the drill, I was caught. My classmates took advantage of the occasion to have a good laugh at my expense. I made sure I paid attention whenever the teacher was talking from then on.

Friday came and we went outside for our afternoon break for physical education, P.E. The classes had been separated into boys and girls. Our group of boys included my class and boys from the other sixth grade class. I hadn't seen some of those guys before, so I was careful to keep my distance. I was in a group from my class that included my friend, Larry. We were the only Negroes in the afternoon P.E. class. Our P.E. teacher, Mr. Conway, was a solidly built man with a strong set jaw, thick brown eyebrows, and piercing eyes. He stood heads and shoulders above us. His manner was forceful. He conducted his class by folding his arms while barking out our exercise instructions like a drill sergeant. I knew we were going to have to get used to his tough manner because he wasn't going to change it anytime soon.

The afternoon P.E. exercise was tag team races. That played right into my wheelhouse. I had always been fast for my age and racing for me came naturally. Our P.E. teacher split up the boys into four teams along class lines. I was on the second team with my friend, Larry. Larry was an easygoing guy. He had a winning smile and came across as a considerate and soft-spoken kid. I liked him a lot. He was confident and didn't need to be loud or boastful to show it. Larry played on our baseball team. He was our catcher. Whenever I looked at him, I could

154

picture his catcher's mask covering his face with his baseball cap on backwards. There were four guys on our team, Larry, Robert, Big Al, and me. We were positioned next to a team from the other class. They had four good-sized guys who looked like they might be hard to beat.

Before we could get started, the biggest one on the team turned towards me and said, "We're going to whip your tails."

Larry led off and gave us a decent head start. Robert, who raced on skates with us around the block during the summer, was next. He ran as fast as he could and increased our lead slightly. Big Al followed Robert in the race. He had earned that title because he was almost as round as he was tall. By the time I got the baton, we were a good twenty yards behind. As I raced to the turnabout, the kid from the other team was already heading home. I reached the line, turned to head home, and caught him looking back at me.

"Last one home is a lazy n....r," he yelled.

I couldn't believe my ears. I had heard the "N...." word used before to refer to Negroes in a derogatory way, but I never expected to hear it coming out of the mouth of a school classmate. I definitely didn't like what I had heard. My blood began to boil. I raced as fast as I could to catch up with him. He crossed the line a few steps ahead of me, turned, and triumphantly raised both his hands in the air. When he did, I hit him squarely in the face. He went down like a big rock and lay at my feet stunned. I stood over him with my fist clenched, ready to hit him again. One of the boys on his team pointed at me, looked at the teacher, and asked him if he was going to let me get away with that. I was certain I had crossed the line. I was ready for the inevitable consequences. To my surprise, the teacher walked up to me, looked down at the kid on the ground, and shook his head. What he said next stunned the rest of the class and me.

He turned to the class and said, "Serves him right. He needs to learn how to keep his mouth shut. We're all in the Army and that means we're all on the same team. "

I couldn't believe what had just happened. A white teacher had stood up for a colored kid in a mixed class in Texas. The other kids just shook their heads and looked stunned. It was a lesson I would never forget. Some members of the Army had learned to treat its military family members fairly because that was the code. The kid got up off the ground and shook off the sand.

Then, he looked at me and said, "Sorry, I didn't mean nothin' by it."

I looked back at him and nodded my acceptance of his apology. The P.E. class was over. We all gathered our things and headed in. It had been a remarkable day, and I had gained a new respect for the Army and the men who serve in the military services.

Back in the classroom, we got another surprise. In the middle of an English lesson, a jumbo cargo plane flew over our school. It was one of the B-52 cargo planes that frequently flew into El Paso, Texas. The noise from its six turboprop engines was deafening. The windows along the far wall of the classroom shook violently. The erasers at the board fell to the floor. The stand holding Old Glory looked like it was about to tumble over. I had never experienced anything like it before and haven't experienced anything as unsettling as that fly-over since.

Our teacher raised her hands to quiet the class. We all looked to her for our next move. She yelled for us to get under our desks and to not make a sound. We scrambled under our desk and peered out at each other wondering what we were expected to do next. It was a good five minutes before the plane passed and the rumbling ceased. The teacher finally told us we could take our seats again. Then, she explained we had just had an air raid drill. I couldn't understand what she meant. Was she afraid the plane was going to crash into the school?

It took a few moments before everyone calmed down. Our teacher told us that if this had been a bombing raid we would have been safer under our desks than standing out in the open. One of the kids wanted to know what kind of bombing raid was she talking about? That was when she dropped the 'n' word. The teacher told us that, in case of a nuclear bomb attack, we were expected to crouch under our desks, put our heads in our laps, wrap our arms around our knees, and stay absolutely quiet until the coast was clear.

I had heard about nuclear bombs, but I wasn't sure why we should be afraid of being hit by one. Was the B-52 cargo plane going to accidentally drop one on us? Years later, I learned that the entire drill was foolish and misleading. At the time, it was the only plan our country was willing to share with us in case a war with nuclear weapons broke out. I know now that the plan was totally inadequate. In the case of a nuclear bomb attack near your school about all you will have time to do is say a prayer and hope you make it to the other side.

Chapter 9: Mid-Year Move to Fort Sill, Oklahoma

Life in Lawton View - Off Post

There were periods in my life when everything around me seemed to move at warp speed. The half-year we spent in Texas was one of those times. My dad was only in Texas for a training mission. He was training to teach the electrical system for the Honest John surface-to-surface rocket. When that class was over, we left. His assignment had lasted half a year. Then, they shipped us to Fort Sill in Lawton, Oklahoma. It was one of two times he would be stationed there. I can't say that I missed my school in Texas since I was there for such a short while. I can say that I missed my lessons in basic geography because I don't recall learning much geography in the classes I took after leaving. That was one of the drawbacks to moving frequently. If you began a subject in one school, but missed it in another, you were out of luck.

Our first few months in Lawton, Oklahoma were challenging. We were unable to move onto the post right away because my dad's quarters were not ready. That meant we had to find our own housing in town. I am certain that it was a stressful time for my mother, but she did her best not to show it. We moved into a small ranch home at the outskirts of the city. It was in a housing development called Lawton View populated by Negroes. It was a relatively new development and still had dirt roads. The rust colored mud got all over my pants legs when it rained. My mother tried her best to get the stains out of my clothes afterwards. We had an old rub-a-dub tub that she used to scrub my pants by hand. I didn't fully appreciate how much work it took on her part to keep us clean.

There weren't many things in the community for youngsters to do. There weren't any parks or playgrounds. There weren't any shopping centers, skating rinks, or amusement parks. There was an outdoor theater that showed movies every Friday and Saturday night. It was close enough for us to hear the sound on a quiet evening. We would sneak over to the grounds to get a peak at a movie when we could. There was a corner store with a small building behind it that served as a recreation center for local kids a half-mile down the road. The center gave kids a safe place to meet and had a good reputation for being clean and alcohol free. My sister and I got a chance to see it with some of the neighborhood kids soon after we arrived. It was a nice place to meet and spend time with kids our own age. Our mother thought so too after her new neighbor, Mrs. Price, introduced her to the store owner and recreation center's director.

Soon after we got settled into our new home, Mrs. Price's niece, Geraldine, came to visit her. Geraldine was older than I was by at least five years. Her aunt thought it would be a good idea if my sister and I to escort Geraldine to a Friday evening function at the recreation center. After I got a chance to meet her, I thought it was a good idea too. In the eyes of that twelve-year-old boy, Geraldine was about the most beautiful girl ever. Maybe it was her light brown eyes, or her long, flowing hair that attracted me. Maybe it was the sweet smell of her perfume, which mesmerized me. All I knew was I wanted to spend the evening getting to know her better. My sister seemed to sense my interest and communicated her disgust with a smirk. I ignored her. I was sure she would leave us alone and join her friends when she got to the center. I was right. She left us in a hurry when she saw her girlfriends standing by the door.

The recreation center had a table tennis set you could check out and play and a small common room where kids could mingle. Sometimes they played music and we could dance, if you liked that kind of stuff. It wasn't my cup of tea. I had tried dancing. So far, I wasn't showing much promise. That would prove to be my weakness and would cost me a wonderful evening with Geraldine.

On the way to the center, I was a polite, perfect gentleman. I asked about Geraldine's family. She lived with their mother and her brother, Charles, in Duncan, Oklahoma. She said her brother stayed at home to work, but she wanted to see her favorite aunt during the school break. I asked her about her school. She told me it was small but she had a lot of friends there. She asked me about my school. I told her I hadn't been there long enough to know many people. She laughed. I would have blushed if I could.

It didn't take us long to reach the recreation center. We could hear the music coming from inside. I motioned for Geraldine to go ahead of me. She entered with a smooth sashay, her head held high. I saw my friend, Earl, standing by the jukebox. I lead Geraldine towards him so I could introduce them. Earl was a shy fellow and meeting Geraldine must have been the high point of his day. His eyes lit up with a bright smile and he nearly fell over with a bow to show his approval. Geraldine was very gracious; she said hello and didn't appear to notice Earl's awkwardness.

After we met Earl, my sister's friend, Connie, came to introduce herself. I knew Connie liked me, but I wasn't interested in her. She gave Geraldine a quick up and down look and then introduced herself. Geraldine smiled and pretended not to notice her staring at me. I told Connie that Geraldine was in town for a few days and that my mother had asked me to show her the recreation center. The explanation sounded all right to me but didn't seem to impress Connie at all. I pretended not to notice.

Just when I began to feel a bit pressed, Geraldine rescued me by asking for a glass of punch. I left her there talking with Connie while I scurried over to the punch bowl to fill up a glass. I didn't notice the older fellow who had entered the hall and now stood by the jukebox. I got two glasses of punch and returned to the far corner of the room where I had left Connie and Geraldine. Before I could say a word, Connie thanked me and took one of the glasses of punch. Geraldine smiled and asked me if the other one was for her. Of course, I said that it was. She reached out her hand and took it.

The music started up again. It was a lively tune and the dance floor began to fill up with kids swinging to the beat. Geraldine looked at me, but I pretended to be preoccupied. When she asked me if I was going to dance with her, I said I would but I wanted to get myself some punch. She nodded and I turned to retrieve another glass for myself. When I returned, Geraldine was gone. I looked around the room and saw her dancing with the older guy. He seemed to be really smooth on his feet and Geraldine looked pleased to have him as a partner. As I stood there in the shadows watching them sway to the music, I got a sick feeling in my stomach. The night was young and I was already out of the game.

Geraldine laughed as they completed their dance and walked over to the jukebox together. She looked down at the music listing while he stood there checking her out. Before I could get over to the jukebox to intervene, Geraldine had selected another song and they were back on the floor. I watched as they slow danced around the floor together. She laid her head on his shoulder and he guided her, step-by-step, from one side of the dance floor to the other. From where I stood, they looked like they belonged together. I was sure I had lost out to a much better man.

When the music stopped, Geraldine whispered something in his ear and then walked towards me. I stood petrified like a stone statue. She didn't seem to notice my frozen state. When she asked me if I wanted to have the next dance, I thawed immediately. As I lead her out onto the floor, I felt an exhilaration that I had never felt before. So what if I couldn't dance? I would do the best I could. My mother and sister had tried to teach me, but I seemed to have two left feet. I put all of those worries behind me and waited for the song to begin. I was in luck. It was a song with a beat like a cha-cha, which I had practiced before.

I swirled Geraldine out into the center of the floor and then waltzed beside her in a one-two-three step, cha-cha-cha movement. She caught on quickly and we proceeded to occupy the center of the room dancing side-by-side in rhythm. I wasn't flashy, but I held my own. Geraldine smiled and waved her hands in the air as we passed each other. I was floating above the crowd. It was wonderful. A few of the kids clapped when we exited the floor. Even my sister smiled at me. I thanked Geraldine for the dance and she gracefully nodded her head in acceptance. Then, I did a silly thing; I asked her about the guy that she had been dancing with. She turned to me, smiled, and replied that his name was Harold. He was a serviceman who was home for the holidays. Before I could ask her another question, she asked my sister to show her where the powder room was. My sister seemed delighted. As Bernadine and Geraldine headed off to the powder room, I joined a few of the guys over by the far wall.

I began talking with the guys. They all wanted to know who was that fine young lady who had been dancing with me. I admit that I wasn't used to getting that much attention, so I spent far too much time basking in my glory. It was quite a while before I noticed that Geraldine hadn't returned from the powder room. I excused myself from the guys, and went over to ask my sister if she knew where Geraldine had gone. My sister was polite, but she didn't answer me right away. When I pressed her for a response, she muttered something about taking a break.

"Taking a break where?" I asked her.

That part of the question, she couldn't answer. I left her standing there talking with the girls and went to look for Geraldine. She wasn't anywhere inside the center, and I wondered if she had gone home. My last attempt to find her took me outside.

I walked along the building until I heard someone laughing. One of the voices sounded like Geraldine's. As I rounded the corner of the building, I saw her leaning against the wall very close to Harold. They were laughing as a gray and white swirl of cigarette smoke curled lazily over their heads. I could have guessed that Harold liked cigarettes, but I was surprised to see Geraldine smoking one too. Harold took a drag, held it, and then puffed out a smooth, gray and white ring, which rose up and up until it disappeared into a translucent vapor. I didn't have to wonder where Geraldine had gone. She and Harold had made a connection and they were enjoying the time they had together. As I turned and slowly walked back to the party, I couldn't help thinking about them. In another place and another time, that could have been me.

Geraldine left the party with my sister and me. Harold walked her home from our house. He was a nice fellow and I wished him well. He was scheduled to be deployed to Germany in a week, but he saw Geraldine every night until he left. She came to our house to say goodbye at the end of her visit. She thanked us for the hospitality and said she hoped to get to see us again. I had wrapped a small present for her to take home. It was a handkerchief that my mother had helped me select at the five and dime store. Geraldine seemed surprised to receive a present from me. She showed her gratitude by planting a kiss on my cheek. I was stunned. That afternoon, a group of us walked her to the bus stop. I watched her get onto the Greyhound bus and then waved as she rode away. I could still smell the aroma of her perfume long after I could no longer see the greyhound on the back of the bus.

The memory of Geraldine was still fresh in my mind when, late one afternoon, her aunt came by our house to see me. She met my mother at the door and they talked for a while. She thanked her for letting me spend time with her niece and told my mom that she wanted to show her appreciation. I thought she would thank me in person and that would be the end of it, so I hung around in the doorway of my room listening to them talk. Finally, my mother called me to come into the living room for a minute.

As I entered the room, I could see that my mother was somewhat excited, but I didn't understand why. To my surprise, Geraldine's aunt greeted me with a big hug. As she squeezed me into her bosom, I realized where Geraldine had gotten her wonderful smelling, rose perfume. The next thing she did surprised me even more. She reached behind her and held up the loveliest guitar I had ever seen. It was a half-size acoustic with radiant walnut laminated finish. She handed it to me and thanked me for showing her niece such a good time. I was elated. I smiled broadly and told her that it had been my pleasure to spend time with Geraldine. Then, I hugged my new guitar and sleepwalked back into my room.

A Fraction Too Fast

We didn't stay in Lawton View for very long. Six weeks after we arrived, our dad was able to find us a town home inside the city. It was a small two-bedroom unit in a subdivision occupied mostly by families of enlisted men in the Army. We were there less than a month before we had met most of the residents.

The women and children were friendly and we felt welcomed in our new home.

It was good that we settled in so quickly because my sister and I started school very soon after we moved. I was in the sixth grade and she was in the fifth. I attended Douglas Middle School, which was near the local Baptist church. It was a neighborhood school that served the residents in the Negro section of Lawton. I entered school with heightened anticipation. It had been only a few months since I had attended an integrated school. I wondered if I would notice anything different. It didn't take me long to find out.

The classrooms were smaller and they held far more students than my previous school. The desks were worn and much older than the stainless steel frame ones we had in my previous school. Other than that, I didn't notice any significant differences inside the building from my previous school. The outside facilities were another story. There were none. Our school did not have a playground or an athletic field. We didn't have a baseball field, basketball court, or any other outside facilities. In the afternoon when we took our break, we played touch football in the school parking lot. It was a rugged game. The parking lot consisted of worn blacktop, gravel, coal cinders, and patched sand areas that turned to mud when it rained. I was shocked by the sparse facilities for the kids in our section of town. That didn't keep us from going at each other hard, however, during our afternoon recess periods in the parking lot.

I liked my sixth grade class. The homeroom teacher was a man who dressed very neatly in a suit every day he came to class. Mr. Morris was a math teacher. He kept our attention by moving around the room like a drill sergeant and engaged students by directing questions at them as he walked. He had broad shoulders and a square jaw. He was cleanly shaven and sported a marine haircut. He also had a soft voice and welcoming smile that kept all the girls in a trance. I liked him because he was smart and he didn't seem to be shy about showing his knowledge.

A few weeks after I had been in his class, we had a contest at the board to see who could work problems with fractions. I had been exposed to fractions at my school in Texas and remembered a few of the tricks our teacher had taught us about manipulating them. One trick in particular was the inversion of the second fraction in a division problem, then canceling multiples before multiplying to get a quick answer. I had practiced before our math contest, so I was ready for the competition.

Mr. Morris started with some easy fractions and then moved on to harder ones. I held my own throughout the first and second rounds. When we got to the third round, we had completed addition and subtraction of fractions. When Mr. Morris gave us our first multiplication problem, I zipped through the exercise in record speed. Within a few minutes, I had eliminated all of my classmates and stood alone at the board. Mr. Morris congratulated me for the job I had done so far. Then, he looked around the class and selected the smartest kids he could find as contestants for the final round. There were two boys and one girl. We worked three problems before the first boy missed one and had to sit down. A few problems more and the other boy dropped out too. The girl proved to be a more formidable contestant. She was able to last five rounds before she finally missed a problem. Once again, I stood at the blackboard alone.

Mr. Morris was impressed. He asked me to wait there a minute and he would be back. As he left the room, I didn't know what he planned to do, but I had an idea. No one said anything to me while he was gone. When he returned he had a cute young lady with him from another class. I learned later she was a seventh grader who was known by all of the teachers as a very bright student, especially in math. She wore a solid pink dress with a white, laced border. Her hair was braided and wrapped with a rubber band into a ponytail. She appeared to be confident and looked a little surprised when she saw me at the board.

"Bernard, this is Amanda Hawkins. She is a student from Mrs. Atkinson's class."

I acknowledged Mr. Morris' introduction and shook hands with Ms. Hawkins. She seemed so polite when I stretched out my hand that I almost thought she was going to take a bow. Mr. Morris explained the contest rules to Amanda and she took her place at the board. Mr. Morris gave us the first problem to work and the competition was on. I started quickly and finished my problem ahead of Amanda. She didn't seem fazed at all. She wrapped up her calculations, and turned to face the teacher. Mr. Morris checked both our problems and nodded his head in agreement with our answers.

The next thing he did surprised me. He turned to the class and said we had both down an outstanding job. The response from the class was a burst of applause. It was at that point that I realized how much this competition meant to Mr. Morris and my classmates. As I surveyed the room, I noticed all the seats were filled. There were quite a few more students in the class than usual. In addition, standing in the back of the room was Mrs. Atkinson and the rest of the members of her seventh grade class. From that moment on I was focused, alert and in the zone. The next few minutes saw us both work problems in record time. Each of us managed to finish quickly and alternated winning by just a few seconds ahead of the other. After five minutes we were tied.

Mr. Morris looked at the clock and announced that the first contestant to finish the next problem correctly would be the winner. I held my head down and looked quickly around the room. All eyes were on us. I could sense the tenseness in the atmosphere. Then, I looked up and right into Amanda's eyes. I could see the anxiety in her face. It was difficult for me to look away. I knew what was going through her mind. If she lost to a sixth grader, she would be a disgrace to her classmates. She hadn't asked to be tested in this manner, and it seemed a cruel reward for someone who had shown such promise in her classes. I tried to shake it off, but I couldn't. When the teacher gave us the final problem, I knew I had an advantage. It was a division problem with large fractions.

The competitive spirit in me took over. I raced to finish ahead of Amanda. I inverted the second fraction and began to cancel to reduce the numbers. It wasn't until I had finished that I realized I had seen a number that didn't actually exist. I had canceled an odd number, 17, dividing by 3, without noticing that it wasn't a multiple of anything. I scrambled to redo the problem. I was running out of time. Amanda was finishing up. It looked like she was definitely going to beat me. I glanced over at her calculations and the answer she was working on was huge. I knew I was way off and didn't have a chance to make up the difference. There was only one thing to do. I finished my calculations and placed my chalk at the board. When I turned to face Mr. Morris, the entire class applauded.

Mr. Morris looked over my work and realized immediately what I had done. He then turned to Amanda and said, "Time's up."

She let out a small sigh and placed her chalk at the board. Mr. Morris turned to the class and proudly announced that we had a tie. He then asked our classmates to give both of us a round of applause. Amanda blushed and looked relieved. I smiled at her. She smiled back. We both turned and took a slight bow. Then, Mrs. Atkinson told all her students to line up at the side door so they could return to class. I watched as Amanda joined her classmates, and they surrounded her to congratulate their champion. I saw the look of gratitude on Mrs. Atkinson's face and the look of satisfaction she received as a response from Mr. Morris. It had been a great day for math students at Douglas Middle School.

Etiquette Is a Lesson

My success as a sixth grade math whiz proved to be very useful for me during my time at Douglas. Both the sixth and seventh grade students accepted me instantly. Their curiosity about my knowledge of mathematics proved to be a great source of conversation wherever I went. I found myself sharing my travel and educational experiences with teachers, administrators, and most of the middle school students. Initially, I was unaware of how limited an exposure to the world many of my classmates had received. I gradually came to understand that I had traveled to more places in my short lifetime than many of them would travel in all of theirs. It was a truth that would follow me throughout my youth. I count it now as a blessing but, during my early years of travel, I longed to be from one place just like all of the other kids.

Mr. Morris proved to be full of surprises. He decided to expose his students to the finer things of life beginning with an etiquette lesson that I will never forget. Over a two-week period, Mr. Morris taught our class how to set a formal dinner table and how to act at a formal dinner. It was an amazing look into a facet of life none of us had any reason to believe we would ever see. I presume that he had to mount a strong argument to get the school board and administration to go along with his project. To this day, I am indebted to him for succeeding at convincing them. It was an unforgettable experience that opened my eyes to possibilities that I would never have realized on my own.

Mr. Morris taught both boys and girls the finer points of formal dining. He introduced the subject to the class by challenging us to recall a time in our lives where we had dreamed about dressing up and dining out. Then, he asked how many of us how had actually realized our dream. There were no hands raised in response to that question. It didn't seem to surprise him at all; he just kept on teaching the lesson. I don't know where the school acquired the fine china and silverware he used to teach us about fine dining. The tableware setting was exquisite. The silverware was highly polished and the crystal glasses, china plates, saucers and cups were more beautiful than any I had ever seen.

Mr. Morris assigned each student a task to perform as his way of teaching us how to set a formal table. We learned the names of the pieces of silverware and where to place each one. We learned the placement and use of each piece of fine china and were queried frequently during the lessons to ensure we were paying attention. We learned the function of a butter knife and where to place it after its use. We learned that the salad fork is placed to the outside of the dinner fork, as is the soup spoon to the outside of the teaspoon. We also learned how to place the dessert spoon and cake fork at the top of the plate, facing in opposite directions of each other. We learned how to use each piece of silverware on the table and how to remove them as the course of the meal progressed. It was a new experience for all of us. We were all learning a very practical lesson at the same pace. I was proud to be a part of such a thoughtful lesson on etiquette, which would prove to be extremely helpful to me in the future.

Finally, when our etiquette lessons were completed, we were rewarded with a formal dinner prepared by members of the school cafeteria staff and served by students selected from our class. The waiters wore white gloves and carried linen napkins on their forearms. We poured water into the tall water glasses and served hot dinner rolls to our excited classmates. We poured sparkling ginger ale into our wine glasses. It was all so elegant, exciting, and uplifting. When the formal meal was completed, all of our classmates stood and gave Mr. Morris a big round of applause. He accepted it graciously. I could tell that he was pleased to have given us a brief peek into a world we would never have experienced so early without his efforts.

I took Mr. Morris' lesson on dinner etiquette to heart. It was a gift that I found would keep on giving. I used it later to obtain a job as a bus boy and waiter at the Fort Sill Officer's Club. The job, which I held for six years, paid enough money for me to pursue my education through the first three years of college. Later in life when I taught high school students math and science, I passed Mr. Morris' gift on to my own class on dining etiquette. Each time I served a formal dinner at the Officer's Club or showed a student how to properly hold a teacup, I would remember Mr. Morris. Through his foresight and kindness, he gave an invaluable gift of dining etiquette to a small class of Negro students who otherwise might never have been exposed to the finer points of formal dining at all.

The Barking Dog Bites

After my success in the math contest, I felt really good about the welcome I had received at my new school. I looked forward every day to my classes. I was in a good place and the transition hadn't been as challenging as I expected. It's during those times of one's life that you just want to hold on to the memories and don't let go. Fortunately, some of us are able to remember a few of the great times in our lives; unfortunately, those times never last. This was one of those occasions.

We had moved into a housing development not too far from my new school. It was in a small two-bedroom house in a subdivision occupied mostly by military families. My sister and I usually walked together to and from school.

A few of the other kids in our subdivision would walk ahead of us. I chose to walk with my sister so I could hear all about her school day before we got home. We usually took the same route home each day. That posed a problem very soon into the school year.

One of our neighbors had an ill-tempered dog that liked to chase the kids who passed in front of the yard. There were no trees or fences. So, if an unrestrained dog chose to confront you, there was no place to hide. With my earlier encounters with dogs still fresh in my memory, I chose to avoid his territory all together. That meant we took an alternate route and got home fifteen minutes later. One day, my sister confided in me that she had to "go," and asked if we could take the shorter way home. I wasn't eager to agree, but she started squirming so I gave in.

We hurried along, as fast as we could, in the hopes that we wouldn't have to deal with the angry dog that day. It appeared that we had succeeded when out of nowhere the dog showed up and started barking at us. It was a major cause for alarm when I realized the dog was a lot closer than I had originally thought. As I turned to get a good look at him, he opened his month wide and snarled at me. I didn't know exactly what to do. I had heard that if you run from a dog it almost guarantees he will chase you, and probably catch up and bite you as well. I hoped the converse of that was if you didn't run the dog would not have a chance to chase you and, therefore, you could avoid getting run down and bitten.

I had only a few seconds to try my theory. I watched as my sister looked back at me with a frightened, pitiful anguish on her face. She had tried to keep moving, but her fear of what might happen next had her frozen in her tracks. I could see she was unable to move. I decided to stand my ground. Somehow I must have conveyed that thought to the angry dog because he stopped dead in his tracks. I took that action to signal that he would not follow us, that my theory had worked. With a new confidence, I turned and began walking towards my sister.

The response from the dog was unanticipated, sudden, and without provocation. He charged at me with a silently cunning stealth that I still do not understand to this day. The next thing that happened was terrifying. The dog bit me squarely on my lower calf muscle. He then yelped as if he had been severely injured and ran back towards the house. I didn't feel a thing. In fact, the yelp caused me to turn and watch as he scampered towards the house and banged against the front door. An unshaven man opened the front door and then stepped aside. The dog scrambled into the house and disappeared into the darkness. The jolt of the front door closing shocked me back to reality and I felt a sharp twinge of pain shoot up my leg. I looked down and saw the blood streaming from under my pants leg. The only thing that kept me from hollering was my sister's reaction to the incident. She seemed to be on the verge of hysterics. I chose to remain calm and to not add to the drama.

Together, we limped home. My sister held my arm and I held my pants leg in an attempt to ease the stinging from the dog bite. When we came crashing through the front door, my mother looked startled at first, but she recovered quickly and rushed to get a clean cloth to dress my wound. She washed it gently and then told me to turn my head because it might hurt a little. I did as she said and tried not to flinch too much as the ammonium peroxide my mother applied flushed the dog saliva out of the wound. She gently dabbed the wound to dry it, applied an antiseptic salve, and wrapped my leg in white gauze. The entire operation took less than five minutes. She didn't ask me a single question until she had finished.

"What happened to your leg?" she asked me finally.

I told her that the big German Shepherd dog at the corner bit me.

She looked straight into my eyes and said, "And what did you do?"

I told her that I stood still so he wouldn't chase us, but he bit me anyway. My mother looked at my sister who had not stopped shaking her head and told her to put her coat away and to meet us in the kitchen. My sister appeared not to hear her, so my mother repeated her command. My sister walked back to the front hall to put her coat away and my mother and I went into the kitchen.

I sat on one of our hard bottom chairs while my mother retrieved a bottle of milk from the refrigerator. She sat the milk on the counter and went to look for the can of chocolate milk mix in our pantry. She poured a big glass for each of us. Then, she scooped some of the chocolate mix into each of our glasses before stirring and placing them on the table. Next, she opened the cookie jar, retrieved two large maple syrup cookies, and placed one in front of each of us. I instinctively reached for mine and stopped when my mother gave me that look. I bowed my head and my sister joined us as we blessed the food.

"Where was the dog's owner?" my mother asked abruptly.

"We saw him open the door to let the dog back in the house, but he didn't come out to see if I was all right."

My mother didn't pursue that line of questioning. Instead, she told me to go rest until my dad came home. He would deal with the man and the dog. I finished my snack and got up to go take a nap. Without warning, my sister rushed over to me and gave me a big hug. It caught me by surprise. I hugged her back and she looked relieved as she stood there watching me head for the back bedroom.

My dad came home around six o' clock every evening unless he had a special assignment to complete after work. That day was no exception.

Dad walked through the door at six o'clock sharp. My mother gave him a kiss and a big hug. My dad looked at her curiously and smiled. Then, he asked her how her day had gone. She filled him in about the routine things that she had managed but did not mention the incident with the dog. My dad sat down at the kitchen table and began to unwind. He loosened the top button of his fatigues and reached for the cool glass of lemonade his wife had sat in front of him.

When it appeared that Dad had begun to settle in from his hectic day, my mother brought up the subject of loose dogs in our neighborhood. My dad eased back in his chair slightly and began to pay more attention as she talked. Then, she told him about the dog biting me. My dad was instantly alert. He asked to see it now. My mother sent my sister to get me. I must have looked disheveled because my dad's face registered concern when he saw me.

"I understand that a dog bit you today. Let me see it."

I reached down to raise my pants leg up so my dad could see the wound. He told me to unwrap it and then he took a good look at the wound. He didn't like what he saw.

"Did the dog have on his dog tags?" my dad asked me.

I told him that I didn't remember seeing any. This didn't sit well with my dad, so he asked me again if the dog had on his dog tags. I flinched at the intensity in my dad's voice, but that didn't persuade him to back off.

"No sir," I responded promptly. "The dog wasn't wearing a collar and I didn't see any dog tags."

My dad turned to my mother and asked her if she knew whose dog it was. She told him it was the black German Sheppard in the house up at the corner. My dad turned to me and motioned for me to follow him. My sister had joined us in the room, but he didn't acknowledge her at all. Dad was on a mission and he wasn't going to stop to explain anything to anybody until he had accomplished it.

I grabbed my sweater and pulled it over my shirt. It was all I could do to keep from limping too badly as we trudged up the hill towards the house. Dad didn't say anything to me as we walked. He didn't look back to see if I was keeping up with him either. When we reached the top of the hill and stood in front of the house, my dad pointed at it and asked if this was the one. I shook my head to indicate that it was. He took me by the hand and walked straight up to the front door. I stood there as he rapped the door knocker in a deliberate cadence to get the attention of the homeowner.

Just when I thought no one would answer the door, it swung open and the dog's owner stood there inside the door frame. He was at least three inches taller than my dad. He had a rough looking face and a small scar above his left eye. He was unshaven and smelled like he had been drinking. The house was dark; there wasn't a single light on anywhere in sight. I stepped back abruptly when the door opened and nearly fell from the pain shooting up my leg. I reached for the leg and then stopped. It wasn't going to feel any better if I grabbed it, so I resisted the temptation. My dad ignored me entirely. He focused all his attention on the man who was standing there in the doorway.

"What do you want?" the half-drunk man barked.

My dad didn't flinch, back up, or take his gaze off of the man. It was as if my dad was sizing him up and waiting to see what he would have to do to get his attention.

"I'm your neighbor from down the hill. Do you have a German Sheppard dog?" my dad asked.

The man looked a little puzzled. He responded by ducking the question and wanted to know why my dad was asking him about a dog. My dad didn't waver in his gaze. He looked the man straight in the eye, shifted his weight to the back of his right foot, and repeated his question. The man became agitated, leaned over, spit on the ground, and then told my dad that he must be mistaken because he didn't have a dog. My dad raised his right hand and placed his forefinger squarely under his chin, leaned slightly back and rested his thumb next to his cheek. At the same time, he balled his left hand into a fist. I had seen a similar pose in the picture of a boxer on the military post at the gym.

Before I could blink an eye, the scene changed suddenly and the next series of moves were a total blur. A wild, snarling dog came charging out of the shadows and leaped for the opening in the door. Just as quickly, the man swung around and stretched out the boot on his left foot, and kicked the dog as hard as he could back towards the hallway. My dad looked startled, but he responded by crouching down and bringing both fists out in front of him. He took a combat ready stance and waited. The dog would not be deterred. He charged a second time and was just as violently repulsed by the man as he had been before. I could see my dad was ready to spring. I stepped back out of his way.

The dog gave it one last try, but the man proved to be too much for him. He retreated to the shadows yelping the same way he had at our encounter. The man turned to my dad and gave him a disgusting look.

"That dam dog is a pain in the…," he spit out. "The kids are always teasing it and I can't do a dam thing with it anymore."

I thought my dad would blow a gasket, but he kept his cool. Then, he asked a straightforward question, "Has your dog been treated for rabies and does he have his tags?"

The man looked back towards the hallway as if he was waiting for the dog to charge again. Then, he turned towards us and refused to answer the question. My dad asked him again, but still didn't get a satisfactory response. My dad informed the man that he was going to report the incident to the post authorities and that he expected them to call on him to check everything out. The man didn't flinch or move a muscle. Instead, he turned abruptly took a step inside and shut the door in our faces.

My dad didn't seem fazed at all. He looked at me, and said, "Let's go home."

I followed behind him glowing with the thought of how bravely he had stood up for me. I had never felt so close to my dad, and I would remember that day long after he was gone.

I wish the rest of the story was as comforting as those few minutes that day, but that's not how real life goes. My dad did turn in the incident report, and the military police came to our neighborhood to check out the dog owner. Unfortunately, they didn't find him there. The dog had bitten me on a Friday. By that Monday, the dog owner had taken his dog and moved. Since the authorities were unable to determine if the dog had been immunized against rabies, I was forced to take a series of ten very painful shots to protect me against the disease.

Every morning for ten days I went to the doctor, took a shot in my abdomen with a very large needle, and then had to attend school for the day. The worse results were how awfully long the pain lingered and how much the injected areas itched. I will never forget fighting back my tears while sitting through five periods of agony. My advice to anyone who is bitten by a dog is to have the animal tested immediately for rabies. Don't let the owner get away with the crime. You are not going to escape the agony if you do.

A Look Back in Time

Chapter 10: Our Church on the Corner

A Fifth Sunday Conversion

Galilee Baptist Church sat on the corner of one of the main access roads into our neighborhood. It was an elegant looking church with Gothic spires and stain-glass windows. It possessed all of the religious traditions that a sound Baptist church is known for. An imposing lady who played a rousing mean piano led the choir. She expected all of the choir members to give her their best and the members didn't disappoint. The deacon board was active and the elderly matriarchs in the amen corner were diligent in keeping the services on point.

Our family attended Galilee Baptist Church after receiving an invitation from a church outreach member who knocked on our door the second Saturday morning after we had arrived. She welcomed us to the neighborhood and spent nearly half an hour explaining the benefits of worshiping with the spiritual family at Galilee Baptist. My mother was impressed with her sincerity and pleasantness. After an exchange of address and telephone numbers, my mother assured her that she would see us next Sunday.

The very next Sunday, we rose early and dressed in our Sunday best. Our dad was a little slower getting up, but he finally joined us. Together we headed for Sunday services at Galilee Baptist Church. When we arrived, we were greeted by an usher who showed us to an open bench near the front of the church. We took our places quietly and waited for the services to begin. We didn't have to wait very long. A lady in a colorful blue dress stepped beside the preacher's pulpit and beckoned the choir to rise. The choir members rose in unison and assumed their places in the choir box. The choir director lifted her hands and the opening hymn began.

I was impressed by the cheerfulness of the choir members. They lifted their voices in harmony and raised a joyful noise unto the Lord. The congregation joined in and the warmth generated by the spirit in the sanctuary increased seven-fold. When the round of spiritual choruses was completed, we were told to be seated. The church secretary rose to read the day's announcements. Following the announcements, an assistant minister welcomed us to the service and asked all persons visiting the church to please stand and introduce themselves.

My dad rose to his feet as if he had been told to stand at attention. We all followed his example. He spoke for our family giving his name, his rank, and current military assignment. Then, he introduced each of the members of our family. He concluded by affirming that we were a Christian family and that we were proud to be worshiping with all the members of Galilee Baptist Church. We stood until all of the guests were recognized and then we took our seats. The assistant minster followed the introductions with a prayer and then one of the choir members performed a solo.

This pageantry was very familiar to our family. We had attended services on the post, which followed a similar program. After the solo, another assistant minister rose to read the scripture followed by another song by the choir. The church sat silently for a brief time after the choir concluded their number and then the ladies in the amen corner began to stir. They joined together to form a chorus of soulful voices. The cadence was drawn out and elongated. The words were strained and difficult to understand. They sounded more like moans than messages. The elderly ladies swayed gently as they sang. A few of them held their hands in their laps and looked towards the heavens. It seemed to me to be more of an exhibition suited for a sorrowful funeral than an outpouring of joyful noises unto the Lord.

The volume of the singing increased gradually as the soulful stanzas were repeated over and over. I had never experienced anything like this before. I looked to our mother to see her expression and reaction to the singing. She was rocking back and forth with the same cadence as the elderly ladies in the amen corner. Her eyes were closed and she seemed to be in another place. I glanced at my dad. He was staring straight ahead with a solemn expression on his face. I had never seen him so calm in such an intense way.

As the ladies raised their voices to the Lord, the entire church transformed into a cathedral of inspired worshipers all repeating the solemn refrain in unison, "Precious Lord take my hand, lead me on, and let me stand…"

I had heard these words many times before, but I had never heard them sung in the tone and tenor of the elderly ladies of the Galilee Baptist Church amen corner. Before they finished singing, some twenty minutes later, the entire church was on its feet and praising God in an outburst of delirious affection. The atmosphere was electrified. The mood was contagious. I watched my mother rise and shout in an outburst that surprised us all. She shrieked at the top of her lungs and then sat down abruptly clasping her arms around her shoulders and rocking back and forth.

My dad didn't move a muscle to comfort her; instead, he looked straight ahead and wrestled with his own version of "coming to the water." Finally the singing abated and the shouting ceased. The minister rose, took his place in front of the pulpit, and exhorted the entire church to praise the Lord with a hearty Amen. I don't remember the title of his sermon. I do remember the fervor with which he preached. I was both inspired and impressed. I could see myself standing in front of a church crowd in a long black robe delivering such stirring oratory as he did. I could feel the power and the glory of such a feat. I knew from that moment on I wanted to know more about the work of the Baptist minister.

A few weeks later, my sister and I attended the church Sunday school where we met a wonderful group of local kids who attended the church services. I gravitated towards a young man named Benjamin who seemed to be very knowledgeable and friendly. We became acquaintances and later we joined the young men's group in the Baptist Training Union, an auxiliary of the church. We did so well leading the discussions in the evening Bible classes that the Sunday School Superintendent enlisted us to deliver the scripture reading on the fifth Sunday when young people were allowed to conduct the opening services. It was quite an honor, and we took the job very seriously.

Benjamin and I took turns reading the scripture and saying the opening morning prayer. We must have been fairly good at it because we received a lot of compliments from our peers and other members of the church. Mrs. Reed, the pastor's wife, told my mother how proud she was to see two young men serving the Lord. My mother passed that message on to me. I placed it in that special place next to all my other unspoken ambitions.

This was also about the time that my mother began questioning my sister and me about our commitment to join the church. She explained that we were getting older now and we needed to consider saving our souls. I knew what she was trying to tell us, but I wasn't ready to take that step. Neither was my sister, so we tried to avoid the conversation whenever it came up. It seemed to be working because our mother suddenly stopped mentioning anything about getting baptized or saving our souls.

Benjamin and I continued to perform as a team for the fifth Sunday opening services. We enjoyed the attention and compliments we received from church members, but we soon began to notice something was missing. No matter how hard we tried, we couldn't get the elderly ladies in the amen corner to go along with us. They always seemed to add another thirty minutes of praise to the services without regards to anything that we had done to warm up the church. One afternoon, Benjamin asked me if I had noticed how long the elderly ladies sang after we finished our opening services. I told him that I hadn't paid attention to them, but I was keenly aware of what he was getting at. Benjamin said that he had a plan to change that. I wondered what it was.

When the next fifth Sunday came, we were sitting in front of the church again with all eyes on us. I read the scripture and Benjamin rose to deliver the Morning Prayer. He seemed focused and very determined. As he began to lift his voice to praise the Lord, a strange feeling came over me. I sensed that this was going to be something different, something very special.

Benjamin reached his arms up to the heavens and pleaded for forgiveness for all the sins that we all knew we carried around with us. He asked for mercy for all those sinners who couldn't help themselves and needed God's grace to rescue them from damnation. He asked for healing for those among us who were sick and infirmed. He asked for divine guidance for those among us who were lost and he pleaded for another chance for those who had given their lives to the Lord but had fallen back in the face of earthly challenges and temptations. Then, he did a very strange thing. He began a personal plea for his own salvation. He chronicled the many mistakes he had committed in his lifetime and asked for forgiveness.

The entire church was moved. You could see the anguish in Benjamin's face. His whole body writhed with desperation. He wavered back and forth and appeared to be in a dizzying trance. I didn't know whether I should hold on to him to sturdy his stance or sit there in awe. When he began to sing, in that slow, methodical moaning incantation, I knew he was no longer with us. The Holy Spirit had descended upon him and he was at that moment in a different world. I had heard about such things, but I had never observed it up close, especially not happening to a friend of mine. I froze in place. I don't recall making a sound, but I found myself moaning along with the rest of the congregation.

When Benjamin sang "Precious Lord, take my hand..." I reached out to grasp him, but I was too late. He fell to his knees and continued singing with even more fervor than before. The members of the congregation began shouting. The amen corner woke up and joined in the rapture. The whole church was aflame with the Spirit of the Lord. That Spirit didn't let anybody go until it had drained every bit of malice, hate, sorrow, and contrition out of us.

Our Senior Pastor, Reverend Reed, walked over to where Benjamin was kneeling and placed his hand on his shoulders. He turned to the congregation and asked them to lift their voices to pray for the salvation of this young man's soul.

Benjamin responded with a hardy, "Yes Lord" and the church erupted in uncontrolled shouting and pandemonium.

The scene resembled a contained riot unraveling in slow motion. Ladies shouted and ran down the aisles. Men turned to each other, grasped hands, and patted each other on the back while repeating over and over, "Praise the Lord! He's Saved!"

When the church eruption finally subsided, Reverend Reed asked for the congregation to be seated. He thanked God for resting His Divine Spirit on our blessed sanctuary and began to preach a mighty sermon. Not a single chorus was heard from the elderly ladies in the amen corner. Benjamin had done it. He had finally succeeded in satisfying the elderly ladies and living up to the tradition of the amen corner. Unbeknownst to him, he also had succeeded in saving a host of lost souls. When the pastor called for those who needed to give their lives to the Lord to come on down to the front of the church and be saved, I jumped up from my seat and, with my sister following close behind, walked into the pages of the Book of Salvation revealed to me that very day by Benjamin, my solemn friend.

A Look Back in Time

Chapter 11: Move to Family Housing On Post

Our Move-In Routine

Dad came home on a beautiful Friday evening and gave us the good news. We had been cleared to move onto the post the following weekend.

We had been on post before, but this time we were going to stay. My dad drove slowly as we approached the main gate. He stopped and showed the Military Policeman (MP) at the gate his army credentials.

The MP looked them over quickly and then said, "You're clear to go, Sergeant."

Dad nodded his head and drove off with a smile on his face. We passed the commissary and Dad asked our mother if she needed anything from the Post Exchange (PX). Our mother said that she would wait until we got to our new home to decide what we needed.

We passed by the firing range, where the red flag was flying indicating that live ammunition was being used and all non-authorized personnel should stay clear. When Dad finally turned off the main road, we knew we were getting close to our new home. I was pleasantly surprised to see a set of tree-lined, barracks style apartment homes unfold in front of us. The formation wasn't in uniform rows like the sets of barracks we had passed. Instead, all of the homes were set back from a circular roadway, which wound its way throughout the complex. There was a spacious field, suitable for playing baseball and other outdoor games, situated right in the middle of the complex. It was not as large as the one we had played on in Texas, but it would do. The entire housing complex was set back from a much more auspicious parade field. I couldn't tell if it had been designed that way, or if our complex had been one of many others planned but not yet completed. The grass was plush in that section of the

189

complex. It would be a great location for our afternoon tackle football games.

Dad asked us to check for our house number on the buildings. We looked at the buildings along our right side while Mother and Dad scanned the numbers on the ones on the left. Bernadine spotted the building first. She burst with joy when she also spotted a group of girls jumping rope besides the building next to the one we would be moving into.

Later when the girls with light-brown complexions introduced themselves, they told us they were from Puerto Rico. My sister wanted to know where that was. One of the older girls explained that Puerto Rico was an island off of the coast of Florida. I had heard about the island, but this was the first time I had ever met anyone from there. I didn't say it then, but they looked a lot like Negroes to me. When we asked our mother later that evening about our new friends from Puerto Rico, she paused to reflect on my observation. My mother told us that they were not from here. She said that they were foreigners, who looked like but were not actually American Negroes. The reserved tone of her voice indicated to me that she was telling us only a portion of what she believed.

Dad parked the car next to our new home. This time, we were assigned to a first floor unit. The keys were in an envelope that Dad carried in his fatigue pocket. He retrieved them and opened the door with his first try. Our mother told us that she thought that was a good sign.

Mother began barking out directions and we all rolled up our sleeves and got to work. A crowd of curious neighbors appeared on the balconies across from us, in the courtyard next to us, and even in the ball field across the street. We had moved into new quarters before, so we knew what to expect. A crowd of curious neighbors greeted everyone when they moved in. The scene was a common right-of-passage for newcomers. We expected it, but it would be a long time before I would get used to it.

Our mother took an inventory of the items we had brought with us and examined the space in the pantry. It didn't take her long to complete the list of items she needed to purchase at the PX and the commissary. Dad didn't need us to go with them to run those errands, but he always took us with him anyway. It was the high point of our move. There is something to be said for the smells, the sights, and the surprises we experienced on shopping trips to the PX and commissary. The PX substituted for today's department store. It included everything you would expect to find in today's Super Wal-Mart, with significantly better prices. The PX sold discounted merchandise priced to fit an enlisted soldier's pay level. It is a military institution that has been scaled back in today's cost conscious environment, but it was an essential shopping value for service men and women at Fort Sill.

After arriving back at our new home following the shopping spree, we sat around the dinner table and gave thanks. Dad offered a prayer full of hopefulness for a fresh beginning for this next phase of our lives in this new place. The sun had set by the time we finished the dishes and began getting ready for bed.

My mother entered the room as I finished my prayer. She seemed pleased to see me rising from my knees. I felt a little embarrassed, so I climbed into bed quickly. I was glad, however, that I was still not too old to get a kiss from her before she turned the lights out. I cherished those moments then. I miss them to this day.

A Look Back in Time

Chapter 12: Hunting With My New Friend

Everyone remembers a best friend from childhood. Since we moved so often during mine, I had a few best friends. The kid next door in Fort Sill was one of my best friends. His name was Richard. We developed a solid friendship after just a few days together. He had a dog that he really loved. It came running toward me the first day I spotted him in the courtyard. It was a medium-sized, black and white, shaggy dog, perhaps an Irish sheep dog. I reached out to pet him, and he scampered back towards his master. When Richard reached out to grab him, he turned and ran back to me. He was enjoying the game, and I sensed that my new neighbor was enjoying it, too.

"What's his name?" I asked.

"Brownie," Richard replied.

I thought that was an odd name for a black and white dog, but Richard didn't seem to think so. I asked him about his family. He described his dad, his mother, and his older brother. When he whistled for Brownie, the dog came running to him and rolled over on the ground.

"Nice trick," I said. "Can he do anymore?"

"Brownie can chase down rabbits," he said proudly.

To illustrate his point, Richard told me about the time Brownie chased a jackrabbit around the firing range for over an hour until the rabbit grew tired and gave up.

Richard said, "The rabbit's ears were over two feet long! They made him look almost four feet tall!"

I liked the tall tale Richard had told me about the rabbit, and I liked him almost from the start. He took to me as well. From the first day we met, we were inseparable.

The very next day, Richard came over to my house and knocked on the door. My mother answered and he introduced himself. When she asked about his family, Richard suggested that we come with him to meet his mom. I was just beginning my day, so I didn't have any other plans. My mother said she would join us after she finished the dishes. Richard and I went outside and sat on the front stoop.

"Where's Brownie?" I asked

Richard waved his hand and said, "I don't know. Brownie leaves early in the morning and comes back later in the day."

I thought that was odd, but I didn't say anything about it. "Would you like to see my marble collection?" I asked.

Richard said that he would, so we went into the house and headed for my room. My mother poked her head around the corner, but didn't say anything when she saw us.

I got my sock full of marbles out of my favorite box and began showing them to Richard. He really liked the Stars and Stripes Boulder. I knew he would. After we finished looking at my marble collection, my mother called and said she was ready to go with us to meet Richard's family. Richard led us around the building, across the courtyard, and into his house. He lived on the bottom floor, too. His unit was designed exactly like ours. As he opened the screen door, we heard his mother call out to ask who was coming in. Richard responded by telling her they had company and asking her to come meet his new friends.

Mrs. Trahan was a pleasant looking woman who wore a light brown dress with a red apron. She had her hair up in curlers and her head wrapped in a kerchief. She stood a little taller than my mother and looked slightly ruddy from rushing to see who was there. Richard introduced us to his mother and then we rushed to his room to see his arrowhead collection. My mother and Mrs. Trahan got along just fine. They exchanged stew recipes and remedies for curing head colds. By the time they finished talking, each of them knew a lot more about the other. They seemed to be comfortable with that arrangement. It would prove to be an asset for our friendship later.

Chasing Jackrabbits with Brownie

When the weekend came and the firing range was clear, Richard and I went looking for jackrabbits. I didn't have a dog, but Richard solved that problem rather quickly. He told me about a stray dog that hung around the neighborhood and sometimes would follow them when they went hunting. We looked near the abandoned home at the end of the next block over and, sure enough, the stray dog was hanging out around the building looking lost and afraid. I had planned my strategy ahead of time to get him to follow us. I reached into the paper bag I had brought with me and pulled out a leftover bone from yesterday's stew. He saw it and jumped up into the air to get a better look.

I coaxed him to follow me before giving him the bone to chew on. He rolled over in the grass playing with the bone when he realized there wasn't any meat on it. I asked Richard what did he call him. Richard just shrugged his shoulders.

"I'm going to call him Rinny, you know, like Rin Tin Tin," I said.

That seemed all right with Richard, so we left with Rinny following us back to our building. Brownie, who seemed to recognize Rinny right away, joined us. They circled each other and sniffed, but didn't get overly aggressive.

"Come on, Brownie," Richard called. Then he whistled and both dogs fell in line behind us.

It was a long walk to the firing range. We watched as the dogs chased each other across the open plains. It was a sight that made me feel so free I wanted to burst into song. I chose not to and I expect Richard was happy about that. There were few, if any, trees on the open plains. There were even fewer on the firing range. The flowing prairie grass waved in the wind while the dogs sprinted after unseen prey. The entire scene was breathtaking.

Springtime in Oklahoma was as beautiful as any place on earth. There were vast collections of prairie wildflowers that rivaled the beauty of offerings in any commercial nursery. The variety and colors were awesome. There were yellow and white sand lilies, blue sage, and blue stem flowers. Across the looming prairie sprang purple Baldwin ironweed, yellow bitter weed, and my favorites, giant Sunflowers. The rare varieties of prairie flowers, found mostly on the plains, captured my imagination.

Oklahoma plains also feature a stunning array of tall prairie grasses, including a variety called Old Turkey Foot. The plant blossoms in three-pronged arrays, resemble wheat stalks. I realized, later in the seventies, that its prongs looked just like today's Peace Sign. Oklahoma also had a species of plant named for its famed buffalo. These massive creatures roamed free on animal reserves set aside by the U.S. Government to protect them from extinction. They enjoyed the freedom and inspired the names of a number of beautiful flowering plants. Those included the yellow Buffalo bur and Buffalo gourd. I personally liked the orange-colored Buffalo grass that dotted the prairie enhancing the majestic look of its vast expanse.

There was prairie grass as far as you could see and fluffy, white clouds floating lazily overhead. A hawk sailed above us in the distance. It was looking for something to pounce on and didn't want to be distracted by a noisy pack of dogs.

Richard reached down to pick up an arrowhead and Brownie, the lead dog, froze in his tracks. His whole body dropped lower by almost six inches as he pointed towards the East. At first, Rinny didn't seem to notice that Brownie had stopped running but, once he saw him crouch lower, he stopped in his tracks and waited for a signal to charge. He didn't have to wait long. A jackrabbit sprang up fewer than twenty feet in front of us and the chase was on.

Nothing matches the splendor of a pack of dogs chasing its prey. It rivals a horse race because the excitement associated with the outcome catches your imagination and runs right along with the dogs. Brownie took the lead and soon had the jackrabbit running in a big clockwise circle. Rinny wasn't to be left out. He charged again and again cutting off the circle and shortening the distance between the jackrabbit and the hunters. I was drawn into the drama of the chase and didn't realize that Richard had left me standing there while he ran wildly after the dogs pursuing the jackrabbit.

"Get 'um, Brownie!" Richard yelled. "Get 'um!"

I joined the chase running behind Richard as we followed the dogs in an ever-widening circle of pandemonium and pure joy.

When Rinny finally got winded and quit running, we were exhausted too. Only Brownie kept at it until even the jackrabbit looked weary. Then, the oddest thing happened. Brownie stopped running and the jackrabbit turned and came to a screeching halt. He pricked his ears up to catch any evidence of danger getting closer and then lifted one leg and began to groom himself. I had never seen such a spectacle. I know I would have never guessed a rabbit would stop in the middle of a chase to groom. In that moment, I learned something very important about God's creatures; they each have a healthy respect for the other's strengths and weaknesses. The dogs had done their best to harry the jackrabbit, and he

197

had bested them at it rather handily. His reward was to stop and repair his tattered fur while the worn out predators lay exhausted only a short distance away. For the dogs and jackrabbit, it was all in a day's work. We were just lucky to be there to see it.

On the way home, Richard caught a horned toad lizard. He held it in the palm of his hand and then turned it upside down. The lizard just lay there as Richard rubbed its belly with his fingers. I had done that with turtles, but I didn't know you could do that with a horned toad lizard. I was learning a lot from this prairie land cowboy. Our walk ended with us spotting a beehive in the trunk of an oak tree. We didn't hesitate to stir things up. The bees weren't happy, and they let us know it by chasing us all over the field. The dogs wanted nothing to do with it. They ran off and left us to fend for ourselves. Richard got stung, and the side of his nose began to swell. I knew I was going to get yelled at by his mom for coming home with him injured. Richard just laughed during the whole ordeal. He thought my panic about his bee sting was the funniest thing. It wasn't until we were almost back at the house that he told me that he got stung lots of times and it never bothered his mother or him. Richard was prone to exaggerate. It was a trademark that he wore like a badge of honor for all to see. I was still glad to know he would be OK.

Winged Masked Marvels

I definitely envy people who can get up early because a lot of fascinating things happen for them. I'm not an early riser but, on occasion, I found myself up much earlier than usual. On those rare occasions, I would dash over to Richard's house and get his mom to let me wake him. Richard also was rarely up early.

One morning, I had a good reason to wake Richard up early. This was the morning that we had agreed to catch some winged creatures.

We had spotted them late the evening before. They were flying around buzzing past our heads until late in the evening. At first we tried to ignore them, but that proved to be a lousy strategy. The more we ducked, the more they seemed to swarm. Richard thought they were swifts, tiny birds that feed on insects. I thought they were swifts, too, until I realized they didn't make any sounds. I was certain then that they were a band of mysterious visitors, and I was determined to find out where they lived. I figured if we got up early enough, we could climb up the big oak tree and get a look for ourselves.

As I rustled Richard out of bed, he tried his best to climb back in. No matter how much I pleaded with him, he wasn't ready to wake up. Finally, I yanked the covers from around his head. He threw a pillow at me. Two or three pillow tosses later, we were both fully awake, and Richard reluctantly rolled out of bed.

"Come on, Richard," I scowled. "We are going to miss them if we don't hurry."

Richard grunted and slowly pulled a t-shirt over his head. When we passed his mom in the kitchen, she asked us if we wanted a biscuit before we ran out of the house. I never turned down anything she offered; neither did Richard. We each grabbed a biscuit, stuffed a piece of ham into it, and then ran out of the house.

Nothing beats an early morning breeze on a warm summer day. The one blowing that morning was really appreciated. Richard and I sat on the porch, chewed on our ham biscuits, and took in the early morning sights and sounds. The leaves on the trees swayed gently as the wind flowed lazily through the branches. If we looked closely, we could catch a glimpse of a spider web left over from the late night hunt stretched between two tall bushes. It was quiet. Even the crickets had gone to bed and the early morning chatter among the blue jays had not yet begun.

Brownie and Rinny were still catching a few winks as the early morning light began to illuminate the summer sky. That was all right since we didn't need any distractions from our special morning mission.

I had spotted the creatures the day before as we sat on the porch and enjoyed the cool breeze that came at sundown. The creatures were flying in and out of the fading late evening light. We could barely distinguish one creature from another, but they were there. I leaned over to alert my pal, Richard, with a whisper, but he had already sensed their presence and seemed enthralled. I tried again to get his attention, but he waved me off and just kept staring at the dome of the large oak tree in the courtyard. Eventually one of the creatures would fly outside of the dome and become illuminated by the moonlight. I waited and watched, too, expecting to get a glimpse of one of these flying marvels.

We didn't have to wait very long. One flew just overhead and flashed a cold, scary wing close enough to cause my hair to stand on end. I realized then we were witnessing a rare phenomena. I became excited about the possibilities for exploring this discovery further. Richard came to the same conclusion, so we made a pact to keep our discovery secret until we could capture one of the creatures and examine it for ourselves. We quickly realized that any attempt we made to climb the tree that evening would be futile. The creatures seemed to sense our presence. They would bolt if we tried to rush them. Instead, we watched them as they executed their spectacular maneuvers and agreed to get up early the next morning so we could take them by surprise.

It was barely six-thirty in the morning when we approached the big oak tree. The courtyard was empty, the dogs were still asleep, and all of the early morning traffic had departed. It was the perfect time to catch a few winged, masked marvels. I had asked Richard if he thought we needed gloves to handle the creatures, but he honestly didn't know. It wouldn't have mattered anyway, because neither one of us owned a pair. I suggested that I be the one to climb up the tree this time, so we wouldn't have a repeat of a prior month's disaster. If Richard's ego was a bit bruised by my suggestion, he didn't show it. I felt comfortable climbing. After all, I was agile and my skinny limbs just naturally clung to tree branches. Richard gave me a boost, so I could get started. I reached for the nearest tree branch, swung my right leg over it, and the hunt was on.

I looked up once to see the tall tree branches ahead of me and then steadied myself. I concentrated on just reaching the next branch. That strategy steadied my nerves and helped me to overcome the fear of falling. I took my time, and Richard held any comments he might have wanted to make until I could capture the prize. The tree trunk grew smaller as I climbed higher and so did the branches. I squinted at the sunlight flickering through the branches as I climbed higher and higher. Finally, I could see what I had been searching for. One of the creatures was hanging from a skinny limb just two branches above me. I would have to ease my way out onto a branch to make the catch. As I proceeded to climb out on the branch, I didn't dare to look down. I was very careful not to move too quickly for fear that I would startle the creature, but he seemed to be mummified or sound asleep.

I stretched out my left arm and very slowly inched my hand along the limb. I held my breath, not wanting anything to alert the creature to my presence. The tactic seemed to work. The creature remained asleep as it hung upside down and totally still. I inched a little farther and then almost lost my balance. I had to place my right leg around another branch to steady myself. I expected the noise to wake up my prey, but he seemed to be oblivious to the commotion going on around him. That proved to be his undoing. I was poised and ready to spring. I grabbed a handful of soft skin and fur, as I clamped down on his small body. His wings were wrapped solidly around him, and I didn't intend to let them go.

Richard hollered up to me as I completed the grab. He was so excited that I couldn't resist looking down at him. That was the last thing I wanted to do. The height was dizzying. I was near the dome of the tree and I could see across the tops of the buildings below. The morning breeze had picked up and a faint smell of eggs and bacon floated up to me as I lay there stretched across the branch. I didn't have any time to appreciate the moment, however, because the creature began to stir. I had to focus on getting down safely. The next few moves were crucial. I eased myself back along the branch, and felt a cold chill sweep across my brow as the branch began to crack.

"Steady," I cautioned myself, "don't try to do it all at once."

The next few minutes seemed like hours. I only had one hand to cling to the branches as I descended. One misstep and I would have tumbled towards the pavement. I held my breath and concentrated with each downward step.

I stretched my way left and right again and again as I eased myself down. It was the only way I could steady myself using one hand. When I finally reached the ground, Richard slapped me on the back and told me what a great climb that had been. I wasn't focused on the climb now that I was on the ground. I just wanted to enjoy the moment. It lasted briefly. I remembered the creature in my hand and looked around for the box that we had brought to put him in. Richard retrieved it for me and I eased the creature very gently into the box. I expected the creature to put up more of a fight than it did. To my surprise, it just spread its wings and lay there. As I closed the lid, Richard looked at me. I knew what was on his mind.

We carried the box to his house and put it into his room. Then, we walked over to my house to see if we could find a picture of the creature in my new set of encyclopedias my mother had bought from a lady who sold them door-to-door. I had skimmed through some of the books mostly looking at the pictures. I knew my mother would be pleased that we had found a good use for them. Richard and I sat on the living room floor and opened one of the big, hardbound books. We searched until we finally found what we were looking for. It was in the section covering nocturnal animals, animals that sleep during the day and hunt for food at night. Our eyes remained glued to the page as we read about the life and habits of our prize.

Our winged, masked marvel was a brown bat that had been resting upside down since early morning in the tall oak tree. We didn't know whether it was a male or female and weren't in a hurry to discover which one it was. It had a pair of broad, gray silky wings and a furry body, which resembled that of a very small rat. Richard believed it was a vampire bat, but I knew from reading the descriptions that very few of those were found in our area. It had been part of a large group of bats that had swarmed all over our neighborhood chasing insects from dusk till dawn. I didn't believe you could get very much blood from gnats, mosquitoes, flies, and brown moths. Richard didn't care that the book pointed to our bat being a non-carnivorous creature. He wanted it to be a vampire bat. That is exactly what we told the girls when we showed it to them.

My sister's girlfriends were always following us around trying to spy on us. Sometimes we would catch frogs and use them to scare the girls so they would leave us alone. If that didn't work, we would pound them with water balloons or spray them with a water hose. Of course, we would get into trouble for that, so most of the time we just ignored them. This morning, we had something really special to show them, our live brown bat. My sister's friend, Margareta, was sitting on the porch watching her siblings play in the yard. Margareta came from a large family. As the oldest, it was her job to watch the little ones. My sister liked her because she showed her a new way to braid her hair. I liked her because she had a pleasant smile.

When we first saw them, the girls were talking with Consuelo and Maria, two girls who lived a few buildings down from us. Richard couldn't wait to show the girls our winged, masked marvel. He ran ahead of me and broke into their conversation. The girls were not pleased at all. They told him to vamoose. Richard wouldn't take no for an answer. He kept trying to get them to come take a look at what we had found. Finally, I thought of a great way to get their attention. I reached into the box and held the bat up by its wings. It just hung there, suspended in mid-air wishing it had never fallen asleep in our tree. I thought it would at least make an effort to get away, but I was wrong. That didn't spoil the show and tell, however. The girls gasped when they saw the creature with its wings spread across my face. Richard was thrilled and he began to tell his version of how we caught the winged, masked marvel.

When he had finished his tall tale, I asked them if they had any questions about the bat. Maria wanted to know if it sucked blood. I answered that it didn't before Richard could mislead her some more.

Bernadine asked, "What does it eat?"

I couldn't resist responding with a lie about it eating nosy girls with pigtails. That drew a laugh from Richard, but none of the rest of the audience thought it was funny. Consuelo asked if she could hold it. I hesitated for a moment, before I told her no. It wasn't that I didn't want her to see the bat; I just didn't want it to get away. Margareta hadn't said a single word the entire time we were showing off our prize. When she finally spoke, she startled me.

"Bats carry rabies," she said.

That got my attention. I asked her, "Where did you get that information?"

She told me she had studied them in her biology class at school. I asked her if all bats carried rabies, but she didn't seem to know. That bit of information caused me to become alarmed. I had already had my share of trouble with a dog that probably had rabies. I wasn't ready to go through that ordeal again. I backed up suddenly. The creature in my grasp began to move. He twisted his body and appeared to be trying to bite me. I panicked and tossed him on the ground. The girls shrieked and ran back onto the porch.

The bat just lay there writhing in the grass. I had expected him to fly away, but I guess he couldn't get enough lift from where he was. I realized that he was basically helpless and out of his element. He would have been so much better off had I left him hanging upside down in the tree. It was my fault that he was stuck in the grass, but I didn't want anything to do with another series of rabies shots so I just watched him flapping around. Richard just stared at him, too.

"Do something," my sister yelled at me. "Don't just stand there watching him flap all over the yard. If you don't do something, he's gonna' die!"

I didn't believe it was that critical, but I began to feel sorry for the little creature. It wasn't his fault that I had panicked. Maybe if I had tossed him into the air, he would have been able to escape with some of his dignity. The thought of him dying in front of all these witnesses made me feel sick. It would be my fault, and my sister would tell our mother what I had done. It didn't take a rocket scientist to determine what I needed to do. I reached down and picked up the bat. He immediately stopped writhing and hung there motionless in the air. I swung him backwards and then forward and up into the air. He caught the wind and sailed high above the trees. He circled once, trying to get his bearing, and then headed east. The girls cheered as the winged, masked marvel flew away. Richard moaned and seemed a bit disappointed, but I knew he would have done the same. It had been a magical morning. We had captured a brown bat and had shown him to our friends. The creature hadn't bitten anyone, and I was alive to tell the tale.

Chapter 13: Learning to Swim

Sometimes we let bad memories from our past blind us to the opportunities that we have that others have not. My opportunity to learn how to swim was one of those occasions. I had to work hard to overcome my bias against being in the water and anything that went along with it. Our mother had told us about the experience she had with our dad trying to teach her to swim. He had approached the task of teaching her the same way others had taught him by immersing her in the water. It wasn't the easiest method to learn, but it had worked for him. He was determined to teach her the same way. We listened as she described, in horror, how he had lifted her up in the water and told her to kick. When she began kicking, he let her go expecting her to kick fast enough to stay afloat. Of course she sank. That episode added to the fear of the water in her that has never left.

My mother's version of that episode was vivid enough for both my sister and I to vow never to go anywhere near the water. My only attempt to overcome my fear had ended in a failure when I found myself terrified of entering the swimming pool with Walter and Freddie in Georgia. The story might have ended there if I had not had the opportunity to try again on my own terms. The Fort Sill recreational facilities available to the dependents of all military personnel, including Negroes, were exceptional. They included a first class, Olympic-size swimming pool where kids could learn to swim for free. It was access to this facility that gave me the opportunity to teach myself.

I had always wanted to learn how to swim. I didn't believe my mother's bias for swimming was the only version of the activity. I had walked by the recreation center and watched the kids kicking and splashing in the water. It looked like fun. I swore one afternoon, as I leaned on the fence and watched some of my friends playing games in the water, that I would prepare myself to join them. It didn't take long for that unspoken pledge to be tested. My best friend, Richard, began asking me when I was going to join them at the pool. I told him that I would soon, and he said that he would be waiting for me. From that moment the pressure was on, for me to tackle my fear of the water.

I began by thinking through the process of not breathing while under the water. I knew I could hold my breath for a while, but I didn't know how long I would have to do that to survive in the water. I set a target of one minute. It might seem like a minuscule objective to you, but it was a tremendous challenge for me. I began by closing my eyes and holding my face in the water in the bathtub. The soapy water got into my eyes and caused me all kinds of trouble. I finally realized I would do better if I practiced before I bathed, so I pretended to wash when I was actually practicing my breathing exercises. I wouldn't have had to pretend if my sister hadn't spent half the time pounding on the door trying to get in, so she could take her bath.

It seemed like it would take forever for me to improve my time under water but, within a few short weeks, I was up to 45 seconds. When I reached a minute, I was so proud of myself that I forgot not to breathe and swallowed enough water to choke a horse. It was all right. I had reached my goal and that mattered a lot to me. The next step was to open my eyes to see where I was going. I wasn't going anywhere in the bath tub, but I pretended that I was swimming across the pool. I tested my newly acquired skills by dropping pennies into the water and reaching down while looking to pick them up. This exercise would prove to be very helpful later. When I was finally able to retrieve all five of the pennies without coming up for air, I knew I was ready for my first test at the pool.

I found Richard playing softball in the square and told him I would be ready to go to the pool with him that weekend. He seemed pleased that I hadn't forgotten about his offer to help me. I was relieved to have taken another step towards overcoming my fears. We started out on our journey to the pool early on Saturday morning. We each had on shorts and t-shirts. Richard had a green towel slung over his shoulder and carried a small sack lunch with a sandwich and a pear. I had a white towel slung over my shoulder and carried a sack lunch with a sandwich and two oatmeal cookies. We shared a cookie on the way to the pool. I asked him what I could expect when we got there. He told me that we would strip to our shorts, and then take a cold shower before entering the pool. I asked him why we had to do that. He said that it was to get us ready for the cold water. Richard laughed when I shuddered at his comment about the cold water.

The swimming pool was already filled with happy, weekend swimmers when we arrived. They all seemed to be enjoying themselves, and I wondered how long it would take me to become one of them. I saw a few kids I knew playing in the shallow end of the pool. They were horsing around dunking each other or, at least, trying to. Just then, a whistle blew and the lifeguard shouted a warning to the boys. They responded immediately by pretending to swim off independently in all directions. I don't know why, but the reprimand and quick response was comforting to my already queasy stomach. I told myself that I was going to be all right this time. I had prepared myself for this. I knew that I could do it if I only gave myself a chance.

Richard showed me where the showers were, and we each got soaked in cool water. I hadn't realized how warm it was that day. The cool water felt good. I watched as Richard twisted his head back and forth to get the water out of his ears.

He laughed as I frowned at him for always being so goofy.

"Come on, Bernard," he teased, "Let's go swimming."

I frowned again and then a big smile came over my face. Richard looked disheveled as always wearing his brother's swimming trunks. It didn't seem to bother him that his own set of trunks had worn out last summer. He was totally without shame or self-consciousness. That was one of the main reasons I liked him. Richard was just a regular guy who wasn't going to let anything get in the way of his having fun.

After we exited the shower stalls, we picked up our towels and hurried to the swimming pool. We came out at the shallow end. Many of our friends were splashing around in the water. Richard waved at a boy from our class and then ran towards the edge to jump in. Just as he got to the edge, he stopped and looked around for me. I was still standing at the entrance to the pool looking around frantically trying to find someone who I could get to join me in the water. Richard must have sensed my dilemma. He waited for me to catch up to him and then asked me if I wanted him to help me get started in the water. When I said that would be great, he smiled and pointed to the shallow end.

We walked over to the ladder and both of us climbed down into the water. The first thing that Richard did was to reach down and splash water all over his face. Then, he looked at me and nodded for me to do the same. It really felt good. I guess he didn't think that I had done that good a job because he began to splash water up at me from the surface of the pool. I could hardly see, but I wasn't going to be outdone. I spread my hands in a fan shape and splashed a ton of water back on him. He laughed, and I realized that I was laughing too.

The next thing Richard did was to ask me if I could hold my breath under water. I told him that I could but that I never tried it at the pool.

He looked at me curiously and then suddenly disappeared right before my eyes. When he surfaced fifteen seconds later, I was still standing there gawking in awe.

"It's your turn," Richard said.

He looked at me with a slight grin on his face, when he said it. I hesitated because I had always ducked my head into the water first. Richard had just sat down and let the water roll over him. I didn't know whether or not I could do that. He sensed my uncertainty, but he didn't rush me. When I finally decided what I was going to do, I motioned for him to move back. Then, I ducked my head under the water. It was amazing. For the first time ever, I saw the bottom of the pool clear as the sky on a summer day. When I finally came up for air, Richard was staring at me. He didn't say anything, but I could tell he finally understood how much work he was going to have to do to actually teach me to swim.

Over the next two hours, we alternated between horse play and practicing our swimming drills. Richard showed me how to cup my hand, and swoosh through the water like a giant turtle. When I tried it, I was only able to submerge myself a few feet, before coming back up. It took me a few more weeks of practice before I was competent enough to go to the bottom and stay under the water as Richard had shown me. During that time, I spent hours practicing on my own while Richard headed down to the deeper end of the pool to swim with the rest of the guys our age. I didn't mind being left behind. I was on a mission, and I knew exactly what I had to do to accomplish it. I extended my time under water until I was finally able to swim the breath of the pool without coming up for air. When I showed Richard what I could do, he was so proud of me that I thought he would burst.

"Follow me, Bernard," he called looking back over his shoulder. I realized he was heading towards the deep end, but I didn't think I was ready for that.

"Where are you going?" I asked him. My voice sounded a little wavy as the words left my mouth.

Richard pointed to the middle of the pool. I threw my hands up in the air indicating that I was uncertain about my ability to handle such a big leap. Richard assured me that the water was only five feet deep and he would show me how to tip toe and stay above the waves. I had trusted him this far, so I followed him to the middle of the pool. When we got there, he told me to watch him dive in. He cupped his hands, leaned over the side, and was gone. When he surfaced, he was on the other side of the pool. He motioned for me to do the same, but I was unsure about my ability to make that move.

Richard swam back across the pool. It was the first time I had really paid attention to him swimming in open water. He looked like a porpoise. He swam effortlessly. When he reached my side of the pool, he looked up at me and smiled.

"Now, let me see you do it," he chided.

I cupped my hands, leaned over, and disappeared under the water. To my surprise, it was as familiar a place at five feet as it had become at four. When I reached the other side, I surfaced, and was shocked to see Richard leaning on the side right next to me.

You can guess what we did next. Both of us stood on the side of the pool, dived in, and raced to get to the other side. He beat me again and again, but I wasn't going to let that stop me from trying to win. Before we knew it, the day had passed and we hadn't been back to the shallow end one time. I was so proud of myself. I didn't even care about

Richard's chiding me for losing all those races. I was determined that I would beat him across the pool before the summer was over. That never happened.

As the weeks wore on, I became bolder and bolder about my abilities to handle myself in the water. I learned to float on my back with Richard holding his hand under it to keep me steady. I learned to float on top of the water with my head down and then to take off like a submarine by kicking both feet wildly. I learned to dog paddle and even tried perfecting a rough breaststroke for good measure. I had really improved over the summer. I could see that Richard was as proud of my swimming accomplishments as I was. That is why what happened on that Friday near the end of the day, was so unforeseen.

I had been horse playing in the pool with Richard and some of the fellows. We had been racing across the pool, and I had actually beaten a few of them. One of the fellows decided to dive off of the board at the deep end. I had never done that before, but I followed the rest of the guys to take my turn. When I got up on the board, I was alarmed to see how far down it seemed. Of course the unwritten rule was that once on the board, you must jump, so the next person can take his turn. There was no provision for turning around and walking back. That was considered to be too dangerous to do, so it was not allowed. I walked to the edge of the board, leaned over, and dove in. It was a long way to the surface. When I hit the water, it sounded like an implosion in both my ears.

For the next fifteen seconds, I was mesmerized by an unbelievable out of body experience. I saw other kids kicking above me and swimming towards the sides of the pool. I saw a huge water drain sucking in the flowing current below me. I looked down and it appeared to be half a mile to the bottom. I wondered how long it would take me to reach it.

Then, I looked up and remembered that the fellows would be waiting for me to surface. I spread my arms and started my accent, when I felt a muscle grab me in my leg. The rank was sudden, quick, and paralyzing. I reached down to see if I could get the muscle to relax, and the pain hit me again harder. I wanted to shout, but I couldn't very well do that while under the water. I looked upward and realized I was sinking downward. I had lost my momentum and gravity was working against me. My mesmerizing out of body experience was over. It was time to recover before something tragic occurred.

I didn't panic because I knew I could hold my breath for more than a minute under water. Instead, I cupped my hands and brought my arms down rapidly to my side, which slowed my descent. Then, I extended my arms upward and pulled against the current the same way I would have in swimming across the pool. When I surfaced, my struggle wasn't over. I slipped right back under the water again.

"It was time to tilt the sub so that it could float." I put my head downward and leaned into the water. My entire body floated to the surface. I took a quick breath, and put my head back down and swam on top of the surface towards the far side. When I reached it, I grabbed onto the ladder and held on. I looked across the pool at the fellows staring at me from afar. I looked up and there was Richard staring me in the face. I could tell he was concerned, but he didn't say anything at first.

"Caught a cramp," I said. I hoped that was all the explanation he needed.

"Great dive," he said, "but you really have to work on your recovery. It sucks."

Chapter 14: Feeling Betrayed over Football

Our housing complex filled up quickly and soon we had enough guys to field two teams of players for touch football. We chose eight-man teams with a captain for each. I usually got picked to be a quarterback because I could make up really good plays. If Richard was on my team, I would agree to be an end because he didn't catch as well as he threw the ball. I used the skill I perfected playing softball, getting to a ball in the air from anywhere.

The guys would start arriving at the ball field around four in the evening. They would mill around and talk about the things that guys talk about, baseball, basketball, football, and girls. I would usually arrive late because I had chores to do before I came. Richard was always good about holding up the choosing of teams until I got there. We tried to be pretty fair about choosing teams. Friends usually chose friends and we balanced the big kids and smaller kids so no one had too much of an advantage. Most of the time, it proved to be a pretty fair contest. Winning was important, but just playing was the really fun part.

Some days we would begin playing around three, and did not stop until late in the evening when the sun began to go down. If I was playing quarterback, I would scope out the other team first to determine which players were the ones to watch. Then, I would match our best catcher with their weakest defensive player and fire away. Each team got at least four plays before turning the ball over to the other team. Since we played on a plush, green, manicured parade field, we were able to use the tall spruce trees, planted approximately ten feet apart all along the perimeter, as first down markers. Out of bounds was outside of the spruce trees. A player could score a touchdown by crossing the invisible line represented by the last spruce tree marked as the goal line at either end of the field.

I had sized up most of the guys after playing with them for a few weeks. Rickey was a lightweight kid who could run in and out of a gang of defensive players without getting tagged. That was a good skill to have. Unfortunately, Rickey couldn't hold onto the ball, so the guys would always slap it out of his hands and ruin our chance to score. Unlike his brother, Warren, Rickey made a good decoy, but he wasn't the one to give the ball unless you wanted to risk losing it.

Bradley was a big kid who could really block, so we always put him up front. Sometimes he would play center and hike the ball. He was a smart kid who knew how to hike it on the correct count and not a second before. He couldn't catch very well, so we didn't often send him out for a pass. He was also a little heavy for a kid his age. That meant he had to take a few more rest periods than some of us. We didn't mind, though. It just gave us a chance to do a little bragging and talking about stuff.

Richard was a good ball player. He had a knack for finding his way through a crowd. I enjoyed playing on his team because he always found a way to win. When he played quarterback, we would run around yelling for him to throw us the ball. He would be running around trying not to be tagged before he hurled it to one of us. My favorite pass route was right across the middle of the field. I would run out as fast as I could and then double back in a button hook pattern. Richard could hurl a ball pretty fast, and I had to be ready to catch it. Some days, I would get one square in the gut and fall out on the field. Richard didn't seem to care as much about my stomach pain as he did about my not dropping the ball.

"Did you catch it?" he would yell and then run towards me as fast as he could to get a look.

I would look up at him and frown. Richard would laugh at the painful look on my face. So would all the other guys.

When we first started playing the pick-up games on the parade field, I wasn't that familiar with all of the rules. It took a while for me to learn the ones peculiar to our neighborhood. You couldn't grab a player without the ball. If you did, you couldn't pull him to the ground. You couldn't tackle a player with the ball, but if you did he couldn't get back up and run. You shouldn't jump on a players back, but if you did and he threw you off it didn't count against you. You couldn't run with the football until you looked for someone to throw it to. If you couldn't find an open man, you were free to run. These and other rules were always popping up during the game. We didn't take them seriously, and no one seemed to let them get in the way of having a good time.

We always chose a referee to keep the game moving and mediate disputes. If there was an even number of guys, we would give the referee job to a physically challenged kid named Eddie. He had one leg that was weaker than the other and walked with a limp. He would hang around the ball field and cheer for one team or the other as we played. No one seemed to mind, least of all me. I thought he was an okay dude, and my mother had taught me to be considerate towards other kids, especially those who were less fortunate than me.

Eddie and I didn't speak much. When we did, he seemed to have a problem acknowledging me. I passed that off as part of his unique personality, but sometimes it would rub me the wrong way. One day, we were halfway through our game, when one of the players on my team had to leave. We didn't have anyone on the side to take his place, so I figured we would play down one. Someone from the other team suggested we take Eddie to make up for our loss. I looked at Eddie and saw that he was just as surprised as I was with the suggestion.

"I don't think so," I responded. "Eddie can't really help us, but he can referee if you want."

Nothing I said seemed to me to be unfair or a direct put down of Eddie's playing ability, but my saying it made the difference.

"I wouldn't play on his team if he begged me to," Eddie spat out. "I think his team stinks."

That wasn't what I had expected to hear. For a moment, I was too stunned to respond. Then to make it worst, Richard started laughing. That caused the other guys to look at him and then shrug their shoulders at me. I wanted to make the whole episode go away, so I suggested we play ball and see whose team was the best.

Richard chose one side, and I chose the other. Eddie flipped a coin to see who got the ball first. We lost. I set my team up, and warned them to watch Richard. I knew he liked to duck under guys and run when he could. Richard wasn't that fast, at least he wasn't as fast as me. The kickoff went well, but I didn't like the call on where the ball went out of bounds. Eddie smiled when I complained. I think he thought he was being funny by placing the ball ten yards further up field than it should have been. I shrugged it off, but it was just the start of a whole series of bad calls by our partial referee.

Richard threw a long pass that was caught by a kid on his team who got behind our defensive player and ran across the goal line for a score. I couldn't say anything about the play, because I had been on the other side of the field covering someone else. Richard took the opportunity to brag a little and the guys on his team joined in. That was to be expected, but what Eddie did next was a surprise.

He threw the football up in the air, and shouted, "See, I told you his team was gonna' stink."

I didn't know what to say in reply. "Let's just play ball," I shot back. "Then we'll see who wins the game."

Richard couldn't resist getting the last word in. "Take a hike, you guys," he chided us. "This end of the field is reserved for the winners."

I walked off towards the far end of the field with a resolved determination to pin his ears to the nearest tree. I knew it was going to be a hard fought battle, but I was ready to prove him wrong. Eddie set the ball up for the kickoff and we turned to face our opponents with a score to settle.

Bradley kicked the ball. It went a lot farther than I had expected. I ran back to retrieve it while the guys on my team came together to form a wedge. I ran towards the middle of the wedge and then, at the last minute, swerved and ran around the right end. I managed to elude everyone except Rickey, who was hot on my trail. When he finally intercepted me, I was half way down the field. It was a good start and we didn't waste any time using it to score. Two plays later, we completed a pass to a kid in the end zone. The score was tied. There was very little celebration on our team. We were in it for the long haul. We knew it was going to be a long, rough day before we could say we had won.

Over the next few hours, we went back and forth trading touchdowns. We had started late, and it began to get dark. The score stood tied at 42 points apiece. It was getting dark, so we agreed that the first team to score 50 points would win. It was our turn to receive the ball. I told our fastest player to get behind me and catch the kickoff. I wanted Richard's guys to chase him to the left side of the field. When they did, he turned and ran in my direction. When we passed each other, he handed me the ball, and I raced around the outside and down the field for a touchdown. I scored! I heard my team cheer and then I saw Eddie limping down the field. He was yelling something that I couldn't understand.

"No fair! No fair! No reverses allowed on the kickoff."

I didn't believe what I had just heard. Eddie had just made up a new rule and it was going to cost us the score.

When the other guys heard him, they complained loudly. I thought that would make him change his mind, but it didn't. He was determined to make it stick, and I was at a loss for what to do to get his call overruled. I stood there with the ball and, when he reached for it, I pulled it away. Eddie lurched forward off balance and nearly fell down. When he got his balance back, he raised one hand and pointed towards the other end of the field.

Then, he gave a really dirty look and said, "You got to kick it again. The score doesn't count."

I stood my ground and so did the other players on my team.

"You heard him," Richard said. "It ain't going to count, so just take your guys and git to the other end of the field. This end is reserved for the winners."

Any other time, I would have continued to argue my point, but hearing my best friend take Eddie's side caught me so off guard that I just turned and walked towards the other end of the field. The guys on my team followed me. We huddled and worked out another play for the kickoff.

Ten minutes later, we had managed to move the ball within fifteen yards of the goal. This time I called for a reverse. Instead of running when I got the ball, this time I threw it to our guy who was standing all by himself in the end zone. Although Eddie didn't look pleased with our successful play, there was no protest from him, at least not right away. We had scored and now were just two points away from winning the game. Normally, a team would take a one point automatic free kick after a touchdown. Not many guys could kick an extra point, and we didn't have a goal post for it anyway.

"We're going for two," I said. That got Eddie's attention.

"No fair, no fair," Eddie shouted. "You got to play on."

"No we don't," I said. "It's getting late and we can barely see the ball. We're going for two."

I expected Richard to jump in and take Eddie's side, but he didn't. The guys on both teams lined up and got ready for the final play of the game. If we scored two extra points, we would be the winners. If we didn't score, the game would end in a tie. We huddled and I called the play. We decided to run the old Statue of Liberty play. Warren took the position behind the center and I moved over to the far left end. When the ball was snapped, I ran towards my left and then doubled back. Warren dropped back to pass and when I ran behind him he dropped the ball into my arms. To everyone standing on the other side, it looked like he was throwing a pass. The players on defense dropped back and looked for the open man Warren was supposed to be throwing the ball to. When they turned their heads, I slipped around the outside and headed for the end zone. Before any of them could react, I crossed just in front of the spruce marked as the goal line. I held the ball up in the air and waved it over my head in the end zone.

Richard looked startled to see me there. The guys on my team began to celebrate. We had won the game on a trick play, but it was all legal. I was pleased, but I should have known the feeling wouldn't last very long. Eddie came hobbling over to me and tried to smack the ball out of my hands. I was taller than he was, so he wasn't able to reach it. That seemed to infuriate him.

"Extra doesn't count!" he exclaimed. "You stepped out of bounds."

I hadn't expected Eddie to be pleased with our victory, but I didn't think he would lie to cheat us out of it.

"What do you mean I went out of bounds?" I countered. "I'm standing right where I crossed the line and it's in bounds."

The other players stretched to see where I was standing, but it was getting dark and harder to see.

"We won fair and square," I said.

My team members chimed in to reinforce my comments. I didn't hear any counter to my claim, so I believed it was settled. That's when Richard opened his mouth. He agreed with Eddie and he said that he thought I was a liar. Then, he began egging Eddie on until he had gotten up in my face. I backed up to put some space between us, but the guys had formed a ring around us. There was no place to go. That's when it happened.

Eddie stepped towards me. When I looked down, he socked me squarely in the jaw. It was a good, solid hit, and I went down face first. I lay there stunned, but conscious. I couldn't believe what had just happened. I knew I hadn't done anything to deserve the punch that Eddie threw and I was at odds about what to do next. I didn't want to look like I was afraid to stand up for myself, but I wouldn't be able to face my mother without feeling ashamed if she found out I had beaten the physically challenged kid over a football game.

I was hurt by the actions my best friend had taken. I was backed into a corner by the limited set of choices I felt I had left to resolve the conflict. I felt dejected, betrayed and confused. I lay there, face down on the ground, for the longest time. Nobody moved to help me. Finally, Richard fell on his knees and began pleading with me to get up. He began by sarcastically urging me to rise. After that failed, he laughed nervously and tried again. This time his pleading was earnest. I could sense the fear creeping into his voice. The other guys sensed it too, and they began asking him what was wrong. I could have lain there for the rest of the night rather than face all those guys.

When I finally rolled over and sat up, most of the guys had gone. I looked around and Eddie was nowhere in sight. I guess he realized what a careless move he had made and wanted nothing to do with finishing it. I rose to my feet slowly with Richard holding my arm. We walked together back towards our housing complex. Neither one of us said a word. I held my head down and stared at the ground. Richard looked straight ahead. We both walked into the darkness.

The following morning I rose very early. I hadn't slept at all and wasn't feeling good. My mother, my dad, and my sister were all still asleep when I slipped out of the house and headed next door. I knocked on Richard's back door. To my surprise, his mother opened it right away. She seemed surprised to see me too. I said good morning and asked her where was Richard. She turned to look over her shoulder and said he was in his room. I took off in that direction. I found Richard curled up in a ball in the corner of his bunk bed. He seemed startled and confused to see me.

"Get up," I said. "We got business to take care of."

He didn't seem to understand what I was trying to tell him, so I began pulling him out of bed. He followed me half-sleep and half-awake as I dragged him through the kitchen and out into the courtyard.

I am not proud of what happened next. I have no real excuse, and I won't give you one. I held him up and then I socked him in his jaw, just like Eddie had socked me. He fell backwards, and to my surprise rebounded almost fully awake. We wrestled in the sandy courtyard, punching each other and rolling in the dirt until I heard my mother call my full name. She tended to do that when I was really in trouble. She ordered me to stop and then she angrily asked me what I thought I was doing. I didn't have a good answer, but I knew she wasn't going to let me get away without giving one.

Richard took advantage of the disruption to scamper for home. I guess he figured he shouldn't have to explain what he was doing fighting at 6 a.m. in the morning with a crazy person like me.

My mother grabbed me by my ears, a favorite technique of strong-willed mothers, and dragged me into the house. By the time she had finished lecturing me, I was worn out, hungry, and wide-awake. She told me I was going to have to apologize to Richard and his mother for my bad behavior. I didn't try to argue with her; she was right. She dragged me across the courtyard and knocked on Richard's back door. His mother answered and asked us to come in. She looked concerned, but my mother put her at ease immediately.

My son has something he wants to say to you, she told her. Mom looked directly at me as she spoke each word. Mrs. Trahan turned to look at me and then hollered for Richard to come into the kitchen. He emerged from the hallway looking like he had been tossed in a bin of sepia colored makeup.

Mrs. Trahan reached out to pull him close to her, and then said, "Your friend has come over to tell us something."

I began by explaining what had happened the day before and then apologized for dragging Richard out of bed. His mother seemed to understand. When I finished, she turned to Richard and told him to shake my hand. He didn't hesitate, and I was relieved to know he wasn't going to hold a grudge.

My mother excused us for disturbing everyone's morning, and then invited Richard's mother over to our house for coffee. Mrs. Trahan was delighted to get the invitation and said she would be over in the next hour. Richard and I looked at each other and grinned. Now that our mothers were talking, we didn't have a thing to say to each other. The incident was forgiven and would never come up again.

I wish I could say that I never lost my temper like that again, but that wouldn't be telling the truth. The impulse to get even is a strong one. If it's not controlled, it can lead a person down the road to destruction. It's easy to reflect now about the reasons why I couldn't control my temper, but there was no excuse for it. In my church school classes, I had learned that if you don't control your temper, you can lose your soul. In today's world if you lose your temper, you can lose your life. And, if you don't learn to control your temper, you can lose your freedom, for the rest of your life.

A Look Back in Time

Chapter 15: A Day at the Races

Living on the post had its benefits. Besides just being a great place to explore, the military community offered a host of activities for soldiers' kids. My mother discovered one of these by accident. She had been shopping at the commissary and on her way out stopped to read a few of the ads and announcements on the community bulletin board. That was when she noticed a posting for a spring athletics contest to be held on the field behind the local recreation center. The contest was open to all boys from eight to twelve years old. Contestants were expected to report to the field the following Saturday by 1 p.m. for registration. The field events would begin at 2 p.m., the running events would be held around 3:30 p.m., and the finals and awards would take place around 4:30 p.m.

My mother tucked a copy of the announcement into her purse. Later that evening, she asked me if I knew anything about the contest. I hadn't heard about it, but I was interested. My response seemed to please her because she sat down in Dad's armchair to explore the topic further. The next few minutes were revealing to me. My mother explained how she was quite a runner when she was my age. She talked about running faster than kids much older than she was, especially when she had to. We laughed when she described a few of those occasions. She then asked me if I wanted to enter the contest, and I told her that I did.

After she described the uniform I was supposed to wear, I went into my room to get my gym clothes so she could wash them for me. My sister followed me. She wanted to know if she could be in the contest. I told her that I didn't think so because girls weren't allowed to run against boys. My sister then asked if there was a girl's contest. I told her I didn't think so. She said that wasn't fair and ran to tell our mother how disappointed she was. I could see that our mother was also disappointed, but she calmly explained that girls were not expected to compete like boys.

"But I can run faster than he can!" my sister cried.

"No, you can't!" I yelled back at her in defiance although, unless overnight I had gotten faster, I knew she was telling the truth. There just wasn't anything I could do to make it right. Girls were treated very differently in Oklahoma, U.S.A., in 1957. On Saturday, my mother drove my sister and me to the field. I grabbed my gym bag with my towel, an apple, and some peanuts in a brown paper bag and ran over to join the other boys who were already there. My mother found a nice place to sit in the viewing stands while my sister leaned on the fence to watch the beginning of the contest. I knew my dad was going to be late, if he showed up at all. I wasn't bothered by his absence when the contest began but, as time went on, I scoured the stands looking for him.

The crowd began to fill the seats. I could still see my mother who was sitting with my sister beside her in the viewing stands. A cadre of local coaches had volunteered to help with the contest. One of the officials gathered all of the contestants into one group and explained the rules. It was going to be a track and field event contest with prizes to be awarded for first, second, and third place in each event. I had never participated in an organized track and field event contest before and was excited.

We were grouped by age and escorted to the registration tables. I recognized Mr. Caldwell, a physical education teacher at the elementary school, at my table. He said hello and then asked me to enter my name and age on the form attached to a clipboard. I was so nervous that my name was barely recognizable. I don't know why I was shaking. The excitement of the event had begun to fade and the anticipation of the challenge ahead of me had started to creep into my consciousness. Mr.

Caldwell smiled as I finished writing my information. He encouraged me to do my best. That helped me to calm down inside. Mr. Caldwell gave me a white patch with my contestant's number on it. I wore number eleven, which proved to be a very lucky number.

Following registration, I was shuffled over to the softball-throwing circle. The official explained the rules of the event and we were permitted to make one practice throw. I began to feel more confident after one of the guys commented on the distance of my practice throw.

He exclaimed, "Don't throw your arm out man! It's only practice." It was a good start to a terrific day.

We completed the softball throw and then moved to the standing long jump. I had never tried this event before, but it seemed like a lot of fun. Each contestant had to stand behind a marker. Then, one by one, each of us gathered both arms behind us and jumped as far as we could in a single leap. The contestants looked like frogs leaping off of a lily pad. I took my turn and then moved on to the next event. The rotation continued for at least an hour. We competed in the standing long jump and the running long jump before moving on to another event. Each time we moved to a new event station, I looked into the stands to see if my dad had arrived. An hour had passed and he was still nowhere to be seen. We took a short water break at the beginning of the second hour and then continued with the field events.

The last field event was the high jump. I looked at the bar, which was set at about 3 1/2 feet, and had no clue about how to clear it. I had not seen many high jumpers clear a bar, so I was at a loss at how to proceed. One kid ran straight at the bar and did a scissor jump over it. Another kid ran sideways and then rolled over the bar head first. I wasn't impressed with either technique, so when my turn came, I ran straight at the bar. When I reached within one step of the bar, I kicked one leg up in the air and followed with the other, just the way a horse with two legs would go over it. I cleared it with half a foot to spare. I brushed the sand off of my shorts and exited the pit. That was when I heard my dad's voice calling me.

Dad was standing next to the fence in the infield. He leaned over the fence and motioned for me to come over so he could talk to me. I was startled to see him there and hesitated before walking slowly over to the fence. I loved my dad, but he could be very critical at times. It was a basic part of his nature. He had been raised without a father or a mother. That had caused him to develop a strong sense self-reliance in him, which he drilled into his own children. It worked for him, but his drill sergeant approach often left me feeling berated and bewildered. I could see he was excited and wondered what he wanted to tell me.

Dad skipped all of the niceties and went right into his lecture. He criticized the approach I was using to clear the high jump. He told me that I would do better if I ran at the bar from an angle, lifted one leg and then rolled the other over. I understood what he was trying to tell me, but something inside me wouldn't agree to do it. When he saw my hesitation, he doubled down on the lecture and berated the way I was jumping straight at the bar. He assured me that I wouldn't be able to clear it at the next height if I didn't change my approach.

I don't know why I ignored his advice. I knew he had been a track and field star in high school and was certain that he knew how to clear a high jump bar. My reluctance to accept the benefit of his experience in such a small matter bothered him, but I would realize later that it bothered me even more. I couldn't bring myself to say I would follow his orders. Instead, I abruptly broke away and returned to finish the contest. As I sprinted back to the infield, I could see my dad walking back towards the stands. He joined my mother and sister and sat there the rest of the day watching me from a distance.

I was more determined than ever to succeed at the final events on my own terms. I rushed ahead in the high jump and tipped the bar slightly. It wobbled, but finally held firm. I had cleared it at four feet. The confidence I gained from clearing the high jump bar carried over to the running events. I sprinted ahead of the other fellows in my class in the 60 and 100 yard dashes. When it was time for the final event, I was feeling really good about myself and how well I had performed. We all lined up for the 440 yard run. I was chomping at the bit and ready to go. I was first out of the pack. I sprinted towards the first curve and settled into the inside lane. I could see the coaches and other officials standing in the infield. They were all watching me. The wind in my face on the backstretch felt really good on that warm, summer day. I ran past the halfway mark and didn't look back.

As I rounded the far curve, I could see all of the families in the stands. They were on their feet cheering for their kids to come home strong. I searched for my parents, but I couldn't see them at first from where I was running. When I did get a glimpse of them, they were standing too. I turned the final curve and blazed my way home. I felt so good inside that I wasn't aware of how much energy I had spent in my effort. When I crossed the finish line, I was 30 yards ahead of all the other boys. I would find out later that my time of 57 seconds in the 440 yard run had broken a record that had stood for quite some time.

In that triumphant moment, I looked up to the stands. I searched frantically for my sister and my parents. When I spotted them, my dad was standing there with his head down. The sadness of that instant crushed every bit of jubilance in me and I dropped my head in shame. How could I have been so thoughtless? My dad had only wanted the best for me, and I had discarded his advice.

At the end of the running events, the officials gathered the athletes in the infield and handed out ribbons as prizes for the lucky winners. I stood there with the rest of the contestants and waited for my name to be called. I didn't have to wait long. I accepted my ribbons for first place finishes in the running events. Then, an official told me to wait right there so that I could receive my prizes for the field events. To my surprise, I had captured first place finishes in all of the field events as well. It was a clean sweep. I was dressed in metals with blue ribbons for first place finishes in all of the events. When they announced my name and the final results, the outcome drew a few cheers and a round of applause from the stands.

I had never had that many people recognize me for anything ever before. I dropped my head and wiped a tear from my cheek. The rush, excitement, and fear of the contest had all subsided. I was so elated that I dashed over to the section of the stands where my parents were sitting with Bernadine and thrust my ribbons into my dad's hands. He handed them to my mother and stood there eying me proudly. I gave him a hug. He hugged me back warmly. Thankfully, I was forgiven for my transgression, but I recall it sadly even to this day.

Chapter 16: The BB Gun Affair

Every boy I know has had a desire to own something that they have seen advertised on television. Often the story goes like this: you wanted something special advertised on television, but your parents got you something like it instead. If you have one of those stories, you are not alone. I wanted a ten-speed bicycle when I was ten years old. I had seen the ads on television and in the newspaper. I just had to have one. The really neat thing about the bike that I wanted was that it had hand brakes. That doesn't seem like a big deal today, but it was a brand new feature when I was a kid.

My game plan for getting my bike was simple. I asked my parents to buy it for me for Christmas. As usual, with such requests, they said they would think about it. Of course, that meant maybe they would buy it for me, or maybe not. The pressure was on them to make good on my wish. I used every opportunity to remind them of how important a wish it was for me. I secretly placed copies of ads about bicycles on the top of the kitchen table. I talked about my friend's bicycle, which I really liked a lot. It was a ten-speed with a real racing seat and racing stripes on the side. My mother humored me by listening to me talk about my friends' bicycles. My father ignored me by hiding behind his newspapers.

You know how this ended, right? I got a big surprise for Christmas. It was a three-speed bicycle with foot brakes, so much for wishes. Now that I am older and wiser, I realize that those disappointments are a part every child's life. If you suffered a disappointment like mine, don't let it get you down. Sure, you can remember one disappointment long after you have forgotten all of the wonderful things you did receive. That's the way the human ego works. However, in time, you will realize that those memories make up a minuscule part of the real happiness in your life. To prove that to you, I'll tell you about a time that I did get what I wanted and how that turned out...badly.

I remember seeing the ads about guns that shot pellets called BBs on television. I didn't pay much attention to them until my friend, Richard, told me he was going to get one for Christmas. Richard kept telling me about how powerful it was and how many quail he was going to shoot when he got it. I knew he was probably telling the truth, and I didn't want to be left out of the hunt. Just as I had done with the bicycle, I began hinting to my parents about wanting a BB gun for Christmas. They both listened and responded as I might have expected.

My mother didn't believe I should get one because she was concerned about my safety and the safety of other kids playing with pellet guns. My dad was more considerate. He had learned to shoot in the military and didn't have as many reservations about guns as my mother did. That was as far as his commitment went, however. He didn't promise to buy me one for Christmas. Of course, that didn't stop me from asking. I kept up the pressure until my mother finally got tired of hearing about my BB gun wish and told me to give it a rest. I became really discouraged when she wouldn't change her mind because I didn't believe I could count on my dad to come through for me.

Of course you know how this ended, right? I got a big surprise for Christmas, a pair of skates and a model airplane kit. I didn't get a BB gun. Needless to say, I was devastated. I just knew my friend would come out to play later that morning with his shiny, new BB gun, and I wouldn't have anything to show for my efforts. I thanked my mother and Dad for all of my gifts and tried to look pleased, but it was hard to pull off. My sister got a doll she had asked for and she seemed to be so excited about it. I knew she would be running out of the house soon to join her friends in the courtyard. She would have her new doll wrapped in a pink blanket to show off. I would have to wait until I had finished building my model airplane to have anything to show. For me, that Christmas, life just didn't seem to be fair.

Later that day, I got together with my friends to show off Christmas presents. One kid had a new baseball glove and another had a new baseball bat. I didn't need a glove to play softball because I caught everything with my bare hands. I was excited about the kid's new bat, however. It was a shiny, new Louisville Slugger marked with the autograph of a real, professional baseball player carved into the bat. I imagined how many home runs I would hit with that bat when we played softball in the spring.

I spent the next few minutes sharing tales about the wonderful things that kids had gotten for Christmas and didn't even notice Richard when he joined the group. He slid in quietly and didn't say anything while the other kids showed off their Christmas presents. He had on a new shirt and, to my surprise, also was wearing shoes. I didn't say anything about my observations. Instead, I waited for him to fill us all in. Richard never did. He stood there listening to the other kids talk about what they had gotten for Christmas, but he didn't say a word.

After all the bragging was over, the two of us walked back to our courtyard to join the girls. On the way back, I took the opportunity to ask him about his mom. He said she and the rest of the family were fine. I asked him if his dad had returned from his army maneuvers. He said that he had. Then, he told me that they were going to visit his relatives in Duncan, Oklahoma, later that day. I told him that sounded like a fun thing to do and that I would see him when he got back. Neither of us talked about what we did or did not get for Christmas. When we arrived at the courtyard, the girls were having fun playing with each other's new dolls. I watched Bernadine brush the hair on her friend's new doll and wondered what her friend would say if she decided to put a hot comb to those curls. At least the girls had gotten what they asked for. Richard and I must have been on the bottom of Santa's gift list.

A few weeks passed and everything went back to normal. I worked on building my model airplane and wished that spring would come sooner, so we could try out that kid's new baseball bat. Richard came over and helped me work on the plane by reading the instructions. He did a pretty good job of it. We seemed to be getting closer to finishing the project. Then, one day he didn't come over when he said he was going to. I waited and watched for him, but there was no Richard in sight. Finally, after wasting most of the morning waiting, I went over to his house to find out what was taking him so long. I found him outside behind the building. He had set up a target and was shooting a BB gun at it. I approached him cautiously. He didn't notice me until I was almost standing next to him.

"Hey, Bernard," he said. "Take a look at what my dad just bought for me."

I glared at the new BB gun Richard was holding in his hands. It was silver with a wood trimmed body and a leather carrying-strap. The barrel was shiny and the wood trim had cowboys riding horses carved into it. It was a beauty, and Richard was really pleased to have gotten it. At first I felt a slight pang of jealousy for my friend's new gift, but that quickly faded. I was happy for him. Richard showed me all the neat features about the BB gun and, after he finished his shooting round, he let me try it. It was a steady instrument with a true sight and a solid barrel. The trigger felt fine when eased back gently and the BB pellets packed a punch. I knew I could bring down a lot of small game with a rifle like this one, if only my dad had bought one like it for me.

The next week was consumed with the two of us finding things to shoot at to test Richard's new BB gun. We set up cans, bottles, and paper targets to try out our skills. We shot at birds in trees and squirrels running to find hiding places. The whole experience was new. We took full advantage of it all. When my mother found out about Richard's BB gun, she cautioned me to be careful and to watch out for little children around the gun. She also told me to respect our neighbor's property and not to shoot at anything that we didn't mean to kill. For some reason, her last admonishment stuck with me. I really didn't know why.

A month later, Richard and I joined some of the other kids in a treasure hunt. Back in the fall, we had found a set of older buildings about half a mile from our house. The buildings used to be barracks for soldiers in the artillery battalion, but they had moved. They looked abandoned, and hadn't been lived in for a while. The guys pried one of the doors open. We plowed inside looking for things we could find. It was an innocent intrusion. We had fun playing hide-and-go-seek among the apartments in the buildings. When winter came, we abandoned the cold buildings for warmer play activities nearer home. Now that spring was just around the corner, we decided to revisit the deserted buildings and look for more treasure.

I didn't notice at first, but many of the windows on the first building we entered were cracked and falling apart. That should have been a clue that something wasn't right. When I pointed it out to Richard as we entered a second building, he just shrugged it off and took off running to find a good place to hide. I chased him and another kid. We spent the rest of the afternoon exploring the deserted buildings.

Early on a Saturday, Richard knocked on my door and asked if I could come outside. I got dressed in a hurry and joined him around the corner from his building. To my surprise, he had his BB gun with him and, in retrospect, he seemed a little nervous.

"What will you give me for my BB gun?" Richard asked me.

I was so shocked to hear the question that I didn't respond right away. When I didn't answer him, he asked me again. I didn't know what to say. Of course, I wanted a BB gun, and the one he was offering was as fine a one as any I had seen. I was, however, a little puzzled by his offer. Richard really loved that gun. I should have been more inquisitive, but I chose to go along with him to see what amount of money he had in mind.

"Will you give me thirty dollars for it," he asked.

That sounded like a fair price to me, but I didn't have thirty dollars. When I hesitated, Richard dropped the price and asked if I would buy it for twenty dollars. I didn't know why he was so anxious to sell the BB gun, but I did know twenty dollars was more than a fair price for it. I told him I would ask my dad and see what he said. Richard told me that he would save the BB gun for me and wouldn't let anyone else buy it from him until I returned with my answer. I was grateful for the chance to buy his BB gun, so I ran back to the house to see if I could convince my dad to give me twenty dollars.

It was early, but Dad was up drinking his coffee and reading his morning paper. Since it was Saturday, he didn't have to be at work until later in the day. He was relaxing which I didn't take into account when I barged into the kitchen and spat out my question before anyone could interrupt me. My mother turned to see why I was in such a hurry and my sister, who had just entered the room, stared at me with a surprised look on her face. My dad looked up from his newspaper and asked me to repeat the question. I asked again boldly if I could buy Richard's BB gun for twenty dollars. My mother looked shocked. My dad wanted to know why Richard was selling it. Was it still working? I told him I believed it was. He sat and mulled over that piece of new information. To my surprise, he asked me when he could see the BB gun. I told him I would find out from Richard and let him know.

I scrambled out of the kitchen, ran across the courtyard, and headed straight for Richard's house. He was inside eating breakfast, but he seemed happy to see me. I told him my dad wanted to see the BB gun before he would let me buy it. I asked him if he would show it to him that morning. Richard didn't hesitate. He said he would come over right after breakfast to let my dad get a look at the BB gun.

I ran back across the courtyard to tell my mother and my dad the good news. I was surprised to find them engaged in a heated discussion. I waited near the screen door listening to their banter back and forth on the question I had raised about buying the gun. My mother felt it was a bad idea and wanted to know why Dad had changed his mind about the gun. To my surprise, my dad defended his position and mine. He told my mom that he believed I was old enough and responsible enough to handle a BB gun. He thought it was being offered at a fair price and just wanted to see it first before making up his mind.

I was so proud of my dad's assessment of me. I had never heard him say how much he trusted me before. I didn't know he was watching to see whether I was grown enough to handle more responsibility. He had come to my defense. It was a pleasant revelation for me. For the first time in my life, I believed my dad trusted me. I was humbled by what I had heard. Finally, my mother gave in. She told my dad that it was his department and that she would go along with whatever he decided to do. Upon hearing her resignation, I pushed open the screen and stood in the doorway with a broad smile on my face. My dad told me to come on in and he asked me when we could see the BB gun. I told him that Richard would bring it over right after breakfast. It was all set. I would have my Christmas wish after all.

Richard came over a half an hour later. My dad examined the BB gun very carefully. He took a shooting stance and raised it to see how it would balance on his left forearm. He opened the chamber and inspected the firing pin and then checked the safety lock. I watched as my dad went over the BB gun checking every aspect of it. Then, he handed it back to Richard.

My dad asked, "Is twenty dollars what you want for the gun?"

I held my breath as Richard said that twenty dollars was a fair price. My dad said that he would have to clear it with Richard's father and agreed to meet with him later that day. True to his word, the men met and my dad bought the BB gun for twenty dollars.

I realize now that Richard had wanted to find a way to hold on to his BB gun. He believed if I bought it, he could use it whenever he wanted to. It makes sense now but, back then, I didn't know the whole story. What transpired a few weeks later would fill in the missing pieces. I was sitting in class at school when my name was called over the public address system. The secretary in the main office wanted me to come down there right away. My teacher told me I was excused. All my classmates stared at me as if they knew something that I didn't. I stuffed my books into my book bag and hurried down to the main office. My heart was thumping wildly in my chest. All kinds of horrible thoughts rolled up inside my head.

What if my mother was ill again? She had been sick a couple of times in the past few months. *What if my father was in an accident?* I knew he worked with guided missiles, but I didn't know how dangerous

240

his job might have been. All those thoughts and more ran through my head, one chasing after the other.

When I reached the office, the assistant principal met me at the door. He escorted me inside where, to my surprise, my father was waiting for me. He thanked Mr. Russell for summoning me. I spoke courteously to the assistant principal and then looked down at my shoes.

My dad turned to look at me and said, "We have someplace to be at 2 p.m., so let's go."

We left the office together, my dad in front with me dragging along behind him. I didn't know where we were going or why he had pulled me out of my science class before the end of the school day. I didn't say a word. When my dad wanted me to talk, he would let me know. He had his way of controlling a conversation. I wasn't going to try to change his approach given the circumstances. We rode along for a few minutes before my dad began to query me about my whereabouts the past few weeks. I didn't know what he was fishing for, but I did understand he intended to get the answers one way or the other.

I told him about our quail hunt with the dogs and our hide and seek games in the old buildings. He asked me if anyone had seen us near the buildings. I told him I didn't think that they had. Then, he looked straight at me and asked me did I have anything to do with the windows being shot out in the buildings. I told him that I didn't have anything to do with it and that I didn't know who did. My dad gave me a stern look and warned me that he would be very upset with me if he found out differently.

I breathed in heavily and held my breath to keep from shaking. My dad was strict but fair. He had a heightened sense of right and wrong, which he prided himself in following. Things were always black or white with him; there was no gray. If you tried to convince him that there was a case for gray, he would only ask you what you were trying to hide. I expect his inflexible stand on morality came from his early entry into the military services. He enlisted in the marines at sixteen years old during the buildup to World War II. He grew up in the military. I can understand now what he inherited from those early experiences.

We reached our destination. I still didn't know where we were going or why my dad had brought me along. As I started to get out of the car, he reached over and grabbed my arm. My dad held onto it tightly and spoke softly into my ear. The words he deposited there caused me to cringe with fear. He cautioned me to tell the truth about whatever I was asked. He would back me up. I had never seen my dad so focused on anything, especially not on me. I didn't want to disappoint him, so I told him I would do as he said.

The building was unfamiliar, but the location was in the middle of the Headquarters Post Command complex. A ring of vehicles was parked out front and men in uniform moved into and out of the building. I didn't recognize anyone, in particular, but I did notice that they all seemed to be pressed and very formal. I also noticed that most of them wore Military Policemen's uniforms that were covered with brass usually reserved for major acts of valor. My dad showed his identification and then told the officer at the front desk that he was there to see Sgt. Conrad. The officer directed him to a doorway half the way down a long hallway.

We shared a long, silent walk to our final destination. My dad knocked solidly on the door. The attending officer opened it and escorted us inside. They exchanged the same set of information my dad had given the officer at the front desk. The attending officer then told us to wait there and that Sgt. Conrad would be with us shortly. Dad sat in the chair next to the doorway. I plopped down into one right next to him. Although we were sitting just a few inches apart, I felt like I was marooned on Mars. My dad was silent and removed. Once again, I felt abandoned.

I had been summoned without any reason given. I was about to enter a room of strangers with a hidden agenda waiting for me to answer questions honestly about who knows what. The officer who had let us into the room interrupted the wait abruptly. He motioned for my dad and me. Dad rose and placed his arm firmly behind my back as he escorted me into the interrogation room following the officer. My feet were numb. It felt as if I was walking without touching the ground. My breathing stopped the minute I was escorted to my seat.

I began to survey the area. The room was mostly bare with just a few certificates on the wall. There was a desk in the far corner with one chair positioned next to it. My chair was in the middle of the room. My dad sat in the one chair next to the desk. The officer who escorted us into the room sat in another chair next to the door. A single light dangled over my head, but it must have been broken, because it was off. Overhead florescent lights shone brightly.

A stocky man entered the room and walked over to the desk. He greeted my dad with a firm handshake and a solemn smile. My dad returned the greeting with Sgt. Conrad, but I didn't see any smile on his face. Afterwards, Sgt. Conrad turned to me and asked me my name. I answered like a good soldier, strongly and directly. Sgt. Conrad looked at my dad and nodded his head. I was directed to sit in the chair under the broken light. Sgt. Conrad sat across from me on a small stool. His demeanor was all business.

Sgt. Conrad began by having me repeat my name, home address, and telephone number. He asked me if I knew why he had requested that I come in to see him. I told him that I didn't. He then informed me that some of the buildings in our area had been vandalized and he wanted to know if I knew anything about that. I told him that I had heard about it, but I didn't tell him that I had been in the buildings in the past few weeks. Then the next question he asked me sent shock waves deep down into my stomach. Sgt. Conrad wanted to know if I owned a BB gun. I told him that I did. He asked me how long I had owned it. I told him it had only been a few weeks. With that answer, he looked over at my dad. My dad nodded his head in agreement. Then, Sgt. Conrad asked me the next question that I had already expected was coming.

"Did you shoot out the windows in Building 134 and 138?"

Before he could get the entire question out on the table, I froze. All kinds of horrible recriminations were running through my head. *Why was he asking me these questions? Why was I singled out for vandalizing those buildings? Who had told the MP's that I was the culprit? Why had my friend sold me a BB gun just a few weeks ago? Did he know this inquiry was coming?* My litany of incriminating questions came to an end when Sgt. Conrad turned abruptly on his stool and I heard my dad yell at me to pay attention and answer.

Sgt. Conrad repeated his question, "Do you own a BB gun?"

I answered him, "Yes," but with a caveat. I told him that I had a BB gun that I bought from my friend next door just two weeks ago. I told him I had not taken it out of the housing complex. I told him that I definitely didn't have anything to do with shooting out windows in those abandoned buildings. Then, when I heard myself talking, I became so frightened that I stopped.

Sgt. Conrad had listened intently to everything that I said. He looked me straight in the eyes for a long while. Then, he motioned for my dad to follow him into his office. They left the room and the officer closed

244

the door behind them. Without looking at me, he sat back down in his chair. Sgt. Conrad and my dad were gone for a while. I nearly fell asleep waiting for them to return. I hadn't noticed how warm it was inside the room until Sgt. Conrad opened the door. When he did, some of the cooler air rushed in from his office. My dad took his seat next to the desk. The officer closed the door and returned to his post.

Sgt. Conrad stood beside his stool and eyed me quietly. Then, he began to walk around the room, seemingly talking to himself. During his one-way conversation, he laid out a series of questions and posed as many answers. He conjectured that some of the kids in the neighborhood had been vandalizing the buildings for some time now. They had broken bottles inside and had broken windows outside. Recently the names of a few of the perpetrators had surfaced. They were now wrapping up the investigation to include BB gun owners in the area. When Sgt. Conrad got to the part about the BB guns, he looked directly at me and then he looked over at my dad. What he said next surprised me.

"Sgt. Lee explained that you just got your BB gun and that he hadn't let you take it out of the house yet. That squares with the intelligence we collected from some of the other kids we interviewed," Sgt. Conrad said.

Then, Sgt. Conrad said something that I will always remember. He said that he had known my dad from an earlier military assignment and that he had never met a finer soldier in his life.

"If your dad tells me you just bought your BB gun, then I believe him. You are free to go."

Those words were both welcome and, at the same time, daunting. I hadn't realized that my freedom was in jeopardy when I went into the interrogation room, but it was. My dad shook Sgt. Conrad's hand, placed his arms around my shoulders, and escorted me out of that hot, humid interrogation room into the cool, afternoon air. I never felt as proud as when we touched solid ground and my dad grasped my hand. We walked back to the car together. On the way home, we talked about our unusual day and gave thanks for all of the things that had gone right for us. I had learned a valuable lesson. Sometimes the things you want the most and believe you have to have are not the things you need in your life. Our wants are not needs; God has promised to provide for all of our needs.

Chapter 17: The Life of Larry

Summer had finally arrived at our Fort Sill housing complex and we were glad to see it. On the weekends, kids streamed into the courtyard early in the morning and didn't go in until dark. We played all kinds of games: marbles, dodge ball, jump rope, steal-the-bacon, red rover-red rover, and, my favorite, softball. The common element in most of our games was how inclusive they were. Anyone could join in and play dodge ball or softball. The oldest kids would usually choose sides and try to balance the talent so everyone had an equal chance to win. The idea of fairness was ingrained in all of us. We were "army brats" and that meant we stuck together. We looked out for each other and believed we were expected to uphold a higher standard of fairness.

The sides would be chosen for the softball game early in the afternoon. We would hit some fly balls in the morning, but nothing serious got started until most of the kids were outside in the afternoon. The kids choosing the sides would select their players based upon their ability to play the game. If a girl could catch a fly ball, she would be selected before a boy who would likely drop it. That was the measurement used to choose. Of course, some squabbling would occur if a team captain refused to balance his team, but, for the most part, we all accepted the results without too much complaining.

If enough kids came out to play, we were able to field teams of six, eight, or nine players. If more kids showed up, we would add them in the outfield and balance the teams when we changed sides. You would think that five players in the outfield would guarantee that every fly ball would be caught. That wasn't the case, however. A high fly ball would be often dropped between two players expecting the other player to catch it. Skills are one thing, but teamwork matters too. Even in professional baseball a fly ball occasionally is allowed to drop because two players

247

can't decide who is going to catch it. Fortunately, we never had a serious collision with two or more players all trying to catch a ball at the same time.

I took to playing softball like a fish takes to water. Something about the rhythm of the game worked for me. I got to be so good at it that teams would require that I bat with one hand on some occasions to give them a better chance to put me out. I was as good a fielder as I was a batter. Sometimes I would play center field and cover both left and right field if we were short of players. I had a very good arm. Most players would be held to a single base hit if I was fielding the ball. If a player was too slow running down to first base, I would throw them out from right field. I got to be so good at it that a rule was finally made to disqualify me from making that play.

If we didn't have enough players to field a team, we would play a game of rotation. Three players would be chosen to bat first and everyone else would take their positions in the field. Upon getting a batter out, everyone would move up one spot with the player at first base going in to bat. If a player caught a fly ball without dropping it, that player would switch places with the batter and join the team at bat. I liked that rule the most. I knew the better players hit long fly balls, so I would take a position in the outfield and wait to run down a fly ball. Once I caught one, I would change places with the batter and, on most days, stay up at bat for the rest of the game.

Our games included a melting pot of kids from all over the country. We had a kid from Pennsylvania who could throw a high pitch ball and strike out most of the batters. We had a kid from Canada who liked to play catcher, so he could harass the batters on the other team. We had two kids from Texas who spoke Spanish and liked to hit ground balls between the bases and watch the fielders scramble to chase them down.

We had a girl from West Virginia, who could swing a bat with the best of them. Team captains would usually fight over who would get to choose her for their team. We had a kid from Oklahoma who experimented with chewing tobacco; he could catch a fly ball with one hand. We had a kid from Louisiana who loved to heckle the pitcher and always tried to get on base with a walk. We also accommodated the kid who was physically challenged. Sometimes he would keep the score. Sometimes he would bat in a round robin and his teammates would run the bases for him. We created a spot for every kid who wanted to play. That was the rule of fairness practiced in our complex. That rule would be tested.

One Saturday morning before any of us were awake, a moving truck arrived on our block. It was not unusual for families to move in on Saturday. When we saw the truck, we all anticipated meeting our new neighbors soon. It was nearly one in the afternoon before the moving truck left. During that time, we had not seen anyone go into or out of the apartment building that we didn't already know. To my surprise, one guy was left behind when the moving truck pulled away. I realized he was not a mover; he was our new neighbor. I watched as he quietly observed the sights and sounds of his new neighborhood. He tilted his head and seemed to be listening for a faraway signal or looking for a familiar sign to use to get his bearings. Finally, he turned and walked into the building, leaving me there in the courtyard to ponder who he was and where he had come from.

A few days later, the moving van returned, bringing the rest of the house furniture. I didn't see the gentleman directing the movers, then. I suppose he was at work. I looked for someone else to have taken his role, but the movers came and went without anyone leaving the house. It didn't seem strange to me at the time, but I would later question it. By the time the next weekend came, the neighborhood was buzzing about the new neighbors. Most of the buzz was based on rumors since no one had seen any of them except me. I listened to the kids exchanging tales of sights unseen but chose not to add to their misguided imaginations. I knew we would meet them soon enough.

Early Saturday afternoon, a family consisting of two adults and one child left their apartment and made their way along the roadway around the apartment complex. The man, who walked briskly, was medium height with a slim build. He had a dark complexion and sported a marine haircut and brown sandals. He wore brown slacks and a camel-colored, short sleeve shirt, which hung elegantly off his body. His wife was tall, with a medium build and dark complexion. She held herself in check, almost rigid, and followed a full step behind her husband. She wore a dark-colored, full-body sarong with a matching headdress and brown sandals. Together they were a matching pair, one serenely confident and the other subdued.

I didn't notice the little kid walking beside his mother at first because he blended almost completely into her side. He had a large head, small hands, and very thin legs. His hair was cut to his scalp and he wore dark green shorts, a purple shirt, and sandals just like his dad. Of all the features that I could have noticed, one stood out. His complexion was very dark. I had never seen a kid as dark as he was. In addition to his large head, his eyes were wide and piercing. I could see that he wanted to get a good look at all of his new neighbors, but he seemed afraid to venture very far from his mother's side.

As the new family made their way along the sidewalk, the kids and their parents watched them from a distance. It was an odd occasion because most families got to know the neighborhood gradually over time, not all at once like this new family was doing. It was strange to see them on display for all the neighbors to view only a few days after they had arrived. That proved to be a problem. As the couple and their small child passed by, I could see the neighbors gawking at them. Then, I noticed a strange response coming from the mother and her child. She was staring back at her new neighbors with a harsh and defiant look on her face. I had never seen anyone greet people they didn't know with such disdain. Her manner was unmistakable. She didn't feel welcome, and her look communicated that to everyone she passed.

My eyes rested on the father. His manner was steady and confident. He walked at a quickened pace looking straight-ahead and made no attempt to engage in eye contact with anyone. I could see that he had already decided his course of action. He wasn't going to let anyone interrupt his afternoon foray. As I turned my head to catch another glimpse of the mother, her son tripped and would have fallen if she had not caught him. What happened next was unanticipated. The mother snatched the young boy up by one arm and proceeded to drag him along the street beside her. He struggled to keep up while she chastised him harshly for being so clumsy.

The episode lasted just a few seconds but, afterwards, all eyes were fixed on the two of them. The father continued to walk briskly without looking back or acknowledging that anything had happened. The boy continued to struggle to keep up. He looked like he was ready to cry. I felt sorry for him. He seemed to be out of place and very frightened by all that was happening. I knew it was wrong, but I couldn't stop staring at the two of them. Then, all of a sudden I felt embarrassed when his mother looked directly at me. I realized that she too had a dark complexion, like her son. As she fixed her gaze on mine, I could see the hatred for me, and everyone else who had been gawking at her reflected in her eyes.

My sister and I ran to tell our mother about the incident we had witnessed. We were out of breath and nearly in a panic as we spilled out the story of what we had seen. It appeared that our mother was a little concerned, but she didn't say anything about it. She told us to come into the house. We ate our dinner and went on with the rest of our evening as if nothing had happened. Later in the evening, the kids in the courtyard appeared to have forgotten about the odd new family when we rejoined them.

The next few weeks were uneventful. We played outside and enjoyed the games as always. One Friday afternoon, we were surprised to see the new kid hanging out near the playground. He was wearing a different pair of shorts and had on a new pair of sneakers as well. We were playing a game of dodge ball. I could see that he wanted to join us. My sister was curious, so she walked over to him and asked him his name. He spoke so softly that I couldn't hear him. My sister asked him if he wanted to play dodge ball with us, but he didn't answer her. Then, before she could ask him again, his mother began calling him to come home.

"Larry! Larry! Where are you? What are you doing? You had better get home now!"

The frail little kid, standing next to my sister, jumped when he heard his mother calling his name. He turned in an instant and began running as fast as he could towards his building. I would never have guessed that he could sprint so fast. All the other kids were shocked to see him running. They stared as he scrambled across the courtyard and down the block towards his apartment building. It was a half a block to his building, and he was struggling to run all the way. When his mother met him at the curb, she had a heavy, black strap with her. We watched in horror as she beat him with it; holding him with one arm and whipping him with the other. She continued the whipping as she dragged him into the house.

We didn't see Larry for a month. When we did see him outside again, he kept his distance and shied away from talking with any of the neighborhood kids. Once during a break in our softball game, I looked across the field and saw Larry leaning against a tree watching us play. He appeared to be afraid to cross the street to join us at the ball field. I could see that he wanted to play, too, but I knew we couldn't force him to join us. The consequences might be devastating for him if he did. That was the last time I recall seeing Larry. I wished I had done more to get to know him, because I believe kids like Larry need friends who care about them more than anything.

It was late in the evening and the sun was dropping behind the clouds. The courtyard was full of active kids playing the games they loved the most. We could never have imagined what was going to happen next. Suddenly, in the middle of a game of tag, one of the kids came running into the courtyard screaming that something had happened to Larry. I couldn't understand all that he was saying, but I knew immediately it wasn't good. My sister ran over to him and tried to get him to calm down enough to explain what he had seen, but the kid was too frightened.

We all ran together to the front of our building. That's when we saw the commotion going on down the street. The MPs were exiting their police cars and rushing towards Larry's building. We could hear voices shouting loudly and a man appeared to be arguing with an officer. A few minutes later, two other officers walked out of the building with a woman handcuffed between them. I was shocked to see the MPs escorting Larry's mother out of the building. She was quiet and subdued.

She didn't look around or try to resist the officers. They placed her in a police cruiser where she sat for a long while before they drove her away.

We ran into the house to tell our mother about the incident we had seen that happened down the block. She listened intently and then told us to come inside for the evening. We didn't want to be left out of all of the excitement, but we obeyed her. She threw a sweater over her shoulders and walked down the block to talk with some of the neighbors. She was gone for a while. When she returned home, she went straight to her room. She closed her door. We knew she didn't want to be disturbed.

My sister and I went into the kitchen and read some comic books until our mother told us to get ready for bed. After we donned our nightclothes, my sister asked if we could have some peach cobbler that our mother had baked earlier in the day. Our mother told her that she would scoop out a portion in a bowl for each of us. She also told us to drink a glass of milk and then go to bed. We didn't ask any more questions. We ate our dessert, drank our milk, said good night, and went to bed.

The following morning the entire neighborhood was abuzz and talking about what had happened the night before. The stories I heard the grown-ups telling about the incident were alarming and impossible for me to fully comprehend. I couldn't imagine the horrors experienced by that frail little kid. He was so young and helpless. I was haunted by the hollow look on his face and the glare from his mother's eyes. I found myself dreaming about Larry and then waking up at night in a sweat, too afraid to go back to sleep. The whole summer had been ruined. I wanted so badly to be able to turn back the clock and do something, anything, to change the outcome. It wasn't going to happen. An innocent little kid named Larry had disappeared and we would never see him again.

Chapter 18: First Year in Junior High School

My First Week in Junior High

I really enjoyed the time I spent at Douglas Middle School. It was a refreshing break from the tension I had experienced in my newly integrated school in Texas. I acquired a few new friends, whom I would reunite with later, when Lawton Senior High School finally integrated in the 60's. I had enjoyed testing myself with students who looked like me who were self-confident and not afraid to take on a challenge. My overall experience had been positive. Memories from Douglas were among the bright spots in my early school years. I would need those positive memories to sustain me through the challenges of my junior high school experience.

Lawton's Junior High School, called Central Junior High School, sat just a few short blocks from Douglas Middle School. It was located right in the middle of the city and had been an all-white institution for as many years as anyone could remember. That changed for the school and for me in 1957. After the 1954 Civil Rights decree following the Supreme Court's desegregation decision, schools serving children of military families had to be desegregated. This meant Central Junior High had to integrate its classes in order to continue to receive funding from the Federal Government. That funding was substantial for any school system served by a military facility the size of the one at Fort Sill. An estimate bantered around at the time placed the financial support at $525 dollars per student. I estimated that at least a third of the students attending Central Junior High were from the military post. That was a strong incentive for the school system to comply.

My mother and father tried to prepare me for what I would experience attending the town school. They cautioned me to keep my mouth shut and my eyes and ears open. They warned me not to expect the town kids to be excited about my attending their school. Nor would they be anxious to become my friend. They suggested that I stay with the other kids from the post and try to blend in. I took all of their suggestions to heart, and then prayed that I would know what to do when the time came. My sister was apprehensive, too. This would be the first time she attended school without me. She would

School Days - 1957-58

still be going to Douglas Middle School as I entered Central Junior High School. We both nervously anticipated these challenges.

I sat next to the window as we rode the bus into town for the first day of school. The bus dropped me off at my school first. I told my sister goodbye. She leaned on the window and watched me as I got off the bus with the other kids from the military post. I waved at her as the bus rolled away. Here I was the first day of school standing outside of this moderately elegant white marble-looking school building. The grounds were tree-lined and covered with lush shrubs and fall plants. I took in the view for a few seconds and then scrambled to catch up with my classmates who were already pressing through the main entrance. We followed the crowd into the cafeteria where rows of teachers sitting at desks waited to help us find our homeroom assignments. I checked into the line for students with last names beginning with "L."

The teacher serving the line was very patient. She asked each of us our name, found us on the stenciled paper, checked off our names, and then handed us a card with our homeroom designation on it. We had ten minutes to find our classes. Outside the cafeteria, a cadre of hall monitors directed us to our homerooms. I found mine just before the warning bell rang. I entered and took a seat next to a red-haired kid whom I had never seen before. He turned to look at me with a smirk. At first I was going to speak, but when I saw the look on his face I chose instead to just ignore him. The class filled up quickly. The homeroom teacher welcomed all of us and began checking us in. To no one's surprise, she began by reading our names off of her stenciled sheet. Each of us responded with a "present" when our name was called. Once that had been accomplished, the teacher went through her list of housekeeping items, which included telling us the locations of the bathrooms, emergency exit doors, and the main auditorium. We were told that we would be attending a mandatory student meeting in the auditorium just before lunch. For some reason that I couldn't explain, the mention of lunch caused my stomach to start churning.

I was still trying to get my stomach to settle down as I searched for the room where I was supposed to attend my third period class. I found the room and quickly looked around to see if I knew anyone. Most of the kids were in the process of putting away their book bags and taking their seats. I didn't recognize anyone from the post in my class, so I hesitated instead of finding a place to sit down. That was the wrong thing to do. I caught the teacher's attention.

She pointed at me and said, "Stop dawdling and take your seat, now."

I was startled by her sternness and halted in the middle of the door to the room. She repeated herself with a bit more emphasis on the word "now." I scrambled to find a seat. Not wanting to be singled out a third time, I sat down in the first empty chair I found on the front row. The teacher looked surprised by my choice, but she didn't say anything else to me. The class began as it had in our homeroom with roll call and housekeeping items. Once those were out of the way, the teacher surprised all of us by asking each of us to stand, state our names, and tell a little bit about ourselves. She began with the first row, so my turn came soon enough. As I stood and faced the class, I noticed a sea of curious faces all staring intently at me. They each seemed to have the same expression of reserved disdain. I chose to ignore that and introduced myself as Bernard N. Lee, Jr., from Fort Sill. I told them that I had arrived recently from a tour in Texas and that I liked to write poems. I don't know why I put that last bit of information out there. I believe I was trying to find a trait that might endear me with my seemingly unimpressed detractors. I don't think it worked because the teacher interrupted me just as I completed my sentence and told me to sit down.

The next few minutes my classmates stood and gave their versions of introductions. I was too embarrassed to turn around to face them, so I listened intently hoping I would be able to place a voice with a face later. I was somewhat relieved when that exercise was over and was pleasantly surprised by the teacher's first assignment. She addressed the class and informed us that we would be expected to learn all about the parts of speech in written language. She encouraged us to prepare ourselves by studying the dictionary and reading articles and books appropriate for our ages.

The next thing the teacher did really piqued my interest. She asked the class if anyone could recite a list of prepositions from memory. I knew I could answer the question, so I raised my hand. The teacher selected a blond-haired girl sitting on the front row two seats down from me. I didn't get discouraged; my hand was still held high. A number of students stood and repeated prepositions they knew in answer to her question. I held my hand up but, for the next five minutes, the teacher ignored me. I listened as one student after another gave their answers to the question. I counted about eight students who volunteered to answer. Only three were able to recite more than ten prepositions. When it appeared that all of the volunteers to my rear had responded, the teacher looked at the front row for additional responses. My arm was getting tired, but my hand was still standing tall. I don't know what made the teacher finally decide to call on me. She may have been curious about what I wanted from her. Maybe she thought I had to go to the rest room. I couldn't read her mind, and I didn't try. I had my chance to show what I knew, and I wasn't going to turn it down.

I rose and turned halfway towards the class. Before I could speak, the teacher informed me that I wasn't permitted to repeat any of the words that any of my classmates had already given. I suspect she thought that admonition would cause me to pause and possibly cut short the obvious interruption. I wasn't deterred at all. I knew I could recite prepositions that I had learned many years before entering the seventh grade because my mother had played a game with my sister and me where we took turns naming things. One of those things was prepositions.

My sister and I had learned that a preposition was anything that a squirrel could do with a tree. He could go around the tree, over the tree, through the tree, under the tree, into the tree and on and on. The winner of the game was always the person who lasted the longest and named the final preposition when everyone else had given up. I loved winning and so did my mother. Our naming contests were fierce and often lasted for quite a while. I was ready for the teacher's challenge. I started slowly and continued naming prepositions one after the other. When I had reached preposition number twenty-four, I noticed a scowl appear on the teacher's brow. She stood beside her desk and stared at me as I recited number twenty-eight through thirty-two. Then, she abruptly interrupted me and told me to sit down. I had expected something a little less caustic for my efforts, but I was feeling somewhat pleased with myself as I took my seat. What came next was shocking and totally unexpected. The teacher addressed the class and referred to my performance as an example of what you can expect from "those people." I nearly fell out of my chair when I heard the words coming out of her mouth.

"See class," the teacher continued. "That's what's wrong with those people. They just don't know how to act. They are always showing off. That's why they will never amount to anything."

When she finished, I dropped my head and slid as far down in my seat as I could. What I had considered to be a solid performance had been shot down. I had been berated in front of all of my classmates on the first day of school. I didn't have any idea of what I would be able to do to recover a small amount of my dignity and self-worth, not to mention my pride. The incident was even more damaging because an adult, a teacher, had criticized me in front of my peers for knowing something that she thought I had no business knowing at all. I felt like a plantation slave who had been caught reading a book. Then I realized that my punishment had been much less than any slave would have received.

It was a dark day for me. I left school wondering what I could do to recover. It was a long ride home. I kept to myself and didn't talk much at all. My sister had enjoyed her first day at school, so she did all the talking for both of us. When we exited the bus, I ignored our friends as they waved goodbye to us and walked toward their buildings. I was in no mood to share my feelings at the time. I just wanted to find a place where I could sit by myself and figure things out. I didn't understand what had happened to cause the teacher to embarrass me in front of my classmates. It was an incident I couldn't fully comprehend with my limited social background. I had spent most of my school days in military schools where all the kids were children of soldiers. The teachers there didn't distinguish between military kids and they definitely didn't refer to us as "those kids." I entered the house pondering those differences and didn't answer when my mother asked me how my first day of school had gone. My failure to acknowledge her greeting caused her to pause. She immediately assessed the situation. She told my sister to go into her room and change her clothes. Then she looked at me and told me to follow her into the kitchen. She pointed to a chair and I sat down.

"Now," my mother said, "why don't you tell me about your first day at school?"

I had held in my feelings for as long as I could. As I began to speak, they all came spilling out at once. I babbled about the awkward introduction I had experienced with my English teacher. I repeated the question the teacher had posed to all of the kids. I tried to explain to my mother what I had done to show I knew my prepositions. I told her how hurt I was when the teacher abruptly told me to sit down. Then, I told her what my teacher had said. My mother listened silently without changing a single expression on her face. When I had finished, she asked me if I had anything else to tell her. I replied that I didn't. She told me to go to my room, change my clothes, and get ready for dinner. She didn't give any indication of what she was preparing to do.

The next morning I rode to school with a sick feeling in my stomach. My mother had told me not to worry about the incident. She would take care of it. I trusted her, but that didn't help me to feel any better about my morning at school. I went through the motions of pledging allegiance to the flag. I wondered if any of those words applied to people who looked like me. My faith was being tested and I was having a really hard time keeping it together. The time ticked by. Soon, I was dreading my next class. I tried to get to my third period English class as early as I could, so that I would have a chance to get into my seat without being confronted by my teacher. I was so glad when I realized I had succeeded. I entered the class and only a few kids were seated already: a heavy-set boy in the far corner, the blond-haired girl who had named ten prepositions, and me. I slid into my front seat and placed my book bag under it. I took out my English book and pretended to read it hoping that would protect me from being singled out again. The blond-haired girl looked at me curiously, but she didn't say anything when I glanced at her. The boy in the back was already asleep. I guess he had a rough night, too.

The classroom filled up quickly as students piled in from their other classes. I wondered where my English teacher was but wasn't overly anxious to find out. Five minutes passed, but she hadn't arrived. I guess the rest of the class was wondering the same thing I was. The class had begun to get a little restless when the teacher finally entered. She looked rushed and somewhat disheveled. I chose not to look at her too carefully; I just wanted to be left alone. The next few minutes went by quickly. The teacher conducted the roll call and passed around a sheet of paper for us to complete with emergency information on it. When that assignment was done, she handed out workbooks on English grammar. We were instructed to write our names in our workbooks and to always remember to bring them to class with us.

What came next was a complete surprise for me. The teacher asked if anyone knew what a conjunction was and if they could stand and name a few. The eager kids in the class raised their hands. I held mine at my side. The teacher looked around the classroom and paused when she came to me. She then pointed her finger in my direction and asked me to stand and answer the question. I was unprepared to respond and hesitated just a little too long. The teacher realized that I was not prepared and started to select another student when I rose to my feet. She looked a little startled, but recovered quickly and told me to proceed. I rattled off five or six conjunctions and then sat down. To my surprise, the teacher said thank you, turned to face the other half of the class, and asked another kid to answer the question. I had passed the second day's test. I had not been berated or humiliated again. I didn't know how I felt about the experience, but I knew it was a lot better than the one the day before. The pattern had been set. I was going to be included. That meant I would always have to be prepared. It was a challenge I eagerly chose to accept.

The ride home was an easy one. I listened to my sister talk about her day and didn't feel any anxiety of my own. She told me about the aquarium that her teacher had allowed the class to visit in one of the high school science rooms and then rattled on about how beautiful the tropical fish were. As I listened to her, I knew she was trying to summon the courage to ask our mother if she could purchase an aquarium for her room. It was a wonderful idea, but it didn't have a chance of going anywhere. On any other day, I would have delighted in bursting my sisters dream bubble, but not on this day. I had received grace and been spared further humiliation. I wasn't going to repay my good fortune by crushing my sister's enthusiasm.

When we got home, I walked deliberately towards the house while my sister ran ahead to meet our mother and pitch her new idea. I was surprised to find my mother waiting in the doorway for me. I had expected her to be engaged in a conversation with my sister trying to convince her to buy an aquarium. When I reached the kitchen doorway, my sister was nowhere in sight. My mother smiled as she greeted me and began asking about my day. I told her about my science class and the picture of the solar system that the teacher had posted over the bulletin board. I told her about my gym class and how I was uncertain that I would ever find a way to climb the rope to pass the class.

My mother didn't interrupt me, but she did interject quietly that she knew I would find a way.

Finally, when I had covered all of my classes except my English class, I stopped talking.

My mother looked me in the eye, and said, "Isn't there something else you want to tell me?"

I responded slowly, so she prompted me by asking about my English class. I hadn't forgotten about it, but I guess I didn't want to spoil the moment sharing my new assumptions about such a painful area of my life. When I did explain what had transpired in my English class, my mother looked pleased. That is when she told me about her visit to the school. She had called that morning and asked to speak with my teacher. They had set up a meeting just before my third period class. The meeting had been cordial but my mother had made herself very clear when she advised the teacher and assistant principal that all military children expected to be treated equally in school and she would accept no less for her son.

The assistant principal assured her that he understood her point of view and that the school had every intention of doing its best to be fair to all of its students, both military and non-military. Upon hearing his response, my mother chose not to elaborate on her earlier remarks. She thanked the teacher and the assistant principal for meeting with her, gathered her things, and left. The meeting had taken longer than planned. That was the reason my English teacher had been late for class.

I really appreciated my mother for her tenacity in standing up for me. I had seen her step forward to defend us on more than one occasion. I knew it wasn't easy for her to do. She had been raised in the part of the country where Negroes were expected to suffer in silence. I couldn't imagine how difficult it must have been for her to go against all that she had learned to fight for her children in an evolving desegregation environment. I admire her to this day for her passion and her courage. She believed in herself, in her God, and in her children. That was all the motivation she needed to take on challenges from forces much greater than herself. For me, the lesson was learned early. I kept my part of the bargain by applying myself diligently to getting my English teacher's work done. The experience was invaluable. I learned more English grammar in the seventh grade than at any other time in my life. It was a challenge I grew to cherish; and it produced a gift that has served me well.

A Night of Miracles

My initial introduction to Central Junior High School was very challenging and kept me occupied for the first few weeks of school. I didn't feel comfortable mingling with the other students and couldn't enjoy my lunches because of my over-active stomach. While the other students chatted during their lunch period and made new friends, I sat alone at a far table and pretended to eat my lunch. It was not exactly how I wanted to begin my school year, but I didn't seem to have any way to change the awful dynamics once they got set in motion. I probably would have continued in that rut if it hadn't been for a kid who broke through my artificial wall.

Jimmy Miller was a rather playful kid who enjoyed telling jokes and goofing off with the guys. He seemed to enjoy the attention. I envied his ability to be that loose in what I considered to be a very stifling environment. In my mind, most of the kids were giving me hateful looks and none of them seemed to be willing to share any time with a kid like me. Jimmy Miller broke through that facade. He stayed behind in the cafeteria one day when I was unaware that most of the other kids had left. As I rose to leave myself, Jimmy confronted me and asked me why

I was in such a hurry. I guess he thought that was a joke that I would appreciate. Instead, I just stared at him like I had seen a creature from outer space. He didn't seem to mind my staring. He asked me directly if anything was wrong. I answered that I wasn't feeling well. Jimmy seemed to recognize right away that I was suffering from some kind of emotional problem.

We walked out of the cafeteria together, Jimmy talking as usual and me with my head hung down. When the first bell rang, I realized I had walked in the wrong direction and had to turn and run to get to my next class in time.

Jimmy yelled as I sprinted away, "I'll see you at the bus, O.K.?"

I slipped around the corner of the building and scooted into my math class just as the second bell rang. I don't know whether Jimmy got to his class on time. I didn't look back to see. My day ended with no new embarrassments. When I headed towards the bus for home, I was so self absorbed that I didn't see Jimmy creep up behind me. When he finally caught up with me, he sprinted a few feet ahead, cut in front of me, and stood there with a smile on his face. "How are you doing now that school is out?" Jimmy asked. "You really were in a funk earlier."

I was so surprised that I didn't know what to say. I mumbled something about feeling better and asked him why he wanted to know. He smiled and told me he had noticed me boarding the school bus earlier in the week. We both lived on the post. He wondered if I had ever been overseas and if I knew any of the guys who had. I told him that I had always lived in the USA, but that I was looking forward to going overseas in the future with my dad. Jimmy seemed impressed that I was interested in traveling overseas. He followed me onto the bus and, to my surprise, sat down in the seat next to me and continued talking.

This was my introduction to the kid who would help me get through my first year in junior high.

Jimmy was an "army brat" like me. He had moved with his family as many times as I had. He didn't seem to mind that I was "different" and that made it easy for me to get along with him. He loved to talk and never turned down a chance to engage in an intellectual discussion. He was well read and informed. He talked enthusiastically about the states he had lived in before coming to Oklahoma. His family was from Vermont. He loved to go skiing in upstate New York. He had an older sister and a two-year-old younger brother. That made him the middle child. I guess he loved finding someone like me who would listen to him. My dreaded rides to and from school turned into a more pleasant experience when we were able to sit and talk on the way.

Jimmy had my English teacher for an afternoon class. He shared some of the stories he had heard about her. She had graduated magna cum laude from Oklahoma University. Her parents were fairly well known in her hometown, and they expected her to do well in her profession. She was teaching at our junior high school, but had been expected to continue her education and teach at the college level. The chip on her shoulder should have been a giveaway. She was used to excellence as her measurement and was uncompromising in those regards. After Jimmy finished describing our English teacher, I had a much better appreciation for her firmness and no nonsense attitude.

Jimmy and I shared at lot of time at school together. We ate in the cafeteria at the same table and rode on the bus together, where we would compare notes about our teachers and the things that happened during the day. I began to ask for his advice and trust his judgment about a lot of things that were new to me. He seemed to enjoy being the kid with the answers and having someone who wanted his advice. In time, I believe we developed a pretty good friendship. We traded comic books and swapped ideas on making paper airplanes. He discovered that I was good at drawing pictures and I showed him a couple of my replicas of prize racehorses. Jimmy liked the drawings a lot. He encouraged me to keep it up. He told me that maybe one day I would be good enough to draw pictures for one our action comic books. No one had ever projected a future for me as an artist. I was astonished to have someone my own age say I had talent.

As the friendship grew, I came to treasure the time I spent with Jimmy in and between classes at school. Jimmy was in my shop class. Together, we collaborated on our end of the year projects. I made matching whatnot stands for my mother to hang in two corners of the wall in the dining room. Jimmy made a beautiful redwood jewelry box for his mother to put her pearl necklace and earrings into on top of her vanity. I learned a lot in our shop class. It was fun to spend time with a friend building things we could use at home. When boys are having fun, the days pass by a lot faster. We would joke with each other and, occasionally, we would horse around. In one class, Jimmy asked if he could see if the color of my skin would rub off with sandpaper. I didn't believe the joke was as funny as he did, but I did eventually forgive him for laughing.

When it came time to select voices for the school chorus to sing in the Holiday Festival, Jimmy dragged me along with him to the try-outs. I was accustomed to singing in the junior church choir, but I would never have ventured to audition for the school chorus if Jimmy hadn't insisted. To my surprise, we were both selected. I was assigned to the tenor section and Jimmy was placed in the baritone section. Practice for that extracurricular activity gave my mother a chance to meet Jimmy's mother. As time passed and my mother got to know her better, they exchanged telephone numbers. Soon afterwards, Jimmy and I were allowed to spend time visiting each other after school. The friendship continued to grow. I was doing well in my newly integrated junior high school environment.

One night around 9 p.m., Jimmy called to talk. It wasn't unusual for him to call me, especially since it was a Friday and we didn't have school the next day. The conversation started out easily enough. I didn't sense anything wrong with him. We talked about the vacation his family had planned for the summer. I told him that I wished my family was going to see the Grand Canyon. We traded ideas about our final shop projects, and Jimmy wanted to know if I had ever built a rocking chair. He laughed when I told him that if I ever attempted to build one, it would definitely rock.

The conversation continued on for nearly an hour, and then he suddenly stopped talking. I could hear him breathing, but for nearly thirty seconds he didn't say a thing. I listened closely and could hear elevated voices in the background. It sounded like someone was angry. I asked Jimmy if everything was all right. He told me to wait a minute. He put down the telephone, walked across the room, and closed his door. The background noise appeared to go away. Jimmy cleared his throat and tried to pick up where we had left off, but he couldn't. He seemed to be upset and not at all ready to continue. I took up the slack by telling him about the home run I had hit the day before using just one hand. He listened and then suddenly interrupted. I thought he was going to ask a question. When he cursed, it startled me so much that I nearly dropped the telephone. I asked Jimmy what was wrong. He pretended that nothing was bothering him, but I suspected there was more going on than he wanted to talk about. A long pause ensued and I wondered what he was dealing with on his side of the world. I finally got up the nerve to break the silence by asking him another question. I realized later that it was an odd subject to bring up then, but I was willing to try anything to get the conversation going again.

"Have you ever wondered who made the stars?" I asked. I didn't expect him to answer right away, but he did. "You mean," Jimmy responded, "how they evolved over time?"

That answer caught me by surprise. I thought carefully about the next thing I was going to say. "No," I said, "I meant who created them and why?"

Jimmy went back into his silent mode and didn't take the bait. I knew he didn't go to church, and we had never talked about the origin of the universe or the concept of a heavenly being. I was patient. I waited for him to mull over his response. Finally, Jimmy waded in with a surprising answer for his response. He admitted that he didn't know how the universe was formed and that he wasn't sure about the role that the stars played in it. I expected him to end his answer there, but he wasn't finished yet. He said that he didn't believe in God and other myths like that and that he knew that no one could prove him wrong.

I took the last remark as a challenge. I was glad that he had found his voice, but I couldn't let his denial of the existence of God go unchallenged. I responded immediately with a flurry of questions designed to see how sincere he was about his assertions. I challenged his easy dismissal of the wonder of the universe and its nightly show of sparkling bright lights. I questioned him again about where the lights came from, if no one created them? His response was that they just existed in time. He submitted the same argument for the existence of the earth and the moon. I knew that argument would be difficult to hold on to. I told him that if I were to agree with his version of the creation, how would I explain the existence of human beings? Did we just appear all at once like the rocky moon, the tree covered earth, and the burning stars?

"Of course not," was his response.

He believed we evolved from tiny organisms that grew and changed over many, many years. Of course, when I heard his explanation, I was curious to know where the organisms came from and who or what superior power had managed such an intricate evolution so masterfully. Jimmy questioned my need to have a God-like force play that role. I took the bait eagerly. I began by trying to imagine how many details had to be managed to accomplish such a task. True, a single-cell animal might be relatively simple, but the similarity in the basic human building blocks called cells couldn't possibly have occurred just by accident. I proposed that not only was there a deliberate pattern to the design of human beings, but that design extended also to the earthly environment they were placed in. The sun provides the energy we use to warm ourselves, the light we need to see, and the fuel stored in plants to sustain all life on this earth. I asserted that surely such an intricate system as that just didn't appear out of thin air. I closed my argument by stating, "Such an elaborate system as our universe was the product of a superior design and all designs have a designer."

Jimmy wasn't convinced. He argued that humans are just a step above monkeys and other animals. He didn't believe the human design was so elegant and, anyway, he was sure that no one had ever seen the "designer" of the universe. Jimmy then admitted that was why he believed that no designer ever existed. It was a classic argument from one who only believes what one can see. I countered with a list of things that you couldn't see, but still knew were there. You couldn't see the wind, but its presence could be felt on your face and its power observed as your kite sailed high into the sky. You couldn't see gravity, but its presence could be observed when you let an apple drop or threw a baseball into the air only to have it return. Jimmy got the gist of the argument right away, but he still wasn't giving an inch on his lack of belief in God.

I decided to try a different approach. I asked Jimmy if he ever thought about where a person goes when they die. I expected him to say that he hadn't thought about it, so I was surprised when he answered. Jimmy told me he believed that our bodies disintegrate and we return to the earth. I asked him then did he believe that God created man from the dust of the earth? Jimmy said that he didn't believe in God, so he couldn't answer that question. So, I asked him then where did he think man came from. He reiterated that he believed man came from microorganisms on the earth.

We seemed to have come full circle. It was 1 a.m. in the morning, but I wasn't ready to give up. Jimmy sensed I was tiring. I expect he, too, was feeling weary from the discussion. I tried to think of something we could agree about, but all I could come up with was more questions. I asked Jimmy if he believed in miracles. He wanted to know what kind of miracles. I described examples of water being turned into wine and people believed dead being brought back to life. Jimmy thought for a while. Then he answered with a yes and a no. He believed you could change water into wine if you knew a trick or two, but he didn't believe anyone could bring a person back to life. "Does that mean you don't believe in miracles?" I asked him again.

Jimmy hesitated and then admitted that he didn't.

"That's a shame," I said.

I told him that makes all of the miracles we see every day seem insignificant. He wanted to know what I meant by that. I explained that his heart beats, but he doesn't have to tell it to. The earth rotates, and the days change like clockwork. The rain pours. The flowers grow and the oceans wash in and out with the daily tides, all on a schedule. Those miracles have occurred regularly for centuries on a preset schedule that none of us controls. It seems a shame that we can't acknowledge that. Jimmy countered very aggressively. He said that he acknowledged everything that I had described, but he just didn't believe those things counted as miracles. He believed they were all a part of the evolution of our world. I seized the opportunity when he said "our world" to make a counterpoint. I told him that we just agreed that we didn't control any of the cycles that I had described, so how could any of those things be just regular occurrences in our world?

I asked him, "What role had we played? When had man done anything significant enough to change even a single, basic equation set in motion so long ago?"

Jimmy didn't have an answer for that line of questioning, so he opened up an entirely new chain of thought. He made the argument that man had actually done a lot to change the world since it began. He cited the advances man had made in architecture, medicine, transportation, warfare, and, soon, space travel. He believed that man was destined to continue to expand his horizons of knowledge and discovery. Then he contended that man didn't need to depend upon a God he couldn't see to protect him or reveal the secrets yet to be discovered in space or here on earth.

I told him that I agreed with some of what he said, but had problems with the rest. I asked him what discoveries he expected man to make that had been created by man. He didn't seem to understand the question. I wanted to know what secrets that man had created would he expect to be found. He acknowledged that man hadn't created any of the secrets he was talking about. So, I challenged him by posing a rhetorical question, "If man didn't create those secrets, then who did?"

Jimmy was ready for my challenge. He countered with a question to me. He wanted to know why I was so sure there had to be a creator. I thought a few seconds and then shared my belief in the power of faith with my friend. I told him about my sickness as a baby and how my mother had prayed for me to live. I described the night she held me as I was choking to death on my own mucus. She rocked me and prayed for me to live. When I continued to choke and then stopped breathing, my mother remembered a passage from the Bible about "the breath of life." She turned me upside down, blew into my airway and sucked the mucus from my nostrils. Her faith in God had saved my life.

When I finished telling my story, Jimmy didn't know what to say. Finally, he asked me if I experienced anything like that myself. I told him that I had. I related the story of my friend in Georgia who had fallen into the quicksand pit after a big rainstorm. I told him that I joined the other guys trying to save him, but we couldn't find him in all the muck. I then recalled how I had prayed a silent prayer and then heard a voice telling me not to give up.

I told Jimmy, "I heard, 'He will provide.' That was when my friend spotted a tree limb that we were able to use to reach the boy and pull him out alive." I suspect that my personal confession made a really strong impact on Jimmy. All he could say was, "Wow."

I let the full impact of the evening's discussion settle in before I spoke again. Then, I asked Jimmy if he believed some power greater than man could have been the catalyst or architect for all of the secrets of the universe? Jimmy wanted to know why I believed a power greater than man had to be the creator. I told him that I believed the creator of earth's secrets had to be a far greater power than the seeker, just as the master builder had to be a far more advanced architect than his apprentice. Jimmy seemed to ponder my premise.

When I asked him again if he believed it would take a greater power than man to design and implement the universe, Jimmy answered, "Yes."

I was shocked and had no idea what to say next. Jimmy must have sensed that I was at a loss for words, so he continued with his newly discovered line of thought. He admitted that he did believe the design of the universe would take a far greater intelligence than man currently possessed. He confessed that he only understood a very limited scope of the problem, but that he couldn't imagine human beings solving it.

I said, "Can we agree that a greater power than man must have existed in the beginning for the universe to have been so intricately designed and implemented?" I paused to give Jimmy a chance to digest what I had just proposed. I didn't expect him to agree right away, so I was completely caught off guard when he said, "Yes, we can agree on the possibility of the existence of a higher power."

I had finally gotten through to him. Jimmy had witnessed the personal connection that a human being can experience with a greater power. He understood the paradox of life and death, and he chose to acknowledge the "Giver of Life." It was 4 a.m. in the morning when we said good night, hung up the phone and drifted off to sleep.

Lunch at Rusty's Downtown

Springtime was an occasion for celebration at school. The kids hung out on the lawn during lunchtime and afternoon class breaks. The guys threw baseballs and footballs around and the girls spread their dainty skirts, sat, and watched. I usually brought my lunch, except on Fridays when the menu included my favorites: Sloppy Joe sandwiches, potato chips, and a warm sticky bun. I ran errands, washed windows, and polished my dad's car just to earn the money for Friday lunches. So, I was surprised one Friday when Jimmy suggested we join some of the other guys and buy our lunch downtown. I had my reservations about the suggestion when it was first proposed because I was aware of the double standard for serving Negroes and whites in downtown establishments. When I voiced my concerns, Jimmy just brushed them aside and assured me it would be all right. I had come to trust his judgment, so I finally said that I would join them.

The guys were excited about going to a fast food place called, "Rusty's." I had heard of it, but I didn't know anyone who had been there before. A short, stocky kid named Martin bragged about how good the place was all the way there. I sort of hung back and listened to the other guys talk about their day. The conversation covered the usual bases. One kid complained about the math teacher's pop quiz that he had failed. I took note because I hadn't had a pop quiz in math yet. I definitely didn't want to be surprised. Another kid rattled on about his new ten-speed bike. He bragged that he could ride up the incline at Mt. Scott, the tallest mountain in our area, at full speed with his bike set in third. We doubted his claim, but no one interrupted him or called him out on it.

It took less than fifteen minutes to reach Rusty's. As we came within sight of it, a tall, skinny kid pointed and began to run to be the first person in line. I watched as some of the other guys took off after him and a lively shoving match ensued. Jimmy didn't join them, so I wasn't left alone to walk the last few blocks by myself. Jimmy's gesture made me feel more comfortable about my new experience. When we finally arrived at the location, I fell in line just ahead of Jimmy and waited to be served. The guys shouted out their orders and then stepped aside to wait for them to be filled. When it was my turn, I stepped forward and checked the overhead menu to see what I might want to order and what I might be able to afford.

I was jolted out of my exercise by a ruddy-faced young man asking me, "What do you think you're doing?"

"Studying the menu so I can order lunch," I replied.

He didn't seem amused. He pulled the screen up higher, so that I could see the whole scowl on his face. I reacted slowly to such an abrupt change in my circumstances. The server became very impatient. "We don't serve your kind out front. If you want to eat, you'll have to go to the back door and wait until I decide to take time to get your order."

I didn't like the tone of his voice nor the command to go to the back door and wait. I must have bristled at his remarks because he seemed ready to punch me through the opening in the window. Before I could speak again, Jimmy stepped ahead of me to find out what was wrong. The ruddy-faced guy told him the same thing he had told me. Jimmy didn't blink at the warning, but he did seem unsure of what to do next. I took his arm and whispered that he could stay, but I was going back to school. He tried to persuade me to change my mind, but I was already on my way. I heard him offer to bring me something back, but I didn't respond to his call. I just kept walking back toward the school.

I was going to be too late to get anything to eat in the cafeteria. I was hungry and my stomach turned over as I thought about what had just occurred. I didn't blame Jimmy for not knowing what was going to happen at the fast food place. I blamed myself. What could I have possibly been thinking when I said yes to the guys' offer to join them? Obviously, I wasn't welcome at Rusty's. Why had I ever considered going? The whole afternoon would be ruined for me. I had to face my peers who would be whispering about my embarrassing incident at

Rusty's. I barely knew half of the guys I had agreed to go with. Now, I probably wouldn't get another chance to become friends with any of them. It served me right. I should have known better. It was 1957 and almost everything in Oklahoma was still operating on a two-tier system. Change would come slowly to the Midwest. I would have to lower my expectations and watch my step until it did.

The embarrassment of being singled out as different was a constant challenge for me during my teenage years. I moved cautiously between the integrated environment on the post, and the slow-changing landscape outside of that safe haven. I rarely let my guard down but sometimes I would forget. On those occasions, I would be harshly reminded by the powers that maintained the color-conscious order at that time. My younger siblings counted on me to show them how to navigate those treacherous waters, and I usually did a very good job of it. It was only when I allowed myself to behave as just another normal human being that I found myself in hot water.

I would never get used to the double standard. To this day, I check myself and don't really trust anyone to treat me fairly until they prove they can. It is a burden many people of color carry with them all the time. It creates instant barriers to honest communication and robs us of the exchange of ideas and good will found in most people. It places us at an extreme disadvantage that we rarely manage to overcome. It is a burden that creates instant hurdles to understanding and acceptance. Now that you know what causes it, maybe you will be able to overcome it and benefit by letting go and moving on.

Chapter 19: Move to Germany

Traveling Across the U.S.A.

Seventh grade went quickly, but I got to spend a full year in Central Junior High School. In the summer of 1958, I didn't know that I would not be returning. My dad had been transferred overseas and was authorized to take his family with him. That family would include a new arrival born in May 1957. Our baby sister, Almaneta Gertrude Lee, was a wonderful surprise. She was named Alma for her grandmother and Gertrude for my dad's sister. Our mother had talked about having more than enough kids to worry about, but I don't expect she meant to exclude Dad's beautiful baby girl. We called her "Dad's baby girl" because, of all the kids in the family, she was the one who looked exactly like him. She had smooth, elegant features and a dark tan that made her his favorite child from the minute she was born.

My mother seemed satisfied to have pleased him. She always reminded him of that on his favorite baby girl's birthdays. The family had expanded to four. My mother couldn't wait to share the good news in person with all of our relatives in Virginia. Dad's transfer to Germany provided just the opportunity she needed.

The transfer process in the military is a mysterious one, especially during times of global conflict. My dad came home one night and told my sister and me to leave the room. We heard him whispering something to our mother as we crunched eagerly against the door struggling to hear. It must have been serious because she responded with a somewhat terse remark.

"How much time do we have before we have to pack up and leave?"

279

My dad's response clearly didn't make her feel better. She gasped and asked him if he was kidding. My dad didn't answer right away. When he did answer, it sounded like he said he was just following orders.

We would have stayed behind the door as we had been told if the next thing that happened hadn't been so scary. We heard a shuffling of furniture. Then, we smelled something burning. That was all the reason we needed to bolt. My sister ran screaming to our mother who caught her by the arm and pulled her close. I stood in the doorway trying to make sense out of what was happening. I saw my dad hovering over a trash can in the kitchen. The can was on fire. He was feeding a folder full of papers into it. The fire grew bigger with each addition. I wanted to ask him what he was doing, but I was too afraid to speak. When he had finished burning his temporary orders, he opened the kitchen door to let out the smoke. My mother, sister, and I left him alone in the kitchen. He didn't seem in the mood to talk.

Later that evening, we got the word. We were going to be moving soon. My dad did the talking. He told us when he began not to ask him any questions. He also told us to keep what he was going to tell us to ourselves.

"This is army private," he said, "and you are expected to keep your mouths shut. Understand?"

We had heard this speech before. It always preceded a move to another location. The whole thing was surreal, especially the part about burning all of his travel orders. I suspected that our dad was in secret intelligence, not army air defense. I am not certain that we ever knew what his real assignments were.

The rush to clear quarters was as hectic as ever. This time was special because Dad hired a few local guys to help us clear quarters.

I really appreciated that since they were responsible for cleaning the kitchen, and the stove. I worked on banging down loose nails, cleaning windows, and scrubbing floors. My sister helped our mother pack, if you can call stuffing lots of things into cases packing. We also gave away clothes, toys, bicycles, and other things that Dad said we couldn't take with us. I had made a bow and arrow set out of a tree limb and select branches. I gave it to a kid on our block. He promised that he would keep it strung tight and that he would remember me whenever he bagged something big.

My sister had to give away her playhouse, her skates, and some of the dolls and things she had collected during our stay. It was all for a good purpose, we told ourselves. We were going to be far away soon. There would be new things to collect. I do remember pleading with my dad to let me keep my guitar. I was so happy when he finally agreed. I also was able to keep my record collection, which I had managed to build one disk at a time. I would be glad that I had kept my collection intact when we arrived at our new destination.

We cleared quarters in July and spent the last night at one of my dad's friend's home before leaving early in the morning for Washington, D.C. Our mother had arranged for us to stay with our cousins in D.C. until we could get clearance to leave for New York City for our flight overseas. I liked our cousins, Yvonne and Arleen. They were a few years older than we were, so we thought they were really cool. The last time we had seen them was a few months before we left for Georgia four years earlier. They were in high school now, and we couldn't wait to find out what it was like.

Our mother had spent the last few days preparing for us to leave. She fried chicken, catfish, and sausages. She also baked a ham that Dad had brought home from the commissary. She made baloney sandwiches, cheese and cracker sandwiches, and, of course, peanut butter and jelly sandwiches. She packed cans of easy to open sardines, tuna, and Vienna sausages, Dad's favorite snacks. She cooked macaroni and cheese because it travels well. We wanted potato salad, but Mother said it wouldn't keep. We tried to get her to change her mind, by suggesting that it could go in the ice chess to keep it cool. Mother told us that the ice chess would have to carry our milk, water, and soft drinks. She said that wouldn't leave any room for potato salad. Mother also packed cinnamon buns that she made from the leftover dough from Dad's Sunday rolls. They smelled so good that we kept pestering her until she finally gave us each a bun.

Our neighbors came to tell us goodbye. They brought hugs, tears, and kisses. Jimmy called and said he would see me at the next outpost. That was his way of letting me know that our paths would most likely cross again before our dads retired from the army. He was right. I would see him many years later while attending a local junior college. My mother said goodbye to Mrs. Trahan and I said goodbye to my best friend, Richard. Richard and I had shared many wonderful adventures together. We would not see them again.

It was unusual for an army wife to ever expect to maintain a long lasting friendship, and the thought of being uprooted again always caused our mother to become melancholy. I watched her sitting in the front seat of the car looking straight ahead as we left. She didn't turn to catch one last glimpse. She reminded me of the story of Lot's wife in the Bible, but, unlike her, mother was obedient to her husband. She expected us to be also. This time, her failure to look back nearly cost our brother, Mercer, who was almost four years old at the time, his ride to Virginia. We had packed the car as tightly as anyone could imagine. When we all climbed inside to leave, no one missed our brother. Dad sat stoically next to our mother in the front seat. He very sternly told us all to keep our hands inside the windows and then he put the car into gear and began to drive away.

My sister and I sat quietly in the back seat neither of us looking at each other for fear that one of us would begin crying. Suddenly, we heard a faint call for help as the car engine began to roar. My sister turned to look out of the back window. She gasped when she realized what we had done. She began screaming our brother's name until our mother turned around to see what was wrong. When she realized what we had done, she yelled for Dad to stop the car. Our brother ran to catch up to us panting as he jumped into the back seat. I didn't care that he crawled over me to get to his place in the middle. We were all just relieved to have him on board. He has never forgotten that incident. It haunts him still.

We left early that evening because my dad loved to drive at night. He would listen to the radio and roll along like a seasoned truck driver. In fact, he knew all the signals to share with truck drivers to make sure they looked out for him. One of his favorite tactics was to flash his lights before passing a truck and wait for the truck driver to flash back at him after he had safely cleared his front bumper. My mother would try to stay up with him and engage him in conversation so that he wouldn't fall asleep. Sometimes, if Mother was too tired, she would ask me to take her place. I enjoyed those times because my dad seemed to like to talk more when he drove than at any other time.

Dad was a fan of the famous jazz singer, Sarah Vaughn. He could talk about her silky, soft voice and his words would seem to float off into another galaxy. My mother liked Nat King Cole and Arthur Prysock, two silky-smooth male vocalists. I didn't prefer either of their choices, but young people always have a different view of what is happening in popular music. Now that I had started playing the guitar, I liked Chuck Berry, Chet Atkins and Elvis Presley. My mother liked some of Elvis' ballads, especially those he sang with the country and western group, the Jordanaires. Dad liked Chuck Berry because he did that "chicken walk" across the stage as a part of his electric performances. My mother and father loved to dance, but my mother hated it when Dad would break off in the middle of a song and do Chuck Berry's "chicken walk."

Our days on the road were pleasant enough. To stay occupied, we would play games like counting cows, horses, or different color cars. The persons nearest the windows had an advantage. Our mother would choose the objects to count, and we would compete to find the most objects within the time limit. We also enjoyed reading the Burma-Shave advertisement signs that we passed along the highway. My mother loved poetry. She got such a thrill from the jingles on those signs. We would help her find them and often read them backwards, as we rolled down the road.

"Our fortune / Is your / Shaven face / It's our best / Advertising space / Burma-Shave"

My mother never tired of reading those signs. She always seemed thrilled when we were approaching them. I believe her desire to write poetry was captured in the simplicity of those Burma-Shave jingles.

Traveling across the country in 1958 wasn't all fun and games for people of color. Although the military services had been desegregated, most public facilities in the Midwest and South were still off limits to Negroes. We couldn't go into a service station to use the bathroom. In fact, we couldn't use the outhouse out back either. That made it difficult to travel any distance across country without suffering a lot of discomfort. Our parents had to plan the trip very carefully and we had to hold our water until we were told it was all right to go.

A young child could go to the bathroom beside the car and most people didn't mind. If, however, you were a girl, or an older boy, you had to wait until dark to relieve yourself like all the adults. Our trip from Lawton, Oklahoma, to Big Island, Virginia, was one of the worst stretches of road a traveler could tackle. No matter how you approached it, we were going to travel 1,200 miles and spend at least three days on the road. Worst still, almost all of that distance we would be traveling through the states of Arkansas and Tennessee. Then, we had the challenge of traversing the rugged Blue Ridge Mountains, which we had to cross to reach our final destination.

I recall our stop on the top of a large mountain near Nashville, Tennessee. It was dark, and we had been holding our water all day. Finally, our dad stopped the car at a bend in the highway and exited in a hurry to relieve himself. It was all we could do to remain inside the car while Dad went. Bernadine complained to our mother, who pleaded with our dad to find a parking spot where we could all go. Dad told her that he didn't know where that would be, but we were welcome to go now if we wanted to. My mother and sister exited the car and squatted beside it to relieve themselves. I followed them and found myself looking down at the bottom of a huge gorge. We were less than three feet from going over the edge. There were no metal or wire barriers to break our fall. I never forgot that episode, and it took me a long time to become comfortable with traveling in the mountains on our country's highways. Even today, I am more likely to select a route that avoids the mountains and includes a stop at a friend's house rather than relying on public accommodations.

The next day was just as challenging as the night before. We had eaten most of our sandwiches that mother had packed for us and were still more than a day away from any of our relatives or friends. Dad told us not to worry; he would go into town to see if he could find us something to eat. I volunteered to go with him, but he told me to stay with the car and look out for everyone. I felt good because he trusted me to do what he asked. I didn't fully realize the danger he was taking upon himself as a stranger walking into an unfamiliar town.

Dad must have left around seven in the morning. He had parked the car near an off ramp of the main highway. By eight in the morning, the roadway began to fill up with cars on their way to other parts of the country or just carrying people to work. When nine a.m. came, I began to worry about our dad. A few cars pulled off to check the air in their tires or take a rest break, but no one asked us if we needed help. I was glad they left us alone.

As the morning wore on and the sun rose higher into the sky, we all began to worry about our dad. I could see our mother was becoming concerned although she tried not to show it. She was still breastfeeding our younger sister, Almaneta, but the rest of us were hungry, too. I finally spoke up and asked if I could go down the highway into town to find Dad. My mother hesitated at first, but then she fell back on her faith. She told us that she knew God would watch over him, and he would return safely. I wasn't worried about God; I was worried about the people in town who might not want a strange Negro walking around asking where he could get some food for his children. My fears were not unfounded. We had heard of stories about Negroes who had gone into towns and were never heard from again. Those stories may have been fables or an exaggeration of the truth. There was no way to tell. We didn't have the Internet to search for answers to those questions then.

As my stomach began to churn and my sister Bernadine began to cry, I opened the car door and walked over to the edge of the railing along the highway. That was when I saw the figure of a man walking up the hill.

He was slightly bent over, but his walk was brisk and determined. He seemed to be off in another world not paying any attention to the cars as they whizzed by him. He looked slightly haggard as if he had been in a rain storm. I stretched my neck to see if I could make out any other characteristics about him, but the trees obscured my vision for the moment. I desperately wanted it to be our father, but I also worried that it could be a loner who might want to cause us trouble. I wished I had my BB gun in the trunk of the car and wondered if I could have gotten it out if I needed it. I stopped wondering right in the middle of that thought.

The figure appeared again through the tree branches and I could actually see his face. I had never seen a more welcome sight than the smile I knew he must have been wearing as he trudged back to the place where he had left his family nearly four hours before. He didn't seem at all to be tired, nor did he seem to be slowing down as he climbed the long way up the winding roadway to reach us. I held my breath as I watched a large truck nearly brush him off the road with the blast of wind from its passing. Still, my dad kept walking. When he finally looked up and saw me at the top of the hill, he looked as determined and proud as I had ever seen him before.

I couldn't wait for him to reach us before I started waving my arms in the air. The others realized that something was happening and began to look out of the windows trying to see for themselves. My sister jumped up and started to exit the car, but my mother told her to sit down and wait. Mother then called to me for an update of what I had seen. I stammered as I told her that Daddy was coming. I know she heard me, but she seemed to go into a trance after my exclamation. I am certain she was thanking God and asking Him to forgive her for any doubt she may have had. As my dad approached, we all felt a great relief as if a huge burden had been lifted from our shoulders.

It had been a long time since we had been forced to wait on the highway until our father found a place for us to sleep, go to the bathroom, or get something to eat. It was a normal dilemma for Negroes in the 1950's, especially for Negroes in the military who were transferred often.

When our dad finally reached the car, he was smiling broadly but looked worn out. I could see the tears in my mother's eyes and I understood how difficult the last few hours had been for her. She had four children to care for. Had she been left without a good man, she would have been hard pressed to succeed at it. There are times when a family comes together and feels united and in one accord. The triumphant return our dad was one of those times. We cheered as he approached the car. My mother opened her door, cuddled the baby in her arms, and ran to meet him. He kissed her and then they slowly walked together to rejoin the rest of us in the car. Bernadine took the baby while our mother surveyed the food. My dad had bought enough hamburgers and french-fried potatoes for us to eat until the next day. He had also gotten some milk for our mother, along with bread and cheese to make sandwiches for all of us. The few soda pops he managed to bring back were warm now, but that didn't matter. We would have drunk them hot just to show him how much we appreciated the risk he had taken to find food for us.

This would not be the last time we would sit stranded on a highway waiting for our dad to find food or other accommodations for the family. In time, the national highway system would include rest stops with bathrooms, fast food establishments, and other services. Those new accommodations would ease the burden of families traveling around the country. They would be welcomed by everyone, but still would not be available to people of color in many places. It would take years of boycotts, protests, marches and finally victories in court, before desegregation of interstate public facilities was accomplished all across this land.

Welcome to the Big Island

The balance of our journey across the country was without incident. We sang songs, counted cows, recited Bible verses, and played rhyming games all the way across Tennessee and into Virginia. This wasn't the first time we had been to our mother's homestead, but it had been quite a while since anyone in Big Island, Virginia, had seen us. Our mother had called her favorite aunt, Gladys Ware. She lived at the top of a winding mountain road somewhere between Bedford and Lynchburg. We loved to visit her because she always gave us such a warm welcome. Her husband, Burnett Ware, was one of my favorite people. He was a tall man who spoke softly and respectfully around my mother and his wife. He dressed like the farmer he was, in long suspenders and overalls. He smoked a pipe, swung a mean ax, and told great stories. We would sit on the back porch and listen to him tell us about his life in the Virginia hills when he was a youth.

I learned a lot about farming from Uncle Burnett. He taught me how to brace myself to pull up the water bucket from the bottom of the well. He taught me how to pacify agitated hens so that I could collect the eggs for our breakfast. He taught me how to milk a cow and how to cool down a horse. He showed me how to stack the hay and how to use the tractor to plow furrows for planting corn. Uncle Burnett was an independent farmer who was proud of his working-class heritage, his humble lifestyle, his Christian faith, and his devoted wife. He was a deacon in the local church, which we visited from time to time when we were there. I don't believe he could carry a tune, but I know he was a capable speaker who never turned down an opportunity to quote a Bible verse or say the evening prayer.

Aunt Gladys was well-known in the neighborhood. She always had a good word to say about everyone and that endeared her to all. She was a wonderful cook. Her pies were famous for disappearing right before your eyes. I loved to eat her biscuits with thick bacon slices or gravy. She taught my mother how to make them like hers so that they were flaky and crisp. I heard her toiling over the hot stove preparing breakfast for us long before most of the house was up. It was my job to bring in enough wood for her wood-burning stove. I would gather it and stack it up in a bin outside of the back door to the kitchen. Aunt Gladys would bring in the wood and start the fire very early in the morning. Then she would place a large kettle on top of the stove filled with water for anyone who wanted to freshen up in the morning. Without her dedication to that task, we would all have bathed in cold water when we rose.

At night, Aunt Gladys would tamp down the fire, so that it would last long enough for all of us to get in bed and be fast asleep before it died. Bernadine and I usually slept upstairs in the room above the vent that caught the heat from the kitchen as it rose. I always wondered how we rated that luxury. I know my mother and father always made sure they had ample blankets and quilts, so that they would be warm during those cold nights on top of the mountain. There was always one place where warm blankets weren't enough to help you. That was in the outhouse, the four-by-four foot bathroom outside.

If you have never sat in an outhouse, then you have missed a real country experience. The toilet seat was made of wood and the doors and windows, if any, were never tight enough to keep out the wind and the cold. I recall lying in bed in agony, trying to wait until the daylight so I could finally go to the bathroom. No one ever wanted to go to the outhouse late at night. Sometimes I couldn't avoid the trip. I recall walking through the snow to use the outhouse with a cold, swirling wind howling around my ankles. It was so cold and dark that I don't recall ever sitting down, but I was relieved to go.

As we rounded the bend in the road where we always made the turn to head up the hill, my dad blinked his lights and honked his horn to let the neighbor at the bottom of the hill know we had arrived. The neighbor blinked his lights off and on to acknowledge our signal. As we wound our way up the hill, the signaling was repeated and my mother began to wake us up to let us know we would soon be at Aunt Gladys'. Flashing lights were not the only signal passed along the road to announce our arrival. The neighbors, who all shared a telephone line, would also signal each other on the line to announce our arrival. The signaling system had been in place as long as the mountain had residents. In a small country town, everyone knows when strangers or relatives come to visit. I expect they signaled each other when wagons were pulled by horses up the mountain as well.

Aunt Gladys' Farm House

291

We had traveled over twelve hundred miles to reach Aunt Gladys and Uncle Burnett's home. They were as glad to see us as we were to see them. Aunt Gladys gave each of us a big hug and then held the new baby. Tears ran down her face as Aunt Gladys admired Almaneta. Uncle Burnett helped Dad and me bring the bags in. He offered my dad a beer and then they went into the living room to talk. We boys chose to stay in the kitchen with our sisters and my mother. It would be warm in there and, very soon, Aunt Gladys would be serving ham sandwiches and warm cherry cobbler. I watched Bernadine holding the baby while my mother helped Aunt Gladys fix us something to eat. We had received a warm and gracious welcome after a very long journey across the country. That night, we didn't have to sleep huddled up in the back seat of the car; nor did we have to go to the bathroom on the side of the road. Tomorrow would bring a new set of experiences, but that night was already perfect.

The next morning I rose early and scrambled to the outside bathroom to relieve myself. It was hard not going the night before, but I really hated going to the outhouse in the dark. Aunt Gladys was already up when I returned. She asked me to bring in some firewood so she could begin preparing breakfast for all of us. It was a short trip to the woodpile. I came back with an armful of choice pieces for her to burn. She thanked me, as always, and told me she would call when breakfast was ready. I decided that I would sling some rocks, so I rumbled through Dad's car trunk looking for my slingshot. To my surprise, I found my BB gun instead, which Dad had placed in the trunk without saying anything to us. I tucked it under my arm and disappeared around the back corner of the house. When I had gotten a safe distance off, I relaxed and breathed in the wonderfully cool morning air.

Nothing comes close to breathing fresh air on a farm early in the morning. I walked lazily through the apple trees and along the

292

back fence looking for signs of early morning activity. I had retrieved my BB gun from the trunk of the car and couldn't wait to try it out. I found an old tin can and sat it atop a fence post on the back fence. It made a challenging target for me to practice on. I walked a hundred feet back to my starting point and took aim at the target. It took me just a few tries before I hit the can. As I walked towards the fence to set it up again, I noticed a rustling in the bushes near the fence post. I froze in place and waited to see what would emerge. I didn't have to wait very long. A small sparrow hopped out of the bushes, turned and eyed me curiously. I took aim and fired a shot in its direction. I missed. The sparrow took to the air and flew quickly out of sight.

I picked up the tin can and placed it back on the fence post. I repeated this a half dozen times and then took a break to sit on the back porch. Uncle Burnett had installed a swing on the porch, and I took advantage of it to break up the lull in my morning. I began slowly and watched the swing rise until the distant clouds disappeared from view. The wind whistled gently through the walnut, oak, and apple trees. I noted the fullness of the walnut trees and decided to pick some walnuts off of the ground to eat later on. As I swung back and forth, I daydreamed about the future and tried to imagine what it was going to be like in Germany on the new post. I wondered if the boys enjoyed playing marbles like we did. I wondered if the girls jumped rope or played hopscotch. I had read that the kids in China flew kites with long trailing tails; I wondered what kind of kites the kids in Germany flew? It was all so new to me, and I was eager to get started on my journey of discovery.

My daydream was interrupted by a loud squawking in the hedges at the edge of the yard. I listened carefully to see if I could identify the source. The squawking continued, and my curiosity grew. I slipped quietly out of the swing, grabbed my BB gun, and headed in the direction of the noise. I didn't have to wait very long to get a glimpse of the culprit. A large blue jay emerged from the bushes still contesting some unknown intruder that had interrupted his early morning nap. At first, I just stared at him. I had never seen a blue jay as magnificent or as angry as this one. It must have taken quite a sizable villain to rustle him out of his hideout. I was wrong. A tiny sparrow, which was protecting its nest of newly laid eggs, came charging out of the bushes with a furry reserved for battle like a big bald eagle. The sparrow didn't stop chasing the blue jay until it had completely surrendered and flown to a perch high up in one of the oak trees. I watched with admiration as the sparrow puffed up its chest and then fluttered back towards the nest to check on her brood.

The blue jay looked confused. It twisted its head towards the porch and then let out a defiant squawk to have the last word. I watched from a distance and a dark and sinister mood came over me. Without even thinking, I looked beyond the beauty of the defeated predator and saw an opportunity to fell a prey. Once the thought entered my mind, it lodged there firmly in the crevices and began eating away at my consciousness. I didn't fully understood the consequences of what I was about to do, and I would never be able to reconcile my actions.

In the brief moments it took me to take aim and prepare to fire off a shot, my whole world changed. I saw the blue jay as it registered the danger stalking it more than thirty yards away. I watched as it rose from its perch caught in slow motion and took to the air in flight. I calculated how fast and how far it would fly before I squeezed the trigger. I held my breath as the rush of air from the muzzle propelled the missile forward on its lethal path. I watched the bird ascend and then plummet as the impact of the missile found its mark. Its magnificent blue and white wings, which had stretched as far as they could, burst into patches of flying feathers. I looked on in horror as this magnificent creature, which God had given the gift of flight, spiraled downward out of control. I knew in an instant that I had done a horrible thing. I felt the impact as surely as if I had received the blow. I knew, beyond a doubt, that I had taken a life that I would never be able to replace. Frozen in that moment was the imagery of a miracle interrupted in flight by my thoughtless decision. There was no redeeming explanation for my action. There was no joy in the aftermath of my callousness. I would never be able to justify it. I turned and ran.

I remembered that Uncle Burnett had left a shovel leaning against the barn door. I used it to dig a small grave for the blue jay. As I bent down to retrieve the bird, the magnitude of what I had done overwhelmed me. There was no stopping the stream of tears that welled up in my eyes. I finally succumbed to the awful sadness that haunts a soul when it watches beauty blotted out by ugliness. As I replaced the dirt and watched the bird's body slowly disappear, I swore to myself that I would never take another innocent life as long as I lived. My aversion to killing an innocent creature has stayed with me and reinforced my decision to live my life free of firearms. If the good Lord wants me to take a life, then He will have to provide the means. That experience helped me to realize you can't replace a life that God has created no matter how much you cry.

Our Stop In Lynchburg

The time we stayed in Big Island passed quickly. Our mother lamented how short it was as she spent the last few days talking with her aunt. They talked about her aunt's church family, her husband's extended family of Wares, and the Mitchells. I always learned something new about our family from listening to them talk about the good old days. I listened to them talk about Aunt Mamie, Gladys' sister, who had three girls named Alberta, Dorothy, and Ruby and one boy named Jasper. Our mother tried to remain close to them by writing and sending post cards as she traveled around the country with our dad. Sending post cards may seem antiquated to us now, but "snail mail" was a staple of GI's and their families wherever they were stationed. In fact, mail call, even on the battlefield, was one of the most treasured periods of the day.

When our time with Aunt Gladys and Uncle Burnett was over, we said our goodbyes and continued on our journey. Aunt Gladys had filled a basket with food and drinks for our trip to Washington, D.C. She gave us chicken and ham sandwiches, apples, peaches, and plums. She had also packed slices of pound cake and her favorite fruitcake, a staple all year round. Not wanting to be outdone, Uncle Burnett had given us a small cooler that held ice and mason jars filled with chilled sassafras tea. We all felt the love we had received from Aunt Gladys and Uncle Burnett and appreciated everything they did for us to make our trip more enjoyable.

The neighbors waved and our dad tooted his horn as we wound our way back down the mountain. My sister and I watched the scenery drift by as we worked our way down the mountain on our way to Lynchburg and then Richmond, Virginia. The Virginia Mountains are known for steep inclines and treacherous hairpin curves. We might have been frightened if we had not already driven through parts of the Blue Ridge Mountain range on our way to Big Island. This portion of the trip didn't seem nearly as hazardous as those earlier challenges. Dad seemed to be comfortable navigating the curves, so we didn't worry.

There was one place we always looked forward to stopping on our way to Richmond, and it would remain a favorite stop for years. It was a small duel pump gas station with a five and dime convenience store that was situated right in the middle of one of the biggest curves in the road. It was the only structure there and impossible to miss as travelers navigated the mountains. The proprietor was a stogy white gentleman, who wore overalls and chewed tobacco. Those traits, however, were not the ones that endeared him to the weary travelers who stopped at his store. He had a personality that overflowed with friendliness and enthusiasm, which he showered on all of the patrons that crossed his doorway. In an era where people of color were most often shunned or pushed to the back, he met them up front with a warm smile, a firm handshake and a lively, inquiring conversation. My dad enjoyed going into his store and seemed to warm up to the area with each trip we took that included a stop in the curve.

There was another attraction that made us kids want to stop at the little store. We always looked forward to stopping at the store, so we could get a chance to see its main attraction, an African lion that lived in a steel caged enclosure on the far side of the building. Over the years, the lion grew and aged, but the wonder he created in the eyes of all the children who begged their parents to let them stop to look at him never dimmed. His magnificent mane, his powerful roar, and mouth full of

Winding Mountain Road

sharp teeth were classic features that lingered with me long after we moved on.

My sister always wanted me to stand in front of her when we went to look at the lion. She would peer around me to get a look, but she never once stood beside or in front of me. I often wondered if the lion understood where he was and why we were staring at him. As the years passed and the aura of this magnificent, caged creature faded, I wondered if all his life had been as miserable as he, in his later years, seemed to appear. The magic of seeing him caged gradually faded for me, and I wished he had experienced a better fate than the one he inherited.

In later years, we rarely stopped when we got to curve in the road with the little store. It seemed that we were always in a hurry to get up the mountain before dark, and the beaten and battered storefront ceased to entice us to stop. The magnificent lion had aged and had been put down. The empty cage, which stood as a monument to his life, was the only reminder that he had ever been there. In time, the wonder of one's youth fades and the attraction that seemed so powerful before takes on a new reality. The lion lived his life caged while I was free. That fact never left my mind and steeled me against the torrents of self-doubt and self-pity that washed over others as we all struggled to realize our God-given potential as free men.

The trip from Big Island, Virginia, to Washington, D.C. included a stop at our mother's favorite beautician's home in Lynchburg, Virginia. Eunice, who had been Mom's favorite beautician for as long as I can recall, was always glad to see her. She lived in a modest home in Lynchburg where she practiced her craft in a small room adjacent to the kitchen. Her husband, Earl, was a considerate man, who always took the time to talk with our dad while our mom was getting her hair done. I admired the way he seemed to enjoy those conversations. They would reminisce about his time in the active services, and Dad would share his most recent experiences with him.

It was evident that Eunice and her husband were devout Christians from all of the religious paintings and renderings of scripture posted around their home. They had the most beautiful painting of *The Last Supper* hanging in their living room. I always took the time to browse through the room and scan the faces of the disciples when we visited. Eunice had a set of beautiful antique lamps with twisted gold and white tassels hanging from the lampshades. Eunice's house was as comfortable a place to be as any of the relatives we visited on our travels throughout the country. Unlike many of the homes of older relatives we visited, Eunice had furniture that you could actually sit on. She didn't cover her chairs and sofas with plastic to keep them looking as new as the day they arrived. She offered our family a chance to relax in comfort without feeling that we were imposing on her or her beautiful decor.

A visit with Eunice was always the highlight of our mother's trip back to Virginia. My mother developed a friendship with Eunice from the time she stayed in Lynchburg with her older brother, Isaiah, and his family. Eunice had the exuberance that all great cosmetologists possess. She was an excellent conversationalist. In other words, she was a wonderful listener. My mother would inquire about all of the people they knew from high school, and Eunice would fill in the blanks during the years they had spent apart. It was a time for our mother to reclaim a connection to her past, and she cherished those hours the two of them spent together.

Earl was a sports enthusiast who kept up with all the Negro athletes on the major sports teams. He loved boxing, too, which was one of the sports my dad followed by attending boxing matches given on the post. Of course, most Negroes admired the successful boxer, Joe Louis. He captured the imagination of every young boy who ever wanted to see his name in lights. Earl admired Joe Louis for his mild-mannered and polite way of talking to his fans. Earl possessed many of the same qualities. He was a considerate and soft-spoken gentleman. He listened intently when someone else was talking. It was his way of showing respect. He was a good storyteller and always managed to embed a positive lesson in the stories he told.

The time at Eunice's house seemed to pass so quickly. My sister and I would sit in a corner and play war, a matching card game, while listening to Earl and our dad reminisce about their time in the service, new developments in national politics, or sports. Sometimes Earl would turn on the radio and we would listen to a sporting event being broadcast over the airways. This particular night was no different. Our mother was busy getting her hair washed and pressed while we found games to play quietly to entertain ourselves. Dad and Earl were in the living room exchanging views over the fifth round knock-out victory of Floyd Patterson over Archie Moore that past November. It was a lively discussion for the two of them, and Dad seemed to be enjoying the round by round details that Earl had amassed. The night could have ended just fine with everyone having enjoyed sharing the company, but an unexpected event changed all of that.

Earl had a son who had just turned eighteen. They always seemed to respect each other. On occasion, in the past, I had watched them shadow box in the kitchen. It was obvious to anyone who knew Earl that he really loved his son. In fact, on more than one occasion, he expressed those feelings to our dad when he asked him about plans for his son's future. He said that he would give his own life before he would ever let anything happen to him. My dad knew Earl to be an honest man, and never had any reason to doubt what he said. Earl was about to be tested.

Earl's son, Earl Jr., had been out joy riding with his friends from high school. It was a weekend night, and no one would have thought anything about a few guys getting together for a little fun. It was getting late, however, and I recall that Earl mentioned some concern over the group of guys his son had been spending time with lately. I didn't think anything about his comment because I knew that all parents worried about their children and their friends, especially when they were out of their sight. This particular evening seemed to be different. As the minutes ticked by, Earl began rising from his brown leather chair and started looking out of the window. My dad tried to calm Earl's nerves by telling him that he believed that Earl Jr. was a responsible young man and that he would know when to shy away from any trouble. Earl wanted to believe him, but he still looked worried about his boy.

It was around 11:15 p.m. when Earl Jr. finally came home. His dad met him at the back door that opened into the kitchen area. As usual, his dad reached to give him a hug, which Earl Jr. seemed reluctant to accept.

"Where you been?" Earl asked. The people in the room next to the kitchen fell silent upon hearing the raised inflection in his voice.

"No where special," was Earl Jr.'s reply.

That didn't set well with his dad, who pressed him for a better answer. The conversation seemed to grow one-sided with Earl asking the questions and a prolonged silence coming from his son. I could just see into a corner of the room, through the crack between the door-jamb and the kitchen door. Earl Jr. appeared to be somewhat distracted. He didn't want to confront his dad, but he wasn't going to be able to do what he wanted to do without being questioned. At that moment, a car horn blew. Someone outside had waited for Earl Jr., and they were apparently getting restless about his delay in returning.

I saw a frightened look in Earl Jr.'s eyes. They narrowed as he stared out into space, as if afraid to focus in on the obstacle standing between him and his friends waiting on the other side of the door. His father spoke in a low, measured tone, no longer willing to hold back his apprehension about his son's plans for the rest of the night.

"Little Earl," he said, "I don't want you going out drinking tonight with your friends. I can't trust them to know what's right and what's wrong when they get they heads bad. I'm sorry, son, but you in for the night."

It was all Earl Jr. could do to keep from punching his dad square in the face. The anger in him welled up so fast; he didn't know what to do with it. In a desperate effort to free himself from the sentence that had just been declared, he flung his body head-on into his dad's chest and drove him backwards towards the door. As the two bodies crashed into the door, Earl realized what was happening and his instinct from surviving in his early years on those mean streets kicked in. He dropped down low and braced himself against the door frame. Earl Jr. did all he could to gain more leverage, in his effort to pry his dad away from the door. Earl wasn't giving an inch. He braced his shoulder against his son's chest and began to drive him step-by-step back across the room.

Earl Jr. knew exactly what he had to do. He dropped his head and dived toward his dad's feet. He braced his shoulder against his dad's lower legs, wrapped his strong arms around them, and pivoted hard to his left. The maneuver caught his dad off guard and Earl went down flat on his back. He looked up from the floor as his son looked down and glared at him, then turned and headed for the door. Earl Jr. got as far as turning the doorknob before his dad grabbed his ankle. It appeared to be a gesture of desperation. Earl Jr. twisted and wrenched his leg to try to free himself from his dad's grip, but his dad held on. Finally, in a last ditch effort to free himself, Earl Jr. kicked at his dad with his free leg. That was exactly what his dad had been waiting for him to do. He yanked the other leg and Earl Jr. went tumbling to the floor. His dad wrapped his arms around his son's waist and held on for dear life.

Earl Jr. wrenched his body one way and then the next. He tried to raise himself up on his two feet, but his dad just swung him around and back down he went. It was a horrific wrestling match with both gladiators going at each other with all they had. Earl Jr. kicked and squirmed, but his dad held on tight. It didn't matter that he had won a junior wrestling championship. His dad had won one, too. It didn't matter that he was pound for pound as muscled and fit as his dad; Earl had a big heart that was fixated on saving his son's life from the mean streets that had almost taken his. He knew the dangers that awaited young men who drank into the wee hours of the morning. He knew the fights that broke out over little or nothing and often ended with a cold body lying in the morgue. He had a scar on his shoulder where an angry man had slashed at him in a drunken rage. He was determined not to let that happen to his boy, not that night, and not ever if he could help it.

The colossal contest went on for more than half an hour with the two gladiators wrestling feverishly, banging against the door frame, and sliding back and forth across the white and blue linoleum covered kitchen floor. Finally, the banging stopped and only an occasional grunt could be heard coming from the kitchen. I lost sight of both of them as they slid into a corner of the room, but I could still tell they were locked in a duel. Neither had the desire to give in. I wondered why Earl Jr.'s mother hadn't come to his rescue. Perhaps, she had seen something like this before and learned it was best to stay her distance. I also wondered why my dad hadn't done something to stop them. Instead, he sat in the corner of the living room, with his head pressed against the radio in an effort to drown out the cursing and grunting in the other room. Maybe he had seen a dilemma unfold like the one unfolding now with Earl Jr. and he knew it was best to stay out of it and let the combatants resolve it themselves. I had time to ponder all of those questions, while Earl and his son lay tied in a tight knot on the kitchen floor.

Long after the honking had stopped outside and long after the kicking had died down inside, the two combatants lay spent on the kitchen floor. The calm was eerie, but welcomed. I listened for any sign of movement in the room, but heard only the faint sound of heavy breathing, coming from the corner outside of my view. I didn't know what to expect or what would happen next.

Earl Jr.'s cry was primeval. It came from deep inside the depths of his soul. It rose unashamedly, unabated, and without any pretentiousness to cover its origins. It caught a draft of the hot and humid night air and then permeated every room soaking us all in a wave of pity. It was a cry for forgiveness. It was a plea for redemption. It was the bleeding from untold hurt and pain, a soul drenched in sorrow and shackled in shame. Yet, there in a corner of the kitchen floor, lay another soul grasping for air, worn and battered but not broken. His cry, though louder, fell silent. It rose from the depths of his heart. It sobbed woefully, tearfully, and with every fiber of its being surrendered totally. Then it sank, unable to rise or climb anymore as if crushed by the hot and humid night air that washed heavily over every fiber of his being. Earl's father was crying for thankfulness. He was praying for salvation. He had flung himself against the Gates of Hell and had been spared the death of all deaths one more time.

Often the true measure of a man's love is that fight in him which refuses to give up on a lost soul. It reaches out for you and refuses to let go. It has no limits, knows no measure, it counts no cost too heavy to bear. It risks all to save a life, to rescue a soul, to stand against all odds facing disaster, for that one instant in time. I count myself lucky that I knew such a man and thank God for the lesson that he taught me. I have seen it demonstrated more than once in my lifetime.

Journey to Washington, D.C., New York and Return

Our journey onward to Washington, D.C. was without incident. Our dad, who had driven a taxi cab as a second job when we lived in Maryland, had no trouble finding his way across town to our cousins' house off of Rhode Island Avenue. We had not seen our cousins, Arleen and Yvonne Nash, since we relocated to Georgia in 1955. They were a few years older and a lot more street savvy than a couple of country bumpkins like Bernadine and me. We sort of looked up to them and really missed seeing them in the years that had passed.

Aunt Hilda was my mother's first cousin. Her mother, Lula, and our grandmother, Alma Mitchell, were sisters. Alma stayed in Virginia, while her sister moved further north, and established herself in the Washington, D.C. area. Her daughter, Hilda, and her son, whom we all called Brother, were born and raised there. Brother was at least six feet and five inches tall. He played basketball in high school and college. We were all very proud of his accomplishments as an athlete.

Aunt Hilda married an outstanding gentleman named Frank Nash. He held a well-paying job as a bartender at a prestigious country club. We all liked Uncle Frank a lot because he had such a gentle spirit and always offered sincere words of encouragement whenever we got a chance to talk with him. Our dad liked him, too, because he could relate to the trials and tribulations that a traveling service man had to go through to feed his family. They could spend hours talking about the military services and the challenges of serving as a Negro recruit in the

Marine Corps. I believe Uncle Frank also drove a taxicab during his working life, and that gave them another shared life experience.

Aunt Hilda and Uncle Frank welcomed us with open arms. They prepared a place for us to sleep in the basement, which doubled as a recreation and guest entertainment area. My mother and her cousin, Hilda, spent half the night when we first arrived catching up and recalling incidents of the past. My mother learned about all the members of her extended family, whom she hardly ever had a chance to see. Aunt Hilda learned about the ups and downs in the past four years of Mom's brothers and their families. She also learned about the many trials and challenges her cousin faced as a young army wife.

Bernadine and I spent the week following behind our cousins and soaking up as much street savvy as we could. We picked up tips on shoes, hairstyles, clothes, and dance steps for current hits on the radio. It was a wonderful time, and we enjoyed every minute of it. Both Arleen and Yvonne seemed to take pride in educating us about the latest and greatest and newest things that we should know. I never got tired of hearing the girls laugh as they told us about the crazy pick-up lines they got from the over-eager boys at school. I was surprised to find out that my sister, Bernadine, also knew a little bit about the games that the boys were trying to play. I gained a new level of respect for her knowing that she was able to hold her own with her older cousins. I also realized that I needed some street savvy experiences myself if I was going to keep up with my peers.

That week at our cousin's house was magical. We bonded with our cousins and found the love and support we had been missing while we were far away with our dad. We hugged and kissed and shed a few tears before we finally left for New York City. The ride from Washington, D.C. to New York was a brand new experience for all of us. We traveled along the newly constructed Baltimore–Washington Parkway, which opened in October of 1954. The parkway was adorned with a magical, tree-covered canopy that sheltered travelers as they made their way between the two cities.

As we drove towards Baltimore on the parkway, the morning sun beamed its golden rays through the oaks, elms, and spruces shading our way. I am sure the glint in our dad's eyes, at times, was blinding, but he didn't seem to mind. We rolled down the windows and breathed in the sweet smell of clean, crisp morning air. Somewhere, from off in the distance, we caught a whiff of honeysuckle in the air. It was as real and inviting as the aroma from the honeysuckle bush that used to grow on the side of our home in Maryland. It made Bernadine and me homesick. For which home I am not sure.

After we traveled a few miles along the parkway, we were in for a treat. We joined a long line of cars waiting to travel through the newly constructed Baltimore Harbor Tunnel, which opened in November of 1957. It was the first time we had ever traveled through a tunnel under the water. It was nearly 1.5 miles long and totally submerged under water. When it opened, the toll road fare was a mere forty cents for the one-way ride. I don't recall wondering whether we could listen to a radio while traversing the tunnel. Today, that is one of the first things people want to know about an underground tunnel. No one wants to lose a call today while traveling. The clickety-clack of the cars crossing the sections of the tunnel reminded me of the train sounds on the tracks at our home back in Big Island, Virginia. We held our breath while we were inside the tunnel, and said a prayer of thanks when we exited on the other side.

We arrived in New York City around noon and went directly to the docks to catch a ferry to Governor's Island. The island was the home to the First Army Administrative Center where our dad was required to report before being cleared for debarkation. The ferry ride was just one more new, amazing adventure that we experienced on our way to Germany. We waited for our dad to return from his appointment in the center. While he stood in line to get his papers cleared, we walked around the grounds and sat on the benches to wait for him.

When he exited the building two hours later, he seemed troubled. He had been told that we would have to wait another week before we would be allowed to board our plane for our flight to Germany. I heard our mother and him talking softly about the new time line and could see the urgency on our mother's face as she listened to Dad explain the delay. We boarded the ferry and traveled back to New York City. Mom and Dad had decided to visit some of our relatives in New York City before returning to the Washington, D. C. area to try to find a place to stay for another week.

Bernadine and I had never met any of our parent's relatives living in New York City. Our mother had a small address book that she had compiled from the addresses on the Christmas cards she received each year. She used it to help Dad find the address of her Uncle James, who worked as a doorman and usher at one of the Broadway theaters in the city. Uncle James lived in a three-story walk-up with a lot of other working class New Yorkers. He was excited to see us. We were as equally excited to know that someone knew who we were in the big city.

Uncle James had pictures of actors and actresses mounted in elegant frames on his walls. He also had a beautiful wooden table covered with a white lace tablecloth adorned with glossy playbills arranged in a semicircular pattern by years. You could tell he was very proud of his current position and length of service as a doorman for a Broadway theatre. His neighbors appeared to be as enamored with him as he was with the theatre. They came one by one to say hello and to pay their respects to his niece and her family from out-of-state. Their loyalty to Uncle James was not misplaced. He introduced each and every one of them by name, told a funny story about his personal relationship with them, and thanked them for dropping by. You could tell they all held him in high regard. I was so proud to be in his family.

Uncle James and Niece Gladys

We spent most of the afternoon with Uncle James and then said goodbye, so we could visit another of our mother's relatives in the Bronx. It was a long, hot ride to the Bronx from Uncle James' Manhattan apartment. Bernadine and I kept asking if we were lost. Dad laughed and just kept driving. When we reached the Bronx, he stopped a taxicab and asked directions to an address Mom had given him. The driver directed us to a row of high-rise apartments a few blocks away.

When we finally reached our destination, our mother jumped out of the car and hurried to the nearest building. She stopped short of the doorway and asked a young man standing on the stoop for directions. He pointed her towards an apartment unit three buildings down. The search for my mother's relatives continued along this ask and point pathway until we finally found the building we were looking for. We were all eager to get out of the car after the long ride, but mother told us to stay and wait until she returned. It was nearly fifteen minutes later when she reappeared and beckoned us to follow her. We eagerly jammed into the small elevator that took us to the ninth floor.

As we exited, you could hear the faint cry of a small child who was probably sleepy for an afternoon nap. We stood in front of a large, white door with a small peephole in the center just above our heads. Our mother rang the doorbell and then stood back from the peephole so she could be seen by whoever came to the door. There was a long silence and then came the faint sound of someone shuffling towards the door. Our mother waited in anticipation. The door opened slowly and then hung on the inside chain lock.

A short, elderly lady poked her head into the crack of the door and then screamed, "Oh, my God! Is that you, Francis?"

The door swung open wide and Ms. Alberta Burks, Mom's cousin, stood there with her arms opened wide. Our mother rushed to hug her and then we all followed her inside. She introduced us to her friend, Raymond Allen, and asked us to find some place to sit. We met her, each in turn, and told her a little bit about ourselves. She seemed to be interested and appeared to be very nice. After the introductions, Alberta and mother launched into an energetic, intense catch-up on the past conversation about all of the relatives in Richmond, Lynchburg, Big Island, Washington, D.C., and other far reaches of the USA. While they talked, Dad and Raymond disappeared into the kitchen. We kids did as kids always do; we found something to entertain ourselves.

A few hours later, we said our goodbyes and departed with Alberta and Raymond waving as we left. It was a much quicker ride back downtown. As nighttime came, we all piled into a corner with a pillow, and blanket and slept peacefully at Uncle James' apartment. We left early the next morning for Washington, D.C. The ride through the newly lighted Holland Tunnel was no longer a novelty, but still was a lot of fun. The Baltimore–Washington Parkway had slowed to a crawl, but we didn't mind since we were going to see our cousins again.

We enjoyed our extra week in Washington, D.C., and our cousins made us feel welcome up until the day we left.

The Night Flight to Germany

The day we left for New York City was cloudy with rain expected later in the afternoon. Aunt Hilda had packed ham sandwiches for all of us. That lunch was going to be delicious. We finished breakfast early so we could see Uncle Frank off to work. He seemed pleased to know we thought about him even as we were preparing to leave the country. He smiled broadly and gave each of us a big hug. Our dad shook his hand as Uncle Frank squeezed Dad's shoulder and embraced him to say good-bye. He whispered into Dad's ear, but I couldn't hear what he told him. I know it must have been some fatherly advice for surviving in a foreign land and returning safely home.

Our ride to New York City was as exciting as it had been the week before. We still marveled at the tunnels and still were in awe of the skyscrapers as we neared the city. We arrived late in the afternoon at a debarkation building for processing before boarding the airplane. I could see the C-130 Hercules transport planes lined up along the tarmac waiting for cargo and passengers to fill their hulls. The C-130 Hercules is a four-engine turboprop military transport aircraft designed and built originally by Lockheed. The C-130, which is capable of using unprepared runways for takeoffs and landings, was originally designed as a troop, medical evacuation, and cargo transport aircraft.

Given its unusual capabilities, I suspect we may have flown out of a restricted airfield on one of the islands in the harbor. A more plausible explanation, however, is that we disembarked from the airfield currently known as LaGuardia, named in 1953 for Fiorello La Guardia who was the Mayor of New York when the airport was built. This would make sense because the airfield at LaGuardia was known for its limited runway capacity. The C-130 Hercules aircraft was designed to compensate for just such a deficiency.

I don't remember the processing procedures or how long it took for us to be cleared for boarding, but I do know that we boarded the plane at night. The airport lighting cast an eerie pall over the wings of the big, tall birds. The shadows that were visible earlier had faded and left just the huge, winged hulls lurking against the overcast night sky. The rain had stopped. It appeared we were going to be cleared soon for takeoff. I don't recall the seating arrangements or whether we walked aboard along a cargo plank or up a steep set of stairs. I do remember sitting next to my sister on the plane. She seemed to be a little concerned about all the commotion, but I tried to stay as calm as I could so that she would not be afraid.

The roar of the engines was deafening. They drowned out any concerns that we might have shared with our parents or among ourselves. I held onto Bernadine's hand tightly, and she held mine just as tightly as we waited to board the plane. Our mother carried Almaneta and held Mercer's hand. Our bags were waiting to be stowed. Our mother clutched the baby's bag closely against her side. I could tell she was a little apprehensive about flying for the first time. I believe we all were in awe of the experience and a little fearful of the looming unknown.

A short, stocky man who wore fatigues led us outside the terminal. He carried a clipboard and a large flashlight. He escorted us to the gangplank and we boarded the plane. A tall, wiry-looking gentleman directed us to our seats and told us to get comfortable and then buckle up. Just like the good soldiers we were, we followed instructions and waited to see what would happen next. After a long wait and a series of deafening engine revs, we were told to check the buckles on our seatbelts and prepare for takeoff. The gentleman who had escorted us on board read his instructions from the clipboard. After he checked our seat assignments, and took a head count, he rattled off a set of do's and don'ts that I was unable to hear. He then turned and proceeded to take his seat in the rear of the plane.

A military airman in work clothes motioned for the plane to begin moving towards its assigned flight lane to prepare for takeoff. He waved a set of long amber lights on the end of batons and the pilot followed him as he backed up and then pointed in the direction the plane was authorized to go. The C-130 Hercules taxied onto an entry ramp and then paused and began to rev its engines one more time. After the drill was completed, the plane engines were lowered to a dull roar as we began to taxi towards the far end of the runway. The lights of the city shone brightly in the distance. I watched from a small window next to my head. Bernadine had chosen to sit as far from the windows as she could.

When we reached the point of no return the plane swerved gently to its right and pointed straight down a short runway, which ended just before the waters at the edge of the airfield. I had never flown before and was unprepared for the heavy roar of the engines or the tremendous shaking of the aircraft as we taxied down the runway. It was an experience I would never want to repeat again. The plane shook as if a huge windstorm was buffeting it. The gigantic rubber wheels might as well have been wooden. They rumbled down the runway causing the plane to feel like it was falling apart. I closed my eyes and began a prayer as we lumbered down the runway. Out of nowhere, a devilish thought entered my mind, *if God had meant for men to fly he would have given them wings.* I brushed the thought aside as quickly as it appeared. I didn't need any negativity to weigh down the aircraft. It was already big and bulky enough. I just wanted this man's bird to fly.

We rose ever so slowly like a gigantic houseboat lifted aloft on a magical flying carpet. The city lights shone brightly through the window and glistened in my eyes as tears ran down my face. We were finally on our way. Memories of all the moves and new neighborhoods flashed before me. I knew this move was different. I would never be the same person once I reached the distant shore. My whole world would be colored by all the wonderful experiences that awaited me, far beyond a small boy's imagination. It would not be the last airplane I would ever sail above the waters in. It would not be the only time I had ever traveled beyond the shores of these United States of America, but it was the first time, and that made all the difference.

I rested my head on the headrest and marveled at how great God's creation was even in the star-speckled darkness of night. I listened to the powerful engines roar as they propelled us forward. They drowned out all my thoughts of yesterday and replaced them with the anticipation of many new adventures to come. In time, I stopped holding my breath and allowed my body to adjust to the frequent jolts and bumps that accompanied us throughout the flight. My mind adapted gradually to the new quarters and slowly put me at ease. I don't know when I dozed off to sleep. I must have been lulled into restfulness by the hum of the engines. They whirred dutifully, and the big bird rose boldly into the sky. Upward it sailed and carried us into the blanket of clouds covering the edge of God's blue heaven.

Citations

"Baltimore Harbor Tunnel." Wikipedia. Wikimedia Foundation. <http://en.wikipedia.org/wiki/Baltimore_Harbor_Tunnel>. Accessed May 30, 2014.

"Baltimore – Washington Parkway." Wikipedia. Wikimedia Foundation. <http://en.wikipedia.org/wiki/Baltimore%E2%80%93Washington_Parkway>. Accessed May 27, 2014.

"Basic Facts about Bats." Defenders.org. Defenders of Wildlife. <http://www.defenders.org/bats/bats>. Accessed March 24, 2014.

"Bat." Wikipedia. Wikimedia Foundation. <http://en.wikipedia.org/wiki/Bat>. Accessed March 24, 2014.

"BB Gun." Wikipedia. Wikimedia Foundation. <http://en.wikipedia.org/wiki/BB_gun>. Accessed March 31, 2014.

"Boeing B-52 Stratofortress." Wikipedia. Wikimedia Foundation. <http://en.wikipedia.org/wiki/Boeing_B-52_Stratofortress>. Accessed February 26, 2014.

"Burma-Shave." Wikipedia. Wikimedia Foundation. <http://en.wikipedia.org/wiki/Burma-Shave>. Accessed March 31, 2014.

"Camp Gordan, Georgia renamed Fort Gordon in March 21, 1956." Wikipedia. Wikimedia Foundation. <http://en.wikipedia.org/wiki/Fort_Gordon#World_War_II_era>. Accessed August 21, 2014.

"Floyd Patterson-Boxer." Wikipedia. Wikimedia Foundation. <http://en.wikipedia.org/wiki/Floyd_Patterson>. Accessed on May 27, 2014.

"Fort Bliss United States Army Post." Wikipedia. Wikimedia Foundation. <http://en.wikipedia.org/wiki/Fort_Bliss>. Accessed February 26, 2014,

"Fort Sill." Wikipedia. Wikimedia Foundation. <http://en.wikipedia.org/wiki/Fort_Sill>. Accessed February 26, 2014.

"Garfield Memorial Hospital and MedStar Washington Hospital History." MedStar.org. MedStar Washington Hospital Center. <https://www.medstarhealth.org/washington/Pages/About-Us/MedStar-Washington-News/Media-Center/Media-Kit/Hospital-Center-History.aspx>. Accessed August 8, 2014.

"Governor's Island: A Silent Sentinel in New York Harbor." National Park Service. U.S. Department of the Interior. <http://www.nps.gov/gois/index.htm>. Accessed May 27, 2014.

"Governor's Island – U. S. First Army Administrative Center." Wikipedia. Wikimedia Foundation. <http://en.wikipedia.org/wiki/Governors_Island#19th_century>. Accessed May 30, 2014.

"Great Depression." Wikipedia. Wikimedia Foundation. <http://en.wikipedia.org/wiki/Great_Depression> Accessed September 8, 2013.

"History of Brown v. Board of Education." United States Courts. Federal Judiciary. <http://www.uscourts.gov/educational-resources/get-involved/federal-court-activities/brown-board-education-re-enactment/history.aspx>. Accessed August 22, 2014.

"History of the Baltimore-Washington Parkway." National Park Service. U.S. Department of the Interior. <http://www.nps.gov/bawa/historyculture/index.htm>. Accessed May 29, 2014.

"Hospital Center History." MedStar Hospital Health Center. MedStar Health. <https://www.medstarhealth.org/washington/Pages/

About-Us/MedStar-Washington-News/Media-Center/Media-Kit/Hospital-Center-History.aspx>. Accessed August 8, 2014.

"Jordanaires, The." Wikipedia. Wikimedia Foundation. <http://en.wikipedia.org/wiki/The_Jordanaires>. Accessed April 23, 2014.

"Lawton High School." Wikipedia. Wikimedia Foundation. <http://en.wikipedia.org/wiki/Lawton_High_School>. Accessed August 21, 2014.

Lee, H. (1945, July 23). Grandpa Mitchell's Death recorded in Family Records of Deaths.

"Lockheed C130 Hercules military transport plane first launched in 1956." Wikipedia. Wikimedia Foundation. <http://en.wikipedia.org/wiki/Lockheed_C-130_Hercules#Operational_history>. Accessed June 6, 2014.

"LaGuardia Airport located in the Borough of Queens." Wikipedia. Wikimedia Foundation. <http://en.wikipedia.org/wiki/LaGuardia_Airport>. Accessed June 6, 2014.

"Map of North Englewood Drive, Hyattsville, Maryland 20785 (ends on Reed Street)." (1951 – 1954 Home located at 5216 N. Englewood Drive, Hyattsville, MD, 20785). Google Maps. Google. <https://www.google.com/maps/@38.911556,-76.916402,15z>. Accessed June 3, 2014.

"Okmulgee, Oklahoma." Wikipedia. Wikimedia Foundation. <http://en.wikipedia.org/wiki/Okmulgee,_Oklahoma#History>. Accessed February 18, 2013.

"Marble (Toy)." Wikipedia. Wikimedia Foundation. <http://en.wikipedia.org/wiki/Marble_(toy)>. Accessed September 18, 2013.

"MGR 1 – Honest John." Wikipedia. Wikimedia Foundation. <http://en.wikipedia.org/wiki/MGR-1_Honest_John>. Accessed February 26, 2014.

"Mount Scott – Lawton's Highest Mountain." Wikipedia. Wikimedia Foundation. <http://en.wikipedia.org/wiki/Mount_Scott_(Oklahoma)>. Accessed August 21, 2014.

"Picture of North Englewood Drive going down the hill towards Reed Street. Fairmount Heights HS on right." (1951-1954 Home located at 5216 N. Englewood Drive, Hyattsville, MD, 20785). Google Maps. Google. <https://www.google.com/maps/search/reed+street+Cheverly+Md+street+level/@38.909931,-76.921087,3a,75y,36.42h,90t/data=!3m4!1e1!3m2!1shAwluOJPvmjMpvYxRTg6O!2e0>. Accessed June 2, 2014.

"Rodin's The Thinker." Cleveland Museum of Art. <http://www.clevelandart.org/research/in-the-library/how-to-research/rodins-the-thinker>. Accessed October 7, 2013.

"Tip Toe Tale, Poem about Walking Fish." Wilson, D. <http://mrsbrower.weebly.com/uploads/1/3/2/4/13243672/poems_for_repeated_reading.pdf>. Accessed October 10, 2013.

A WORD ABOUT THE AUTHOR

Bernard N. Lee, Jr. is the oldest son of a career veteran of the US Army. Together with his sisters, Bernadine and Almaneta, and his brother, Mercer, he traveled throughout the United States and Europe during his childhood. The places he traveled, the people he met, and the stories he remembers are shared in this memoir.

Bernie, as his friends call him, grew up in the fifties and sixties, when the United States was experiencing the aftermath of World War II and the Korean Conflict. That historical period shaped many of the perceptions that we have today of shared sacrifice and love for our country during times of war. Those times had a profound impact on Bernie's family and on his father's career in the US Army. They also shaped the personal perspective the author has of his childhood and memories of the places he lived and the people he met.

Bernie kept a mental diary of people and places he experienced during his father's tours at various military bases throughout his childhood. Taken together, those stories form the basis for A Look Back in Time. They also give the reader a window into the world of an African-American youngster growing up during the years of the civil rights struggles and America's unique journey towards equal opportunity for all.

Now approaching the age of seventy, Bernie can look back over a life of educational achievements, corporate accomplishments, and commendable community service. Bernie attended Cameron Junior College in Oklahoma and Howard University in Washington, D.C. While at Howard, Bernie joined the Army ROTC Program and pursued his father's dream of him becoming an Army Officer. As an ROTC cadet, he obtained a private pilot's license, a regular army commission and retired as a Captain from the Army Reserves. After graduating from Howard University in 1969 with a degree in Electrical Engineering, Bernie joined the family of Bell Telephone System companies, where he worked at Western Electric, AT&T Long Lines, AT&T Headquarters, and various subsidiaries until his retirement in 2003.

Following his retirement, Bernie obtained a Master of Arts in Education and taught high school classes for four years at Somerset Vocational & Technical High School in New Jersey. During that time, he volunteered to lead a Central New Jersey group of parents sponsoring the Program for the Acceleration of Minority Careers in Engineering (PACE) for high school students pursuing advanced placement in STEM college programs. Bernie also served as a coach, manager, and director for children's athletic programs in Franklin Township. He recalls his record of fourteen years as the "Voice of Pop Warner Football" in Somerset, New Jersey, fondly.

Bernie currently resides in Conyers, Georgia, with his wife of thirty-eight years, Edwina Lee. He spends his time volunteering in Deerwood Subdivision and teaching "Chess for Beginners" in an after school program. Bernie and Edwina have two children, Erik A. Moses and Angela F. Bostick. They also have three grandsons, Evan and Ethan Moses and Roman Bostick.